DED

This book is dedicated to the families of America, the basic building blocks ... the foundation of this great country.

ROYALTIES

All royalties created by the sales of this book will be contributed to Camp Blessing Texas, known as "A Special Place for Special Kids."

http://campblessing.org

ACKNOWLEDGMENTS

My many thanks to the following important people who helped make this book come together:

Maureen Peltier, wife of my brother Peter, lawyer for families, an English teacher in her early adult life and Chief Editor of this book. She spent countless hours correcting my run-on sentences, punctuation, and other grammatical errors. Without her help and support, this book would have never gotten out of Chute Number One.

Steve Rife, my great friend and banker, who also read over my material and guided me in many ways.

My son Josh, who has been resourceful in putting together the cover and all the picture images.

Gerald Peltier, grandson of Joseph Peltier (who brought the first Peltier's to Texas), who contributed some of the written history from his family and pictures of the stationary thresher of the Joseph Peltier family.

Thank you, all.

AWARDS

Reader Views, LITERARY AWARD WINNERS 2016/2017
(For 2016 Copyright Books) *The Thundering Herd* won:
    First Place in the category of History / Science,
    Best Regional Book of the Year in the South, and the
    Richard Boes Award - for the Best Debut Book by a Veteran.
    Conversations Award for the Best Regional Book of the Year

2017 Next Generation Indie Book Awards, *The Thundering Herd*
Won:
    Finalist in the MEMIORS (Historical/Legacy/Career)
Category.

2017 Colorado Independent Publishers Association, CIPA EVVY
Award, *The Thundering Herd* won:
    Merit Autobiography/Memoirs Category
    2nd Place in the History Category.

    It surprised me that *The Thundering Herd* won the awards as a history book. I've always considered it a memoir, but I have always been a student of history and after considering the content I can understand why.

CONTENTS

Acknowledgments i

Prologue 1

1 La Connexion Francaise 4

2 The Scottish Side 13

3 The Flames of Love 30

4 "I'm in the Army now..." 47

5 G.I. John 68

6 Combat Medical Training 91

7 Good Morning Vietnam 107

8 Winning Hearts and Minds 138

9 More Than You Ever Wanted to Know about Cattle 172

10 Hurricane Carla: Howling Winds 197

11 Short Timer 213

12 Back in the Lone Star State 241

13 A Herd of My Own 250

14 Peltier Brothers Construction 265

15 A Rattlers Tale, May 11, 2007 278

16 An Essay on Grass and Water 284

Epilogue 289

JOHN E PELTIER

PROLOGUE

Welcome to the history and stories of the "Thundering Herd," the name my mother pinned to my family. I must admit we wore it very well.

I am John Eldridge Peltier, the fifth of the twelve children who are included in this "herd". Having taken up the challenge of memorializing our family history, and what it was like growing up in the 1950's on a rice farm / cattle ranch and serving time in Vietnam during the 1960's, I've felt compelled to expand this into an update on my family, the family business and other stories.

The two sides of the family are the Peltier's and the Keillor's. The Peltier side had a known linage going all the way back to France, but no stories to speak of. The Keillor side was just one generation away from Scotland and had many stories. My mother and her brother Peter (referred to in this book as "Uncle Pete") told us stories and wrote a lot about their years growing up in the high and dry Escalante Desert of Southwestern Utah and they have been a rich source of information.

As you will see, I have used my time in the United States Army from June of 1967 to January of 1969 as a backdrop to introduce many of the stories of our growing up. I tried to get most of the stories vetted by my brothers and sisters, but that was like "herding cats". I couldn't get them to read and comment on all of the stories, but they were always available for specific questions. We found that none of us could agree on many of the details – we all seemed to have oddly different versions, so these are stories as I recall them.

My siblings' birthdays were stretched over eighteen years and can be broken down into groups that are basically time periods when we did many things together. Peter (1942) and Kay (1943), born before Dad served in World War II, are one group. Louis (1946), Kenneth (1947), me (1948) and Becky (1949) were born after he returned are a group. Stephen (1952) and Paul (1953) were the next group. Leo Patrick (1955) left us after only seven days. Arthur (1957) and Richard (1958) are another group. Molly (1960), the youngest, was a loner.

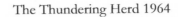

The Thundering Herd 1964

Back Row: Kenneth, John, Mom, Peter, Kay, Louis, Dad
Front Row: Becky, Molly in front, Paul, Stephen, Richard, Arthur

As we all got older and had more common interests and experiences, the lines drawn in the groups faded away, but you will notice that Louis, Kenneth, and Becky were a much bigger part of my life growing up than were Peter or Molly.

Over the years I have been involved in various businesses with my brothers and sisters, with the exception of Kay, Becky and Paul. Most were successful; all were interesting. We as a family were always inclusive and seldom exclusive.

When I began this project, I realized that if someone didn't commit my family's history to paper, future generations would lose a large part of their heritage. That has been my constant motivation. For that reason, I consider this book a gift to my siblings, children, grandchildren, nieces, nephews, many friends and other interested souls.

In the early family history, Chapters One and Two, the stories of my mother and father's early lives and courtship, I have taken literary license in filling in the gaps. For many of those stories I had some information; for others I just imagined what might have been. Also, in the Vietnam stories, some of the names are real and some are made up, as it's been nearly fifty years and I've slept too many times to remember them all.

I hope you find this journey and its stories interesting and, hopefully, enjoyable. It's been a fifteen year project with many ups and downs and twists and turns in the writing of it.

Writing is not one of my natural abilities.

1

LA CONNEXION FRANÇAISE

The Pelletier Family

The Pelletier Family

The Peltier side of my family traces its earliest roots to my ancestor Pierre Pelletier. He was born on August 24, 1634, in St. Martin de Fraigneau, Poitou, France. The Poitou area of France is on the far west central coast and is today known for its abundant seafood. Its significance for us today here in the United States is that most of the Acadian and Cajun settlers in Louisiana and the eastern part of Texas came from that area.

Much of France in the 1600's was devastated by a great plague and severe famine, causing many residents to immigrate to present day Canada seeking better living conditions. At the same time, France was entering into an era known as the Age of Enlightenment and Expansion. The French were beginning to colonize large portions of North America, beginning with the area around the Saint Lawrence River now known as Quebec. The area where Pierre settled was called Neuville, a picturesque village founded on the north shore of the river populated then by 372 people, including 63 families. Today it is still a small village, populated by around 4,000 people whose first language is still French.

To strengthen the colonies and to correct an imbalance of men to women, King Louis XIV offered to send to New France single women between the ages of 15 and 30. They came to be known as the "King's Daughters". The King, that is, the French government, offered to pay their

4

1920

Roy, Walter, Annette, Dora, Ronald, Mitchel (Buck)
Sister Gerard, Rosa (Mother), Ruby, Joseph (Father), Bill

Stationary Threshing Machine 1935

My grandfather Telesphore, later saddled with the nicknames of "Tellie" and "Dud", was born on October 9, 1875. There are stories of his having rheumatic fever as an adult and of his living with his brother Wilfred around 1910. When he was 37, on September 8, 1912, he married Matilda Louise Lambert. She was fifteen years younger than him, having been born on August 7, 1890. They quickly began their family, consisting of five children: Aldia, born on June 25, 1913; Wilburn (my father), born on April 23, 1915; Romelia, who lived from March 3, 1916 until September 18, 1917; Alrose, born on March 10, 1919; and Ellen, born on February 6, 1921.

My father Wilburn grew restless in Kansas, like a caged animal. Like many other children in that era, he ended his formal education in seventh grade because he was needed to help work the family farm. He knew there was still a lot to learn, as he continued his education in the school of hard knocks, where cause and effect were the teachers. Farming was all he knew because his family raised wheat. He learned that being a farmer required knowledge of many subjects and many decisions, like when to plant the seeds, how and when to care for the crop, when to harvest and how to arrange help for those tasks. The better the planning and knowledge, the better the crop. Farmers also had to know how to improvise to keep their machinery running. They had to become very inventive in the face of necessity; many times equipment was held together with baling wire and bubble gum, plus hope and a prayer.

The Peltier family farm was a small farm just outside the town of Concordia, Kansas. The power required to run the farm was provided by the strength of horses and men. Dad's siblings were girls, so he was required to provide most of the manpower. But, after a number of years, the family found itself struggling under the pressure of Mother Nature's *Dust Bowl* and the national economy's *Great Depression*.

Beginning in the early 1930's due to drought conditions and very poor agriculture land practices, topsoil was literally blown from county to county and state to state. Dust storms, dark clouds of hot and dry earth spread by howling winds, blocked out the sun as they skipped and howled over the Midwestern prairies and croplands. It seemed that dust permeated everything, including the very souls of the people who lived through them. Wilburn tired of the dust he took into his lungs with each breath and the grit in his mouth with every bite of food. After thoroughly scrubbings, his skin still revealed dirt in its pores. Nobody could get really clean.

Like that of many of its neighbors, the Peltier family farm failed and his father was forced to sell. The failure was a bitter pill for the family, but for my father it offered a welcome opportunity, a chance to strike out and find out what might be, instead of what was, a chance to find out if his dreams were made of fact or fiction.

At the age of 24, Wilburn had also started to dream about the woman he might marry, the girl of his dreams, and there were few available young women wandering around Main Street and the back roads of Concordia.

Added to that, he was beginning to tire of the freezing cold and biting snow of Concordia's winters and the terrible migraine headaches the conditions caused him. Restless, pent up and at a crossroad in his life, he felt a new chapter of his life opening and the excitement of the possibility of new adventures.

He knew that some of his cousins had relocated years earlier to the Texas Gulf Coast to farm rice, though he himself had never ventured further than a hundred miles in any direction from the house in which he was born.

Armed with an adventurous spirit and a great desire for change, he resolutely shook off as much dust as he could, packed his bags, and headed south in his old junker Plymouth. Like thousands before and after him, he was going to Texas!

His journey ended in the small southeast Texas town of Danbury, where he happily connected with his Peltier cousins. These were the cousins who had banded together in a cooperative partnership known as the Peltier Brothers for their farming operation, as mentioned earlier.

As in most farming operations there are times when things are slow, and other times, like preparing the seed beds, planting and harvesting, when work goes from busy to frenzied. For such times, the Peltier Brothers needed him and he was happy to help and gain an education in rice farming at the same time. He found a room to rent and settled into the Danbury society, which was mostly St. Anthony's Catholic Church on Sunday's.

The windy Kansas wheat fields had taught him one thing very well and that was how to work. Dow Chemical Company in nearby Freeport was building its plant infrastructure aggressively in 1939 and Dad found additional work there. He began saving for his grubstake in future farming.

He was hired first by one of the construction companies in the area that built the plant that produced magnesium (in what was known as the "mag cells"). Later he was hired by Dow Chemical as a transfer operator to work in the facility. As a transfer operator his job, using a steel dipper, was to skim molten magnesium floating on top of a boiling red hot salt bath and pour it into a crucible where it was sent to be cast into ingots.

Although happy with Texas and his work, he was saddened with the news of his mother's death, April 1, 1940. He made a pilgrimage back to Kansas for the funeral.

Wilburn was single, working the dirt and at Dow taking all the overtime it offered. He was also happy, tired, and dirty most of the time, but very content, like he was finally getting ahead of the curve.

2

The Scottish Side

My mother's side of the family, the Keillor's, traces its roots back to Peter Thompson Keillor, my grandfather, called "Papa" by my mother. I will also refer to my grandfather as "Papa" in this writing. Much of the family history related about the Keillor's is gathered from stories and writings of my mother and her brother, Peter Thompson Keillor II, who I will refer to as "Uncle Pete" in this writing.

My grandfather was born in Stanley, Scotland, on Christmas Day in 1881. Stanley was a small village on the right bank of the River Tay, just north of Perth. Its main industry at that time was a cotton mill on a bend in the river. Today the historic cotton mill has become its main attraction and it is a suburb of the large city of Perth. The late 1800's in Scotland was the time of the Industrial Revolution and the Boer War raging in South Africa.

At the young age of twelve, Papa became apprenticed to a tailor in the nearby village of Blackford, but as many young apprenticed boys at that time and now, he longed for adventure. He abandoned his apprenticeship and signed on to work on a freighter that traveled all over the world. We know that around 1904, at the age of 23, he landed in Vancouver, Canada. There he met and married Gertrude Mabel Horrell. She was born on July 17, 1884, and they were united in marriage July 15, 1906.

The couple moved to Baxter, Kansas, in 1907, where Gertrude had family connections. Returning to his earlier learned skills, Papa worked as a tailor in Kansas, but he really didn't like that line of work.

They had a daughter named Esther May (my "Aunt Esther") on June 19, 1908. Shortly after Esther's birth, tragedy struck when Gertrude died of heart failure on June 6, 1909, at the age twenty-five.

Papa learned there was abundant work and opportunity in Los Angeles and the surrounding area. Soon after Gertrude's death Papa decided to head to the Golden State. He made arrangements for Gertrude's kinfolks to take care of his young daughter Esther until he was settled in California. He sent funds back to Kansas to pay her expenses and, within a couple of years, was able to take her with him to California.

On March 17, 1916, Papa was at a St. Patrick's Day party in Los Angeles when he met my grandmother, Sarah Katherine (Kate) Wright, born in Kentucky on May 29, 1885. Papa kept Esther in a boarding house while he worked in various places to support her. We know that he often stayed at YMCA's, as he received postcards from his friends addressed to various YMCA's in different towns around Southern California. As Papa and Kate got to know each other, he moved Esther into a boarding house run by Kate's sister Ida. Both Papa and Kate had good voices and sang together in the local church choir. Kate took a definite "shine" to Papa, and once told her sisters, "He's mine, even if I never get him."

At that time, Kate had an uncle, Columbus Hobbs nicknamed (Lum) , who was making plans to homestead land in Utah. He painted a rosy picture of the place and influenced Papa to also apply. They could homestead a half section of land, 320 acres, by living on it, clearing and cultivating it for five years, and then receive a clear title. This land was in the high and dry Escalante Desert; the half section they chose was adjacent to a Union Pacific railroad line. Water was only available when homesteaders hand dug wells, which they did.

Papa rode out with Uncle Lum in his 1912 Oldsmobile to Nada, a tiny town adjacent to the railroad right-of-way. Together they built Lum's house.

Papa made application for his own homestead, about a half mile away, with the Department of the Interior on March 22, 1917. On May 3 of that year he received his official "Notice of Allowance", the Department of the

My mother described Granny Keillor as a short little woman, always dressed in black, with only one visible tooth in her mouth. She arrived with two wooden cases which carried many of her keepsakes. In the desert of Utah, she was happy to meet her grandchildren and be with her son again but was unprepared for the rigors of desert life. After several months she had a stroke and died; they buried her in Milford, about 20 miles away from their homestead.

Many homesteaders tried and went bust. Others left the desert soon after they had proven up their homesteads. What on the surface looked like "free land" was in fact a five-year sentence to hard labor in a sometimes very harsh and inhospitable environment.

But Papa and Kate did not leave so quickly.

On February 10, 1922, the land became officially theirs with the receipt of the United States document granting them their chosen 320 acres of homestead land. The document stated, "*On the tenth day of February, in the year of our Lord one thousand nine hundred and twenty two, Peter T. Keillor has been established and duly consummated, in conformity to law, for the east half of Section eleven in Township thirty-one south of Range thirteen west of the Salt Lake Meridian, Utah, containing three hundred twenty acres.*" They had done it and were the legal landowners.

In 1925 Kate bought their first motorized vehicle, a used Ford Model T. Papa didn't want the car, but Kate did. The old axiom "If Momma ain't happy, ain't nobody happy" proved true.

In nearby Cedar City they found a car which had been recently purchased by a doctor for his wife. It had a number of "fancy extras" for that time. It was equipped with a speedometer that was operated from a little sprocket on the inside of the front right wheel. It also had a heater, which sent heat through a little grille on the right floorboard, with the heat fed into it from a sheet metal cover over the exhaust manifold. The steering wheel was made with a fancy wooden rim with a metal ring inside for the horn. Best of all, the back of the front seat was cut down and hinged so that it could be made into a bed. It was an "open" model, meaning it had a canvas top which could be folded back. Clear flaps were zipped or tied down for windows. However, Mrs. Crouch, the doctor's wife, didn't like it. She wanted the more luxurious "closed" model, with a molded steel body and rollup glass windows in the doors to protect from the wind and rain. Both wives got their wishes and Kate was very happy.

Papa did not like having a car and refused to learn how to drive it for a long time; every time something went wrong with it, he cussed Henry Ford!

Besides the family's getting its first motorized vehicle, 1925 was also a year of other changes in the desert. The local school board decided to open a school in Nada. There was an unused school building in Latimer a few miles away, and local men in the area pulled the old school building to Nada with their wagons. With a few modifications it was soon ready for classes. There were about fifteen students in the school, including Mom, who was seven, and Uncle Pete, who was five. The new school was about two and a half miles from the homestead; Mom and Uncle Pete walked there and back nearly every day. Occasionally they would get a ride in the closed Model T of the Crouch family, who lived about three and a half miles further from the school.

If the temperature got down to around zero, they stayed home from school. One morning there were several inches of snow on the ground and it was continuing to snow heavily. Kate encouraged Mom and Uncle Pete to stay home that day. Though they were only seven and five, they thought they could make it all right.

Shortly after they set out in the heavy snow storm, they realized that they were not following the road, so they took what they thought was a short cut through the sagebrush on a path that led to the railroad tracks about a mile away. Almost immediately they lost the path in the snow and went in an arc to the left. After walking and walking, they finally reached the railroad track at a point twice as far away from Nada as they were supposed to be. Fortunately they made it to school, because there were few houses and no fences or other landmarks in the desert at that time. If they had not run into the railroad tracks, those two little children would have likely perished, lost and wandering in the snow. They certainly couldn't have survived a night in the desert under those conditions.

Another memorable story my Uncle Pete recalled was the celebration of Memorial Day in 1925 when his teacher invited a war veteran to speak to his class. The veteran's name was Mr. Stevenson and he lived near Nada. With his long white beard and gray hair, he looked to Uncle Pete far too old to have served in The Great War that ended in 1918. He told them that he joined the

Army of the Confederacy when he was sixteen and spoke of the perils and ugliness of the Civil War.

After Kate bought the Model T, they found that they needed their horses Queeny and Topsy less and less; finally they let them loose to run with the wild herds that ran out of the mountains and through the valley. Their two mares delivered three colts over the years. It was a wonder, but their horses would still come to Papa when he needed them. Herds of wild horses ran loose and stayed pretty close to the mountains most of the time, but they spent some time in the valley just galloping freely through the desert, truly a sight to behold, my mother exclaimed.

Sharpshooting wranglers would stalk the wild herds to capture young colts to tame and sell. When they were in close proximity to one they wanted, the wranglers would attempt to knock it out by shooting it in a very specific area behind its neck to make it temporarily lose consciousness. The procedure was called "grazing". After the horse was knocked out, they would tie it up and capture it. If the shot was an inch low, it killed the horse. Papa never had a chance to train any of the colts that Queeny and Topsy had, as his shots were always a little low.

When Aunt Esther turned sixteen, she went to live with her Aunt May in California to finish school. In 1926 she graduated from high school and fell in love with Eldridge Backus, whom we called "Uncle Edgie". Uncle Edgie was Kate's sister May's son, whom Esther met when she was visiting her Aunt May.

(Note: they were not blood kin, as Esther's mother was Gertrude Horrell, Papa's first wife, who had died when Esther was very young.)

Uncle Edgie had served in the U.S. Navy, where he learned sheet metal work and how to be a "tin bender". He married Esther shortly after she graduated from high school. They then moved to Palestine, Texas, where he set up a sheet metal fabricating shop. In 1927 they were blessed with a daughter, my cousin Alice Mae.

Papa quit the railroad in 1926. He wanted to work on and live off the homestead. He milked seven cows twice a day and ran the milk through a cream separator hand cranked by Mom and Uncle Pete. The cream was then shipped to Salt Lake City on the railroad in five gallon milk cans; the creamery would then send the empty milk cans back with a check. The rest of the milk was used to make cottage cheese. They all drank their fill and fed what was left to the pigs and chickens.

May and Ida went to visit them in Utah one summer with a load of delicious fresh California apricots. They decided to dry the extra fruit for winter. After slicing them in two and pitting them, they put them on the flat roof of the house to dry. The drying worked well and they looked good, but Mom said that the finished product tasted like tarpaper.

Mom says that they always had a garden growing near the house, where they grew sweet corn, peas, beans, potatoes, carrots, and squash. They canned all the vegetables that would not keep and put the carrots, potatoes and squash down in the cool root cellar. They butchered calves and hogs and canned most of the meat because there was no refrigeration available. They also had currant bushes, gooseberry bushes and a rhubarb patch which provided jams, pies, and sauces for the year. Kate drove the Model T to nearby Lund nearly every week to sell whatever she could, which was usually butter, eggs and fresh seasonable vegetables.

Things changed in the summer of 1929. Word came that the school in Nada would be closing. Mother had been suffering from hay fever and the hard life was getting harder. So after struggling in the desert for twelve years, they decided it was time to move on. Uncle Edgie and Aunt Esther reported to them that they had been able to scratch out a living in Texas and invited them to go out for a visit and check it out. So they decided that Texas was their next destination in continuing their "pursuit of happiness".

They packed up the belongings they wanted to ship by rail and loaded the Model T for the trip. They sold the cows, buildings and tools to their friends and neighbors and gave away the rest. Queeny and Topsy were left to gallop wild and free among the herd of wild horses in the area. As they were leaving, Kate looked over her shoulder to see the west room of their house being dismantled by neighbors to be relocated and was saddened by the finality of leaving, as a little sad tear crept from her eye. Her family had built that little home with their bare hands and had invested twelve years of toil and anguish with few dividends to show for it, but despite all the hardships, the place would always occupy a warm spot in their hearts.

(Note: as my mother and Uncle Pete grew in age, we have gone back with them to visit Utah. They always loved to return to the place that held so many memories for them. My brother Peter and I now own those 320 acres. We have found remains of the old house and well; we have camped among the dusty dry sagebrush and slept under the same beautiful dark sky and bright stars and viewed the distant mountains. Experiencing it with modern day campers and tents, though, we wonder how they lived there for so long. In the spring of 2017, on Memorial Day weekend, ten of us siblings and our spouses camped out at the Homestead and experienced the rugged beauty and its harsh environment . It was amazing to us how our grandparents endured life there for twelve years.)

As they began their journey to Texas, the Model T turned out to be not only transportation but also a camper. The running boards were modified to carry a toolbox, and some of the old five gallon milk cans were carried for extra gas and water. Each front fender held a bedroll, while another was strapped to the spare tire. The back seat was padded with quilts and pillows, leaving just enough room for a nest for Mom and Uncle Pete.

They started out around the 1st of September of 1929, driving down through Cedar City and reaching the Virgin River the first night. There they camped and the next morning went into Zion National Park where they stayed three days. That was the only time they ever took the top down on the old Ford. With the top down, they could drive along and look up at the cliffs.

Then they went down to Rockville. At the time they were just building the tunnel leading to the east entrance. Out of Rockville the road ran up out of the Virgin River valley at a steep incline. Two strangers helped them to the top because the old Model T couldn't make it under its own power. Papa, Uncle Pete and the two men pushed, while Kate drove and Mom carried a rock to wedge behind one of the wheels when they stopped. They made it to the top. The men told them that theirs was only the second Model T they had seen make it up that hill.

The Model T had a ten gallon fuel tank which gravity fed the meager twenty horsepower engine. Therefore, the procedure for attacking the steep hills was to drive in reverse because in doing it that way the fuel tank was higher than the engine. That hill, which rose 1500 feet in two miles, was the first of a lot of pushing. During one climb, a rock flew out from under the rear tire and hit Papa on his calf, crippling him for a couple of days.

After they left Jacob's Lake, Arizona, they had a number of hard travel days. The Kaibab Plateau was cut with gullies that gave them a lot pushing to do. Once they had to unload the car and carry everything to the top before they could push the car up. When they got to the edge of the Plateau, the road down was a real challenge for the brakes. Many people cut trees and dragged them behind their cars to control them. Kate and Papa decided to try it without a tree, but Mom and Uncle Pete were so scared they walked down. The road, such as it was, just dropped from one rock to the next. They got down without incident and spent the night at House Rock, Arizona.

The next day was spent on the road between the Vermillion Cliffs and the Colorado River. The road would run a short way and then drop into a dry wash. It would turn down the wash a short distance and then shoot up. Mom, Uncle Pete, and Papa would jump out and push when the engine bogged down. It was slow going, but they finally arrived at the newly completed Navaho Bridge where they camped on the north side. The Navaho Bridge crosses Marble Canyon where it is eight hundred feet deep. It was a beautiful and memorable sight. By that point in the trip, it had taken nine days to go 130 miles, as the crow flies. They surely must have been exhausted, but they had just begun.

As they approached Flagstaff, Arizona, the Model T encountered the first bit of paved road they had ever driven on. They thought it would be smooth sailing for the rest of the trip, but when they got to Springerville, Arizona, Route 60 was washed out and they had to detour through the mountains. They went through one canyon with a flat bed and vertical walls so close together that Mom and Uncle Pete felt like they could touch both sides at once. They met a bus on its way to California that had made it through, but did not see how it was possible. That night they came to a ranch house that was built like an adobe fort. The people there had an empty room and let them camp in it. The next day was spent working their way through the mountains on another primitive road. By dark it was cold and rainy; they took out the side curtains and put them up when they arrived at Pie Town, New Mexico.

The roads got better when they crossed over into Texas. As they neared Fort Bliss, near El Paso, they passed what seemed like miles and miles of soldiers on horseback, the U.S. Army mounted cavalry.

student tripping and causing her to fall towards the fire turned out to be a fortuitous encounter for both of them, in more ways than one.

It seemed like forever to him before Barbara broke the silence between them when she turned to him and said, "Thank you so much. That fire was starting to feel really hot!"

She later thought to herself, "As stunned as I was by this whole ordeal, it almost seemed providential in how it happened. I didn't feel shock or fear. I almost felt comfortable with this man."

"Well, my name is Wilburn Peltier and I was glad to be there. Plowing into that fire wouldn't have been a very healthy experience," Wilburn replied.

She simply replied, "And I'm Barbara Keillor, the new librarian and English teacher here at Danbury."

And that is how my parents met.

Growing up in the desolate and isolated Escalante Desert in Utah had caused my mother to be a little bookish. Although attending high school and college in Texas had broken down many of her walls, she was still a little shy. For the first time in her life she was on her own, away from her family and feeling a little homesick. Her brother Pete, who had supported her through college after their parents died in 1938, was at the University of Texas taking his turn at getting an education, and her sister Esther was in Palestine, Texas, raising her daughter Alice Mae and keeping her husband Edgie in line.

So the fall of 1940 found her in the little town of Danbury, on the Texas coast, with a real job as a librarian and English teacher and part of a new school and community, a life she had long dreamed about. But it was all still very new to her and she had not quite adjusted to it. Then, in the midst of it all, this man named Wilburn Peltier entered her life by saving her from a near tragic accident.

Wilburn was more settled there and prospering on the work front, but he, like Barbara, missed his family. In addition, he was feeling that it was time to search for a partner to share his lifelong hopes and dreams. When the new teacher, this lady named Barbara Keillor, almost fell into his arms, it seemed like his dreams might possibly be coming true.

But how could he garner enough courage to actually ask her out?

After struggling a few days with how to approach the problem, he decided to do the only thing he had ever known when tackling an issue, confront it directly.

Barbara lived in what was called the "teacher's cottage", a one bedroom efficiency across the street from the school.

The day immediately after deciding to ask her out, he found himself gently tapping on her screen door. After work, freshly showered, with school having been out for a while and the sky starting to darken, he felt about as comfortable as a fish out of water flopping on the ground.

Barbara came to the door smiling and said, "Why, Mr. Peltier, what a pleasant surprise."

"Please call me Wilburn," he replied, warmed by her smile. Then he added, "I thought I would come by and see how you were doing after that little scare the other night."

"Please call me Barbara. I'm well, but I learned that I will be much more careful the next time I'm around a bonfire," she replied in a very friendly voice.

He went on, "On a different note - our meeting the other night was a little awkward and abrupt when we were both taken by surprise. I was hoping we could meet in a more social way and get to know each other a little better, so I was wondering If you'd like to go to dinner with me Saturday night?"

She smoothly replied, "That would be nice. I'd love to go to dinner with you."

Then, nodding at the two metal chairs on her small porch, she added, "I just made some ice tea. If you would like to sit and talk out here awhile, I'll make us a couple of glasses."

Starting to feel ready good about his decision to go see her, he could hardly contain himself as he blurted out, "That would be very nice!"

"Do you like lemon and sugar in your tea?" she asked.

Barely controlling his delight so he wouldn't look too eager, he answered, "A little sugar, please."

There was no moon as the dusk soon turned to darkness, but the stars offered a beautiful array of light sprinkling across the sky and, before either of them were aware of the time, night had fallen. They had talked for several hours, but it had seemed like just a few minutes.

Wilburn glanced at his watch and exclaimed, "Where did the time go? It's 10:30!"

Also surprised, Barbara replied, "Well, I guess we better wrap this up since we both have to work in the morning. "

With that, they stood up; he took her hand in his and thanked her for what had turned out to be a very nice evening for both of them. She told him what a pleasant evening it had been for her, too.

Afterwards, they both realized that the evening had been a giant icebreaker in their relationship. They had gotten to know each other's backgrounds and, even with the realization that they were raised quite differently, they felt a pull towards each other. Like the poles of a magnet, their opposites attracted.

32

After that, Wilburn and Barbara spent much of their spare time together. They attended most of the Danbury High home games, plus church and many other community events. They quickly became known as an "item" around town.

In their little community, one of the favorite pastimes for young couples, married or unmarried, was getting together on weekend nights and playing a domino game called "42". It was a partners game, with two teams of two couples filling each table. Generally there were four or five tables at each gathering. Once the games started, the losing couple stayed at the table and the winning couple moved to the next table. At the end of the evening the winners of the most games won a prize provided by the host. In early 1941 Wilburn and Barbara were invited to join a group of teachers and farmers that played regularly. They promptly accepted the invitation, met many new friends, and enjoyed more and more evenings together.

Hollywood movies were also a big entertainment for them; Grapes of Wrath with Henry Fonda was a bitter-sweet movie they had seen together. They both had felt the pinch of the Depression and reliving it on the silver screen was not all together pleasant. Charlie Chaplin in The Great Dictator was entertaining, but with Adolph Hitler's rise in Germany, it also gave pause and a little concern for the future. The Maltese Falcon with Humphrey Bogart, The Philadelphia Story with Cary Grant, James Stewart and Katherine Hepburn, and The Shop Around the Corner with James Stewart and Margaret Sullavan were also big hits that they enjoyed.

There was no television at the time, but when they got together, the radio was frequently in the background playing Big Band, Jazz and Swing music for their pleasure. They like hearing Frank Sinatra, Bing Crosby, Ella Fitzgerald, Nat King Cole, Louis (Sachmo) Armstrong and many others. The radio was the source of most of their national news, too. They, like most other Americans of that era, regularly listened to President Roosevelt's Fireside Chats and comedy shows like Ozzie and Harriet, Amos and Andy, Jack Benny, Bob Hope, and Fibber McGee and Molly. Detective radio shows like The Shadow and Sherlock Holmes provided many additional hours of entertainment.

Wilburn read the local and regional newspapers, while Barbara was always reading a book or grading papers.

As the days and months went by after their first meeting at that fateful bonfire, Barbara and Wilburn found themselves in a familiar and comfortable place, with happy times and regular routines which ultimately led to their reciting of the familiar words that would bind them together permanently in this life, "till death do us part".

Not surprisingly, by the end of the school year in the spring of 1941 they began discussing marriage.

At the same time, their couples' domino group was planning an end of the school year party. Wilburn had secretly bought Barbara a modest, but beautiful, diamond engagement ring. Then he decided that he wanted to surprise her with a proposal of marriage in front of all their friends at the party. For that purpose, he enlisted the aid of the host of the party, his friend and one of Barbara's fellow teachers, Robert McMillan (also known as "Mr. Mac").

After conferring with Mr. Mac and finalizing the details, not surprisingly, the shy Wilburn began having second thoughts about going through with his plan. He realized then that he had never liked being the center of attention or in the spotlight and that all eyes would be on him.

One day he dropped by the school to see Mr. Mac to share his increasing anxiety.

"Robert, I don't know if I can propose to Barbara in front of everyone," he truthfully confessed.

His friend encouragingly replied, "Oh, you'll do just fine. It'll be over before you know it." Mr. Mac addressed people every day as part of his profession.

Bravely, Wilburn decided to stick to his plan until, finally, the day of the party arrived.

Wilburn had been nervously practicing, "Barbara, will you marry me? Barbara, will you be my wife?"

He also was having thoughts like, "Wilburn, you are going to screw this thing up and embarrass yourself and Barbara. You're a real idiot for even thinking you can pull this off!"

On the day of the party, Wilburn had been frustrated working on a tractor engine that he never did get running. But he quit early anyway, taking time to carefully and thoroughly get the dirt off his hands and the black grease from under his nails. Then, in a new green shirt and nearly new blue jeans, he was finally ready and went to pick up Barbara.

As his luck would have it, as soon as he turned the corner onto her street, it started raining, a real downpour, and he didn't have a slicker or an umbrella in the car. He got thoroughly drenched running from his car to her porch. Nevertheless, with water dripping from his clothes, he knocked on her door.

In contrast, Barbara came out nicely dressed, in a freshly ironed white blouse and an attractive blue skirt, wearing a raincoat and carrying an umbrella. With Barbara politely sharing her umbrella, Wilburn helped her into the car, looking and feeling like a drowned rat. The car felt too warm, humid, and stuffy to him. His wet shirt stuck to his back. He was miserable and becoming more and more nervous at the thought of the proposal he had carefully planned for that evening. His spirits had been totally dampened by the downpour.

By the time they arrived at the McMillan's house, the downpour slowed down to a drizzle and Wilburn was feeling a little better.

During the time when everyone visited and caught up before they started the games, his shirt dried out a little and he began feeling more relaxed. They talked with their friends, had some coffee and punch, and enjoyed the hostess's little cakes. Then everyone took their assigned tables under the guise of preparing to concentrate on the domino games.

Everyone except Barbara was aware of the planned proposal as Mr. Mac rose and tapped his glass three times with a spoon to get everyone's attention, the prearranged cue for Wilburn to begin his proposal.

At that moment Wilburn felt his face turning red, but, nevertheless, he rose from his chair and then got down on one knee in front of Barbara, as he fumbled clumsily to get the ring out of the little box he had been hiding in one of his pockets. The box fell to the floor, but he took the shiny golden ring between his forefinger and thumb. With his hands shaking, he held the ring up toward her and was barely able to get the word "Barbara" out of his mouth before his felt his eyes begin to water. He found himself unable to get another word out of his mouth. He later told Mr. Mac that he felt like his whole face froze at that moment.

"Yes, I will!" blurted out Barbara, as she excitedly took the ring from his hand, bent down, gave him a huge kiss and wrapped her arms around him. He could not have been more delighted.

The room spontaneously erupted into applause, congratulations, and laughter.

Wilburn felt great relief as all of his embarrassment turned into happiness. They were engaged! The hard part was over for Wilburn. He was on a cloud, the happiest he had been in his whole life.

They soon choose September 20, 1941, as their wedding day, a date which they both wildly anticipated. Barbara handled most of the details, arranging to have the wedding at the home of Roy Peltier, one of Wilburn's relatives.

The attendance list was short because their families were small, but they were happy to have Wilburn's dad Telesphore, his three sisters Aldea, Alrose, and Ellen, Barbara's brother Pete, and her sister Esther with her husband Edgie and daughter Alice Mae. There were also close friends and a number of cousins attending the small wedding. Wilburn was greatly relieved that his public speaking part would be small. He wanted no possibility of a repeat of his embarrassing proposal performance.

While Barbara was arranging the wedding details, Wilburn began work on their first home, outside of town near Austin Bayou.

Danbury was (and still is) in an area of the Texas coastal plain that is as flat as a pancake and at a very low elevation from the Gulf of Mexico. When a major tropical storm or hurricane blasts through the area, the tidal surge pushes the water from the Gulf up into the bayous and out into the low lying areas. In addition, as the storms go inland, they may drop tens of inches of rain; the runoff drains back down the bayous, often creating flooding from the opposite direction. Those caught in the middle experience the greatest flooding.

In late 1940 and through the summer of 1941, three of the Peltier Brothers, Roy, Ronald, and Buck, built new houses about a mile and a half south of Austin Bayou. The purpose of the move was to be closer to their fields, but far enough away from the bayou so that their homes would be protected from floodwaters when the bayou rose. At the same time, another brother, Walter began building a new home totally away from the bayou in Danbury.

Wilburn made a deal with Walter to buy his older house, a real "fixer upper", near Austin Bayou. The house had cold running water to the kitchen sink but no permanent bathtub or indoor privy, only an outhouse about one hundred feet southwest of the house.

Construction began, with Wilburn ready and eager to fix up the house where he would live with his beloved bride. He knew the structure had been flooded several times, so after checking the elevations of the past flood waters, he calculated that the house would need to be raised at least twenty inches. At the time the crawl space beneath the house was only about eighteen inches.

There were 32 piers supporting the house, so he figured out a sequence to reduce the stress on the existing beams under the house as the house was being raised. With short pieces of leftover construction lumber, a twenty-ton hydraulic jack, and two eight inch concrete blocks for each pier, they started phase one, raising the house.

Barbara and Wilburn were excited about having their own house and they met after work as much as they could to work on the project. Wilburn did all the jacking and under house work, while Barbara moved the blocking around the perimeter and kept the water cold and flowing. They lifted the house at each pier one and a half inches at a time, then repeated the process until Wilburn could get one of the concrete blocks under each pier. After two weeks, they had two blocks under each pier and were at exactly the desired elevation on the southeast corner pier. Wilburn then made a "water level" out of a fifty-foot hose, with one foot of clear hose on each end. He attached the level mark on one end of the hose at the top of the pier on the southeast corner and shimmed the rest of the piers to match that elevation.

The next phase was building a six-foot wide porch along the west wall of the house to accommodate a bathroom, water heater, washing machine and some storage. The porch was one step down from the floor of the house. This plan was to create a mud room for cleaning up and depositing dirty clothes before entry into the rest of the house.

World War II Europe

Atlantic Wall Cannon

Downed German Aircraft

Wilburn wasted no time. He had a family to provide for and he hit the ground running. He needed a job, just like many hundreds of thousands of men separating from the military. He wanted to farm rice and raise cattle and be his own boss, but that would take capital they didn't have, so he decided to work on the fronts available.

Dow Chemical put him back to work. On his off time, he started looking for land to farm and for a used tractor and implements to prepare the land. By the end of 1945, things were coming together on the farming front. As a veteran, he took advantage of the government guarantee of small loans for farming. He found about 100 acres he could sharecrop and purchased an old Model L Case tractor with a plow, disc, and harrow. He planned to put in a rice crop in the spring of 1946.

He also happily found out that they were expecting another baby in July.

Wilburn and Barbara stayed very busy growing their family. Over time, they had twelve children, including Leo Patrick, who lived for only a week. Dad worked hard at farming and Mother contributed as the librarian for Danbury schools. After leaving the employment of Danbury Independent School District, she successfully ran and was elected to the school board. They continued to be hardworking and respected members of their community and church, as well. They survived droughts, hurricanes, failed crops, and other calamities.

Mom summed it all up very well when she said more than once, "When you get to the end of your rope, tie a knot and hang on."

4
"I'M IN THE ARMY NOW..."

The lights come on. I hear the crashing sounds of two metal trash can lids exploding in the dark, reveille playing in the background, then a loud bark, "Fall out in front of the barracks in ten minutes."

"Do what?" I ask myself.

"Where am I?" is my next question.

As I roll out of the top bunk, the cobwebs in my brain start to dissolve. It's 04:00 and my second day of basic training at Fort Polk, Louisiana. I look up and down this second floor; there are rows of bunk beds lining both walls, with about forty young men I don't know milling about. They seem to have the same glazed over look on their faces that I noticed on my own face in the mirror just moments ago.

"What am I doing here?" I whisper to myself.

It is of my own doing, I know. Just a few weeks ago I was still in high school. A few months before that, I had analyzed my life's situation, which needed a good dose of forward planning.

*   *   *   *   *

It was early 1967 and I was nearing the end of my senior year of high school. I knew that I had to try and figure out how I was going to spend the next few years of my life because if I didn't, it would be done for me in an order that I more than likely would not like. One thing was obvious: I was not a candidate for college. My SAT scores would get me in, but being one of twelve children living on a farm that barely fed the family, there was no money in the till for college. Anyway, I was tired of school in general, and I

47

probably ranked 11th or 12th in my class of sixteen. I was weary of the small town atmosphere that had shaped my life for the last eighteen years. I needed and wanted a change in my life.

It was a stormy time in America. The Vietnam War was in our living room every night, in living color, up close and personal. It seemed to have an insatiable appetite for the young men of the day. Men were burning their draft cards in protest of the war. Many went to Canada and elsewhere to avoid the draft. Women were burning their bras in protest of their unequal treatment as compared to men. The federal government mandated integration of schools in order to get certain required racial proportions, and a plan of bussing students to different schools was implemented, creating racial unrest. The mood of the country was starting to heat up; tensions were high on several fronts. There was change in the air and I knew that whatever plans I made, my life's path would be impacted by those winds of change blowing through the nation.

The main choice I had to make was how to address the issue of my military service. Every American male of service age had to make a decision to serve in some capacity, or not to serve at all. Cassius Clay, better known as Muhammad Ali, received his induction notice in April of 1967, the same month I did. He did not serve based on the precepts of his newfound Muslim religion.

Dad had entered Normandy on D-day plus a week; he served as a cook in the 93rd Medical Battalion. He had offered no advice in the matter, and I requested none. I had always felt a duty to my country. Maybe I had recited the "Pledge of Allegiance" so many times it was as much a part of me as an arm or a leg.

I didn't really relish the thought of going off to war, but I also knew that I wouldn't avoid serving.

As I evaluated my choices, I saw them as relatively simple. I could get a job and work until I was drafted into the military, which was inevitable. I could enlist in the Army for three years or the Marines, Navy, Air Force, or Coast Guard for four years and have some choice in my job description. I could volunteer to be drafted for a two-year hitch and take my chances on the type of duty I might draw. (At that point in time, draft numbers did not exist.)

My brother Louis had been drafted the prior September, had trained at Fort Hood, Texas, and Fort Ord, California, and was then serving at Fort Hood with an artillery battalion. Peter, my oldest brother, was then serving in the Naval Air National Guard in Dallas, Texas. They both seemed to have earliest memories it always seemed in need of a coat of paint. It was heated with three Dearborn space heaters and cooled with a box fan and two heavy black oscillating fans that were moved around as needed. There were only two doors inside the house, the bathroom door, which latched with a screen door latch on the inside, and Mom and Dad's bedroom door which had no lock and wouldn't close all the way because the house had settled. Of course, none of the entry doors to the house locked or even had locks on them. We weren't in a high crime area and there was nothing there worth stealing, unless slavery became legal.

What we called the back porch had been added by my parents in the early 1940's to modernize the house with indoor plumbing. It consisted of a six foot wide enclosed porch along the whole length of the west side of the house. Its main use was as a mudroom. If you were covered with mud or other farm generated materials, you were required to take your clothes off on the back porch and go straight to the bathroom and clean up. If you were not a good judge of how clean you were, Mom would let you know with a swift bop on the head to let you know that you didn't pass muster. The house might not have been much, but it was still her castle and tracking mud or other debris inside was highly frowned upon. The back porch also housed a large freezer, sometimes two, the washing machine, and later a gas dryer. The bathroom had not held up very well because of the high humidity. The fake tile surrounding the bathtub had mostly deteriorated and peeled off to the point that on a windy day a candle wouldn't stay lit on the inside. There was one bathroom to serve this herd, with the unwritten rule that the boys peed outside behind a tree.

The old unused outhouse was still standing in the weeds near the edge of the back yard. The vertical wooden planks that made up its outside walls looked like a couple of haggard old men standing in a storm holding up a piece of rusted tin to protect themselves from the rain. The planks were weathered so deep between the grain you could see light through the seams. We stayed clear of it because it was covered with dark gray clods of dirt which housed dirt daubers on the outside; yellow jackets had hung their white puffy nests on the inside. They were always looking for a target to buzz or sting.

Life on our farm was full of hard work, lively games, close quarters, cool spring rains, scorching summers, wet fall hurricanes, and freezing winters.

I was the fifth of the twelve children born to Wilburn and Barbara Peltier who populated this home. Sometimes I felt like a character in the nursery rhyme about the old woman who lived in a shoe. The pecking order of this herd in name and year born was Peter 1942, Kay 1943, Louis 1946, Kenneth 1947, John 1948, Becky 1950, Stephen 1952, Paul 1953, Leo 1955 (only with us for a week, but not forgotten), Arthur 1956, Richard 1957 and Molly 1960.

Home was out on the flat Texas Gulf Coast salt grass prairie where mosquitoes, rattlesnakes and cottonmouth water moccasins reign over the land. My family lived off this land raising rice, cattle and very large vegetable gardens.

Summer days were mostly dry, hot and humid and the winter seemed icy cold much of the time. Spring was the most beautiful of the seasons with endless sweet smells of wildflowers in every color of the rainbow and rainbows that showed up with the spring rains, dancing around in the sun from horizon to horizon. In the fall, hurricanes invaded from the Gulf of Mexico every few years, disrupting and threatening our livelihood and our very lives.

We knew summer was over in October or November when a mass of bruised, bluish and black clouds formed in the northern sky. A slow breeze started gaining speed and as the clouds came nearer they seemed to roll like a giant rolling pin low in the sky with streaks of brilliant silver lightening shooting through and all around. The temperature would plummet from the upper nineties to the mid sixties in just a few minutes. The ozone filled air smelled new and refreshing and energized us as the wind picked up speed. As it bore down on us, protected only by ragged cutoff old blue jeans, big fat drops of rains started pelting our bare bodies. It felt good at first, but soon we had to run to the cover of the front porch as this first "Blue Norther" of the season engulfed us.

We are so acclimatized today that we hardly notice these happenings. Back then, air conditioning existed only in a few stores and restaurants, but not in schools or many homes. We had no place to hide from the extreme changes that the seasons delivered to our doorstep, so we experienced them all.

Baby boomers were filling schools, Dwight Eisenhower was President, and the economy was booming as America delivered to the world goods and services to rebuild Europe and the Far East after World War ll.

John, Mom, Kenneth, Dad, Louis, Kay, Peter 1950

Mom, Stephen, Peter, Kenneth, Louis, Dad, Becky

Kay, John

c. 1953

I loved the peaches. Mom would halve them and can them in a light sugar syrup and/or make jam with them. We helped her, too. First we would blanch them so their skins would slide off effortlessly. We would then cut them in half to remove the pits. If they were going into jam, we diced them into small cubes. That was the start of the canning process and it continued on until the lids started to pop.

When Dad arrived home from those trips to Houston we generally attacked the car to see what he had brought home. We all shouted, "Did you rob the bakery?" That was code for, "Did you stop by the Mrs. Baird's Thrift Store?" Most of the time, budget permitting, he would go by there and get day old bread, raisin bread, cinnamon rolls, or whatever they had that sounded good at a bargain basement price.

The cinnamon rolls were our favorite delight. For breakfast we would heat up four or five packages, "butter them up good," and then see who could eat the most before they were gone. We always washed them down with cold milk.

As an added attraction, sometimes Dad would butter them up and sear them on the skillet like pancakes.

We always had one or two milk cows (depending on the number of young babies that were around) and that meant they had to be milked in the mornings before school and in the evenings, seven days a week. That also meant we had nurse cows to feed the milk cow's calf and her own.

We split up the chores around our various schedules. Occasionally, when everyone's schedule was messed up, we had to work out who had to do what. A pecking order, which was generally the oldest to youngest, developed. Occasionally that was not satisfactory and someone would try to prove his manhood by trying to bump the order. That generally didn't work out too well for anyone who tried.

We all did our share of milking the cows, feeding the hogs and nurse cow, and tending the chickens. Those were everyday chores.

Kenneth, Stephen, Billy Joe, Kay c. 1966
Arthur, Richard, John, Molly, Becky

Uncle Admore LeClair, Aunt Aldea

Paul, Mike, Molly Bob, Richard, Arthur

In the winter we also had to hay the cows. (A cow is a female that has had one or more calves. A heifer is a young female that has not had a calf).

In November we rounded up all the cattle that were pastured around the rice fields a couple of miles from the house "as the crow flies". That was usually right after the first frost that ended the forage growth. We saddled the horses, Paint and Tony, and drove the herd from those pastures to the pastures around the house for winter feeding. When the winter grasses started showing up in late February, we had a "cattle drive" back to the rice field pastures.

We "worked cows" every spring and fall. That included drenching for worms, administering various injections, castrating the bull calves, branding all the calves, and culling old and nonproductive cows. We sent the culls, along with the older steers over 500 pounds, to the sale barn. The income from the fall roundup provided us with shoes and clothes for school every year.

There were seasonal chores to be done, too. In the spring, when we were in high school, Dad would meet us at school at 2:30. We would skip out of the last hour, which was conveniently scheduled as PE, and go to the fields and drive tractors until dark. That worked fine until 1964 when Dad bought a new diesel Case 930 Comfort King tractor which had lights and power steering. Compared to the old LA Case tractors we also drove, the Comfort King was a Cadillac. Many a school night one of us drove until around ten o'clock.

Kids were in season most of the time, and more often than not there were two in diapers. I can vividly remember seeing many bright sunny days with two of the three clotheslines full of white diapers flapping in the wind. To bring them in, Mom would have us stretch out both our arms and load us with double armfuls as she unclipped them from the lines. We took them to her bedroom, flopped them on the bed and then folded and stacked them by the baby bed. Clothes washing and drying was a never ending chore at our house.

It wasn't all work and no play. Like our parents, we were mostly all "gamers". Each of us had a coffee can containing our pennies, nickels, dimes, and a few quarters. We played lots of moon dominoes and poker and kept the money circulating like a booming economy.

We were also encouraged to hunt and fish, which we all loved. The results of our efforts were always a welcome addition to the food on the table.

While not the setting of most normal families, a large farm family struggling to survive was not unusual for that time and place, and there was never a dull moment. All the people, conditions, and happenings combined to form the glue that held my family together through a lifelong journey of love, respect and support for each other. It was the glue that served us all well in the trials that we all eventually faced.

Growing up on a rice farm in Southeast Texas, the fifth of twelve children prepared me for what? In the midst of growing up, I thought, "Nothing". In my rearview mirror I think, "Everything". Everything came in increments, bite sized pieces I could understand and achieve .

The first chore I can remember was gathering eggs. When I was five years old, Dad took me out to the chicken coop and showed me how to carefully pick the eggs out of the nesting boxes and place them in a wire basket.

Dad explained, "As you go through the coop, do it quietly without exciting the hens."

Then I carried the eggs to the house, cleaned them and packed them into cartons. It was fun and I was glad to be part of supporting the family. We sold all the eggs we didn't use. It was like graduating from babyhood into boyhood.

Gathering eggs was a chore shared with my older brothers Louis and Kenneth, two and one year older than me, respectively. The chicken coop was a dark, dank place and reeked with the odor of chicken droppings. Picking eggs barefooted was done at your own peril.

Not too long after being assigned to the egg gathering team, I was in the coop one day making the morning round, picking eggs out of the nest. I grabbed for an egg and suddenly the box came alive with a six-foot chicken snake.

"AAHHHH!" I yelled as I bolted for the door.

The coop came alive with cackling hens, the yellow and brown snake slithered away, and I got into trouble for cracking a half a dozen eggs while making my escape.

Louis and Kenneth thought it was so funny they laughed until they cried.

Then they showed me the broken shovel handle hanging by the door. It was fashioned into a club made especially to discharge chicken snakes, rats, or anything else disturbing the hens.

Milking cows was a twice daily chore Louis, Kenneth, and I shared from twelve years old through high school. It was a plain and simple task that could be achieved in about twenty minutes.

Most the time the milk cow was waiting at the corral pen gate. She knew the routine. If we were not on time, we could call the cow up in just a few minutes. Then, we deposited a ration of food into the trough, sat down on a stool or bucket with the cow udder in front of us and cleaned the udder and teats as needed. If the teats were dry and flakey, we administered a little udder balm to heal and moisturize the skin. Talking and singing to the cow all the while kept her settled down. Then we leaned towards the cow, putting some pressure into her flank with our heads to reduce her ability to kick the bucket. We would hold the milk bucket between our knees, grab two teats, one in each hand, squeeze the teat first with a thumb and forefinger, then tighten up our next finger, then the next finger, until all our fingers had squeezed the teat. We pulled downward gently as we squeezed. Soon we developed a rhythm with each hand as the milk flowed into the bucket in a continuous stream.

Sometimes during the process the cow managed to kick her foot into the bucket. Then we had to decide what to do with the milk. If it was really bad, we had to throw it out. Most the time we just hoped the strainer would adequately clean it up. There were other times when the cow ate something bitter and the taste got into her milk. Generally we didn't find that out until we drank it.

Many times I had company while I milked. The dog and cats all liked a squirt or two. Louis told me one time a skunk walked by and wanted a squirt. The only problem was the dog in the vicinity, which excited the skunk, so it sprayed the dog and stunk up the area. I think the cats were the most fun to watch. They sat on their hind legs, trying to pull the milk into their mouths with their front paws, while licking up a storm.

We often had cousins or friends in on weekends who always thought it novel to watch the milking process. They didn't like it too much when I squirted them, but how could I not? It was just too tempting! I have to admit the milk was kind of nasty and sticky as it dried. I knew - I'd had the experience of being squirted many times.

After the milk quit flowing, we'd get up with the bucket in our hands to protect it. If we didn't, the cow would kick it or the dogs or cats would attack it.

The outside part of the work was done when the cow was let out into the pasture.

After bringing the pail of milk into the house, to insure the milk was free of any debris (mostly dirt, hair, dust, or chaff), we always strained it. We set up the strainer on the counter, secured a filter in its bottom, and poured the milk through the strainer into porcelain-coated pans about the size and shape of a shoe box. After filtering we would put the matching porcelain lid on the pan and slide it into the refrigerator. After we washed the bucket and the strainer, the chore was completed.

Even the feed bags served a purpose on our farm. When we bought feed for the milk cows and chickens, Mother told whoever was picking up the bags what print she wanted on the feed bags. The prints came in many colors and designs. A fifty pound bag measured 34 X 38 inches and a one hundred pound bag measured 39 X 46 inches in a heavy durable cotton material which was used to make some of our clothes.

If we were on the feed run, we would occasionally get to choose the bag design for our next set of shorts, shirts, or dresses, for the girls. Mom made mostly shorts for us boys with a strong elastic band at the waist and skirts for the girls with the same strong elastic band at the waist. She also made shirts, but they took more time and were harder to make. With the scraps she made kitchen hand towels, quilts and work cloths for the barns.

In the summers, shorts (also called "jams") would be all of us boys had on our bodies. The skin on our feet grew thick and callused from being bare footed all the time. Our hands also grew callused from all the shoveling, hoeing and other work we did year in and year out.

Gardening, to me, wasn't nearly as much fun as some of the other chores, but it was very necessary to our existence. I would guess that over half of what we ate came from the garden. All the shoveling, hoeing, and raking the dirt into hills, beds, and rows was hard work, but there was always something growing in the garden as a result. In the garden, everyone could contribute something. It didn't matter if you were five or twenty five.

Planting started in early spring. Then we fertilized, watered, and hoed between the rows to keep the weeds at bay. We fought birds, bugs, coons, and rabbits that were always trying to harvest the vegetables before we had a chance get the produce on the table or canned and on the shelves.

Spring was always a busy time of the year.

It was also baseball season, though Louis, Kenneth, and I never played organized baseball. Most of the other kids collected baseball cards and knew all the major league standouts. (Throughout my life the only time I really wanted to see a baseball game was when one of my kids was playing.)

There were tractors, combines, trailers, cars, and endless other things that were continuously breaking down. Many times we used whatever was available to keep things going. I remember Dad telling us more than once, "If men made something, it was likely that we can take it apart and fix it."

Our parents were always reminding us that we could achieve anything if we applied ourselves, with the help of God and much hope and a prayer.

Over the decades there were many opportunities to learn, provided by hay fields, rice fields, gardens, varmints, cattle, pigs, hurricanes, freezes, droughts, cars, tractors, combines, and on and on. Our fragile lives, too, were always in need of repair. All we needed was the right sized hammer and copious quantities of baling wire and bubble gum.

*   *   *   *   *

Note: Earlier I mentioned that I had never smoked before. That wasn't exactly the truth. One time Larry Springfield, a couple of years older than me, decided to show Michael, Ronnie, and me how to smoke cigarettes. Larry lived in Shadow Bend, a small development on Austin Bayou a quarter of a mile down the road from us, with mostly weekend homes built on poles to avoid flooding.

Larry took us out into the woods, gave each of us a cigarette and then lit one for himself. He first demonstrated how to take a small puff and suck it into our lungs. Then he lit up our cigarettes and watched as we did what he had done. After a lot of hacking and coughing, we got the process down. Then he gave us another one and told us to smoke the whole thing.

After smoking that day, at first I didn't feel anything but a little green around the gills, but the next thing I did was started puking. I didn't stop until long after I had nothing left.

I have not smoked another cigarette since then. Thank you, Larry.

*   *   *   *   *

Life on the farm seems quite foreign to this new lifestyle as a private in the Army. I long to go back there, but I know I have a few hills to climb before that can happen.

5

G.I. JOHN

This is the beginning of an era in my life that seems to have turned into a series of never-ending lines. Coming from an environment where a line of ten is considered a long one, I am now in an arena where the typical line could be a hundred people long. I am amazed at the speed and efficiency with which these lines move.

As we stand in the various lines, no talking is allowed. With the exception of short smoke breaks and off-time in the barracks, there is no speaking unless we are spoken to. We are assigned to training companies with names like Alpha, Bravo, Charlie, Delta or Echo.

I'm in Charlie Company, generally referred to as "C" Company. We are assigned to barracks that are the remnants of 1940's WW II training facilities. The two-story wood frame buildings on concrete blocks house a platoon of about forty men on each floor. Bunk beds stick out like fingers down the walls, each with a footlocker at the end of the bunk and another against the wall between bunks. The shower-latrine area, built on a concrete slab, is situated on one end of the first floor. The Army must have found a great bargain on beige paint because almost every building on the base is painted that same color.

The line is long, but I finally enter the main door of another long building in need of some of that beige paint. "Quarter Master" is written on the sign in front of the building. As I enter the building, the first thing I am handed is paperwork. I fill out my name, rank, serial number and the date; the rest is a checklist of all the gear I am to be issued. The line inside is nearly as long as the one outside. There are dozens of men behind a counter nearly as long as the building.

The first station is socks. "What size?" yells the clerk.

"Twelve," I reply. He throws six pairs of green wool socks, size 10-13, at me and I check them off. The next station is underwear. He just looks at me and slides out six white boxer shorts and six white tee shirts. The process continues through boots, belt, OD (olive drab) fatigue pants, OD blouses, OD cap, all class A dress attire, and a duffle bag to put it all in, until we are completely outfitted with everything we need to survive basic training.

By that time, I also have a new and complete understanding of why we are commonly referred to as "GI's" – every single thing I will wear or touch now is "Government Issue."

I thought that in our willingness to serve the needs of the country this gear would be a gift, but no, the cost comes out of our first month's pay of $95.70.
After all the clothing costs are deducted, there is barely enough left to pay attention.

Returning to the barracks with our newfound treasures, we are assigned bunks and footlockers. We are instructed by Sergeant Mitchell on how place all the gear into these footlockers according to regulation. Next we take off all our civilian clothes ("civvies"), put them in our civilian bags, and are shown how to properly wear our new clothes. After we are instructed to leave the bags with our civvies on our footlockers, we are marched over to the barbershop.

In 1967 long hair on young men is coming into style. The standard at my home demanded my hair be cut short, but some of the new recruits have shiny manes that hang down well below their shoulders. I am in line beside one of the longer haired guys. Gazing up and down the line, I see long hair, short hair, Afros, and everything in between, in all the colors of the rainbow and a few colors that I don't recognize. I can also see the exit door of the barbershop. Without exception, the haircut of every single guy as he makes his exit is the same, an eighth of an inch long all over, tapered at the edges.

As I enter the building, I observe ten barber chairs. I take a seat in a barber chair as I am directed. I overhear the barber at the next chair asking my longhaired neighbor, "Would you like to keep your hair?"

With a glimmer of hope on his face, the guy answers, "Yes!"

The barber smiles and says, "OK, hold out your hand."

The process is short and sweet. Each haircut takes less than a minute. There is only one style and all the electric trimmers have the same very short attachment. There are two full time recruits constantly sweeping up the floors.

I wonder if they have a market for all that hair and if they are going to deduct the cost of the haircut from my pay.

Upon our return from the barbershop, we discover that our civvies have disappeared. Sergeant Mitchell explains to us that we won't be needing them until we have completed basic training and that they will be returned to us after graduation. We all know the real reason is to keep us from going AWOL (absent without leave). The Military Police (MP's) are constantly on the lookout for skinhead recruits anywhere they're not supposed to be.

We are all quickly made to look and feel as if we have no past or future; there is only the here and now. It's the first time for most of us to be away from home, and after a few days with Sergeant Mitchell, everyone is getting pretty homesick.

Our days in basic training start at 04:00; I am thankful the clashing of trashcan lids has been eliminated from our wake-up call and that now it's just the bugle and blinking lights. Nevertheless, I still don't think it would be a good idea to ignore the call.

The first thing we do is make our bunks, then we shave and fall out in front of the barracks into squads and platoons till the company is formed for inspection. After everyone is present and accounted for, we're off for a one-mile run before breakfast.

We are always getting inspected. Anytime Sgt. Mitchell thinks someone is getting lax, everyone gets a surprise inspection. If your area, including inside your footlocker, isn't up to snuff, you get demerits, extra duty, extra PT or some other special assignment. Soon we figure out that if we keep our areas in tip-top shape our lives will be a little more bearable. At least once a day we are lined up shoulder to shoulder in the company compound and have to police the compound for every visible piece of trash from cigarette butts to toothpicks. Order and cleanliness are always expected.

Before each meal, we have to complete a short obstacle course, consisting of running through tires, jumping a ditch, and negotiating a seven and a half foot high horizontal ladder by "walking" with our hands.

The chow line is one line that I don't mind waiting in. There is always plenty of food. It isn't the same as Mom's, but I don't find it so bad. Uncle Sam wants us to get eight hours of sleep most nights, so it's "lights out" at 20:00.

There is fire watch each night that requires four recruits in each barrack. When you draw fire watch you're on one hour and off two, so the next day you're usually "dragin' wagon". One night, in the second week, the firewatchers discovered two recruits being overly friendly in the showers. We never saw those guys again.

The days are filled with calisthenics, training, and marching, interspersed with classes and testing on various military codes and procedures. Anytime we move around the company compound out of formation, it's at double time. In the beginning, we constantly work on close order drills, learning first to always start marching with our left foot. Soon we are responding to commands as Sgt. Mitchell barks them out, "dress right dress", "left face", "right face", "about face", "right shoulder, arms", "present arms", "order arms", "parade rest", "to the rear, march", "at ease", "eyes right", and my favorite "fall out".

We march everywhere, singing cadence songs like:

"Around her neck she wore a yellow ribbon,
She wore it in December and in the month of May,
And when you asked her why the hell she wore it,
She wore it for her lover, who was far, far away,
Far away, far away,
Oh, she wore it for her lover who was far, far away.
Oh, she wore it for her lover who was far, far away".

There are numerous other tunes and melodies we sing to keep in step. As the time passes many new verses are added reflecting the happenings of the day. Many of these verses have much to do with the mysterious "Jodie". He is the guy back home who is trying to take over the affections of your wife or girlfriend. "Dear John" letters are common, but not for me as I left home very unattached.

In my big "bullish" plan for the rest of my life, I don't consider all the ramifications as they affect my "hummingbird ass," my description of total unpreparedness. A small detail like "summer"? Who in their right mind would devise a plan that included completing basic training in the military in June, July, and August?

It is hot as hell in these piney woods of Louisiana. The temperatures we train in hit the century mark almost every day. These hot days are not strangers to me, growing up on the banks of Austin Bayou with no air conditioning offering relief from the heat and humidity. However, the smell of the pines is new and refreshing to me. I may be better prepared for this heat than most of the troops, but that doesn't make it any less hot.

A few weeks into basic training I am ordered to report to the company commander. I enter his office, stand at attention in front of his desk, salute, and announce as previously instructed, "Private Peltier reporting as ordered, sir!"

Captain Baker looks up, returns my salute and says, "At ease, Private Peltier. Your scores on the testing you took qualify you to attend Officers Candidate School (OCS). Is that a track that would interest you?"

"I haven't thought about it. Can you tell me what would be required of me if I went in that direction, sir?"

"It's a three month program. You would have to finish basic training and then you go right into OCS with the temporary rank of Sergeant E-5 during training. Upon successful completion of the course, you would receive the commission of Second Lieutenant and be required to serve two years active duty from that time."

"How much time do I have to think about it, sir?"

"I have to turn in my recommendations by the end of the week."

"Thank you, sir. Is that all?"

"Yes, you are dismissed."

I salute, do an about face, and exit the room.

I give OCS a lot of thought over the next few days and talk it over with my brothers Louis and Peter, who both have had service experience. It would add a year to my service, which I don't like, but it could be a great leadership development tool that I think might help me in the future. After making inquiries I find out that many OCS graduates, also known as ninety-day wonders and "butter bars" (because their insignia was one bronze bar) get duty as squad leaders in infantry platoons. That doesn't sound good to me at all, being that the Vietnam conflict has been steadily escalating. I also talk to several other men in my company to whom the offer had been made. It is an attractive option that many accept, but I tell Captain Baker that I must respectfully decline the OCS offer.

This is my first time to be on fire watch. I have the fourth shift, which means my first watch is from 23:00 to midnight. Even though lights go off at 20:00 when fire watch begins, there are still small groups of guys talking throughout the building until 21:00 or 22:00, depending on how physical the day has been. Soon all there is to hear is heavy breathing and a few snores emanating from the bunks. Also it's barely dark outside at 20:00, but it's still hot as hell.

Knowing I have guard duty, I lay down as soon as the lights flick off. The sheets stick to my damp skin and I close my eyes, lie as still as I can and wait for sleep to wash over my body like the tide. Within a minute of 23:00, I feel a hand tug on my foot. On one of the first nights at basic, a guard shook the relief's shoulder to wake him and took a fist upside his head as the relief's first reaction. Since then it's been keep your distance and shake a foot of the guy relieving you.

I roll out of my bunk, quickly dress, and relieve the guard on his next round.

No one likes guard duty, but I find it refreshing to have a little quiet time alone to think. I understand why fire watch is important. If one of these old wood frame buildings ever caught fire, they would go up like a box of matches. The fire watch guard's routine is to walk through the building, looking at each bunk as he passes making sure it is occupied, and if it's not, to find out where the recruit is or report him missing to the sergeant of the guard in the orderly room. No one is supposed to smoke inside the barracks so we are also on the lookout for that. A round through both floors and the latrine takes just a few minutes and gets very monotonous. Nearing the end of my first hour I am feeling tired and weary. I grab my relief's foot, make sure he's getting up, make a final round, and seconds later I'm asleep in my bunk.

No longer than a few minutes seems to have passed and I'm startled out of bed again with a yank on my right foot. It's 03:00, and I have the final shift for the night. It's 04:00. When I hear the bugle sounding reveille, I will flip the lights off and on several times, and then leave them on as the barracks groan to life. I think back over the years on the farm. Most days we were up before dawn while it was still and black as pitch outside. Somehow this reminded me of the mischief that used to go on in our own bunk house.

*　　*　　*　　*　　*

I remember that once Louis and Kenneth were at an "away" basketball game on a fall Friday night. I was fast asleep in the Little House when they came in. I guess they saw me peacefully sawing logs and their mischievous minds felt I needed to be disturbed. Knowing that we were planning to go duck hunting the next morning, they stripped to their underwear and started putting their clothes back on. Kenneth shook me until I was awake and said,

73

"John, it's time to get up and go hunting."

Groggily I got up and started getting dressed, looking forward to the hunt. Then Louis said, "Mom said be sure and get her up and she'll fix us some bacon and eggs before we leave".

I hadn't noticed how slow they were putting on their hunting clothes and headed into the main house. I turned the light on in the kitchen, stuck my head into Mom and Dad's bedroom and said, "Mom, it's time to get up."

Mom ambled out into the kitchen, looked at the clock, then at me, and said, "Are you crazy? It's one in the morning!"

I looked at the clock and I knew that I had been had. After apologizing to Mom for the prank my stupid brothers had pulled, I headed back out to the Little House. Louis and Kenneth were howling with laughter as I opened the door. There was no sense in creating a ruckus that night. They had successfully pulled a good one on me. I would just have to bide my time for a payback.

* * * * *

I chuckle to myself as I make another round and my mind goes back to an even earlier time.

* * * * *

Shortly after Peter, Louis, Kenneth and I moved into the Little House, Peter had a date with Pat Cleaver. She was the prettiest girl in the junior class; Peter was a senior and thrilled to take her out. When he arrived home after the "hot date", he was beside himself; he must have gotten his first kiss. He was also locked out; the screen door latch could not be unhooked from the outside.

Kenneth and Louis were fast asleep in their double bed and I was asleep alone in the other double bed. Peter tried knocking on the door, but we were dead to the world and it was going to take a lot more than a tap on the door to wake us. The moon was full and shining brightly. It was almost like daylight outside; the air was a little heavy with fog near the ground, and

Peter had a plan to get inside.

He found an old rubber boot and filled it with water from a mud puddle on the ground. He gently slid the window open over Kenneth and Louis's bed and dumped the boot of water right on top of them. A great commotion erupted immediately. Kenneth was trying to beat the hell out of Louis because he thought Louis had just peed on him in the bed. Louis was busy just trying to hold him off while he was trying to figure out what was going on, and I was just dazed, bewildered and clueless.

Then we heard laughing outside the window, and Peter, who could barely utter a word because he was laughing so hard, said, "Open the door so I can go to bed".

I let Peter in. He hopped into the dry bed with me, and Louis and Kenneth dried off as best they could and went back to bed. Kenneth was happy just knowing that nobody had peed on him.

For a time after that we watched each other very close to make sure one of us didn't decide to retaliate and start a water war.

*   *   *   *   *

I am jolted back into today with the sound of reveille. I hurry to the light switch, flip it a few times and holler, "Roll out!"

The barracks immediately come alive with activity that reminds me of a freshly kicked fire ant hill.

*   *   *   *   *

Growing up on a farm, I had the opportunity to participate in many cattle drives and roundups. After we got the cattle rounded up in the corral, we branded, castrated, vaccinated, dehorned, and drenched them.

Generally we used our own horses to move the cattle between pastures. The distances could be as short as through a gate into an adjacent pasture, or as long as a five mile cattle drive over the salt grass prairie or down a county road.

Once I got to see a man on a horse with two dogs round up a herd of cattle and put them in the corral single-handedly.

The particular incident occurred on a hot and humid day in mid-July, one of those dog days of summer. The mosquitoes were so thick I had to breathe through my nose to filter the air. Our neighbor Galin Flora showed up in a beat-up old Ford truck with two dogs in the bed and a horse already saddled up in the trailer he was pulling. As he was unloading and bridling his horse, my brother Louis and I walked over and asked what we could do to help.

He said, "Stay in the truck and out of the way."

He mounted the bay mare; his dogs, a black and white male and an ugly brown/gray bitch, sped out beside him as he headed towards the far end of the 50 acre pasture. I was in awe as I watched the performance from the comfort of my front row seat.

Cattle don't generally like to follow instructions, especially if they've been on the open prairie for a while without contact with people or horses. The heat, flies, and mosquitoes had the herd more on edge than normal. Galen made a wide circle around the herd, motioning and talking to the dogs. The dogs were well trained to follow the almost indiscernible gestures he made from his perch on the back of his horse as he approached the herd.

One of the lead cows that tried to break out from the herd got the first lesson. With no more than a nod from Galin, the male dog immediately went into attack mode and encouraged the animal to return to the herd. The dog's methods were simple, fear and intimidation. He accomplished that by getting between the cow and open pasture, then barking and biting the cow's nose, neck, or whatever was handy, all the while staying clear of its horns and hooves. After the cow had enough of that torment, she returned to the herd, her left ear gashed and bleeding. That black and white dog looked like an acrobat as he flew through the air, firmly attached to her ear.

The bitch used equally persuasive tactics. After a few of the lead cows made unsuccessful attempts to break out, a cluster of cows started to form. Soon the herd was in a compact knot. Not one of those cows wanted to take one step away from the safety of the herd. Those dogs had earned the respect of the cows, or perhaps the cows were just plain terrorized. Nevertheless, the whole herd became very attentive to the mongrels' every move.

When the wrangler had the herd formed to a manageable size, he worked them right through the corral gate and into captivity.

I believe if Galin had wanted those cows to move through the gate on their hind legs dancing the Texas Two-Step while mooing "Dixie" they would have tried to oblige.

The U.S. Army must have had some general who was familiar with that process. Instead of dogs to instruct us, they used well-trained drill sergeants.

*   *   *   *   *

Our memorable first drill sergeant, whose last name is Mitchell, gives us our initial indoctrination quickly and to the point when he barks, "Since your mother, father, wife, or girlfriend is not here, I will be taking their place."

Pointing at a man in the front line, Sgt. Mitchell asks, "Where are you from, boy?"

The new recruit answers, "California, sir."

In a tirade, Sgt. Mitchell says, "I understand there's nothing in California but steers and queers, and I don't see no horns on you!"

Then he went on to add, "I am not a 'sir'". I work for a living. You may address me as 'Sergeant' or 'Drill Sergeant'". (Enlisted men are referred to according to rank; and officers are "sir's".)

Because of the draft, which crossed all socioeconomic lines, the U.S. Army is the new melting pot of America. Basic training is even more so because the participants consist of a mix of draftees, regular Army, National Guard, and Army Reserve.

We call the National Guard and Army Reserve recruits "weekend warriors". Most of these units are not taking new recruits; their ranks are full because of the high probability they will not serve in Vietnam. Senator Hubert Humphrey's nephew is in our company training for the Guard. He is a likable, overweight guy and wants to get his weight under control during basic training.

Basic training is mentally and physically draining, but I am surprised at how quickly this strenuous routine becomes somewhat bearable. We are not taught to think about what or why we do what we do. We are taught to react quickly and precisely to many different commands. The days are long and hot. The barracks are open, impersonal and offer no privacy; this reminds me of my own up-bringing.

*   *   *   *   *

There were many large families of over ten children where I grew up in the rural Gulf Coast of Texas, and it was very normal for them to be packed into their homes like sardines in a tin. Of course there were also those who were born into smaller families of only two or three children. I would hear from them about being punished by being sent to their rooms to "think about what they had done" or them running to their rooms and slamming the door to avoid a brother, sister, parent or whomever. There were no mind games like that at my house; justice was quick and painful. After a good cry we had to just shake it off and get on to the next event.

Over the years, I've given some thought to these circumstances as they pertain to doors (or the lack thereof). Doors offer protection from the harsh elements that Mother Nature continually throws at us; they keep the heat, cold, and dampness in, or out, as the situation dictates. But they also offer us an easy separation from others with whom we may have unresolved issues.

I can speak on this lack of doors with some authority. Being from a large family of eleven children plus friends, my sister Becky says she always set the table for seventeen when we were in high school. There was only one operational door inside the house, that one being to the bathroom. Without doors to separate me from my older brothers, the settlement phase of problem resolution was generally sharp and to the point. I learned this early on and would generally give my older brothers, who were larger, stronger and more experienced, a wide berth. My younger brothers and sisters had to pay more attention to my wants and needs. Darwin's theory on the survival of the fittest came into play in determining the pecking order around our house.

On any big issue, anything illegal or immoral, Mom or Dad would take control and dictate a resolution. They must have grown weary of feeling like referees at a basketball game, having to resolve a problem every time someone yelled foul. They would tell us to work our problems out amongst ourselves, and we did. Things like sitting in the living room- if I wanted to retain the place or chair where I was sitting and if I had to leave the room, I had to announce before leaving, "My place when I get back". When we were going places in the car and I wanted to sit by the front door passenger side, I had to be the first to yell, "shotgun!" (Generally that was the prime spot in the car, unless we were going through several fence gaps because that position also had to open and close all the gates.)

An occasional bloody nose gave us a healthy respect for one another. Any fights we had were out of the sight of Mom and Dad. If we were to get caught fighting, we'd receive a harsher punishment from one of them after the fight. We learned that it was easier to give each other a little space and get along, than to crash into each other at every exchange and cause misery and discomfort for everyone.

*　　*　　*　　*　　*

From almost the first day of basic training Ronnie Kemp, from New York City, is jawing at me constantly with disparaging comments about my rural upbringing, my size, and anything else that might come into his mind. Have you ever walked into a room and took an immediate dislike to someone before they've even uttered a word? I'm sure that's exactly the way Kemp feels about me. Sitting around the barracks in the evening, we wind down and get to know each other. I am an oversized kid, 6' 4" tall, about 220 pounds and fresh off the farm. Kemp is about 5' 10", 160 pounds and considers me a dumb country bumpkin who deserves to be treated like a doormat. He is right about the country bumpkin part but wrong about the dumb and the doormat part.

I've never been a runner and those mile runs each morning are tough on me. During a run that first week Kemp yells at me as he breezes by, "Peltier, you run like a cow."

"How would you know? Have you ever seen one?" I answer, heaving out the words between breaths.

Later in the mess hall, Kemp takes a plate, waves it at me, and says, "Do you know what this for, or do you eat at the trough with the rest of the pigs?"

I ignore him, but I am getting fed up with being the butt of his comments. At the first opportunity I take Kemp aside and ask him, "What am I doing to piss you off?"

With a blank look on his face, he looks at me and says, "breathing", as he turns and walks off.

I am at a loss. I have never had a problem getting along with anyone. There were people in my life I didn't care for, but the answer had always been give them a wide berth, be civil, coexist, and it usually worked out just fine. There is no avoiding Kemp. He is an "in your face" kind of guy and he is relentless in his pursuit.

He is walking up the stairs to the second floor behind me. Passing me up, he gives me a little shove and says, "Get out of my way!"

Off balance, I grab the line of buttons on the front of his blouse, turning him around, pushing him down backwards against the risers, landing hard on top of him, and pinning him to the stairs. It all happens in a split second and looks like it has been choreographed. He has a surprised look on his face as I lean down with my face inches from his and spit out, "I've had enough of your shit. Lay off."

Kemp doesn't say a word, but the look in his eyes tells me he understands. We never become friends, but the harassment ends then and there.

After mulling over the unexpected incident, it reminds me of throwing a calf. I had thrown them hundreds of times growing up on the farm.

*   *   *   *   *

As the training continues, we are issued M-14 rifles. Again we have another serial number to memorize. The first time someone calls the rifle a gun, the drill sergeant explodes with a premeditated tirade. He grabs the rifle, gets everyone's attention, and sings out, "This is my weapon (signifying the M-14) and this is my gun (grabbing his crotch). This is for fighting (M-14) and this is for fun (crotch)."

So our indoctrination to the M-14 rifle has begun.

Growing up, I did a lot of hunting, mostly duck, goose, and rabbit, so I have a good basic understanding of rifles and safety. I am astounded at the lack of knowledge or even common sense that many of these men have as they deal with these weapons, things like pointing a rifle towards another person and treating it like a toy.

Soon we discover that Sgt. Mitchell has zero tolerance for any mishandling of our rifles, either actual or imagined. Early in the training Private Birdwell drops his rifle; I think Sgt. Mitchell knew this was going to happen to one of us sooner or later and when it does, he is all over Birdwell like a chicken on a June bug.

"Birdwell!" Sgt. Mitchell barks.

Birdwell, scrambling to retrieve his rifle, says, "Yes, drill sergeant!"

"Is this how you take care of your girlfriend?"

"No, drill sergeant!"

"I want you to think about her and run circles around the platoon carrying your rifle over your head as we march back to the compound. Can you do that?"

"Yes, drill sergeant!"

"And Birdwell, I want you to sing out loud and clear over and over as you run, 'I'm a shit bird.'"

"Yes, drill sergeant."

As we are marching with Birdwell carrying his rifle over his head constantly declaring, "I'm a shit bird. I'm a shit bird", no one is laughing. After about fifteen minutes, the man is totally spent and the rest of us are extra careful with our weapons from that point on.

We learn every part of our weapon: its name, what it is for and how it works. Then we learn how to clean it, disassemble it, and put it back together again. Then we learn to disassemble it and put it back together blindfolded.

That evening as I lay in my bunk, I looked over toward Birdwell two bunks away. His bad luck reminds me of another incident with the mishandling of a shotgun from my not so distant youth.

* * * * *

It was a fall morning in 1962. Gary Raney, Louis, Kenneth and I were in the Little House.

Gary, who was a senior in high school, had been staying with us during the school year for the past two years. Elizabeth Raney, Gary's mother ("Aunt Elizabeth" to us) and my mother had been best of friends and roommates at Texas Women's University during the late 1930's. The Raney's lived in the city of Bellaire, a suburb of the big city of Houston. Gary had been going to Bellaire High School, but he didn't like it. Gary wanted to go to a small school, so Aunt Elizabeth and Mom made it happen. He stayed with us in the Little House.

Louis and Gary had just returned from duck hunting and the shotguns were standing by the door inside the Little House. (Note a House Rule: all weapons inside the house were to be unloaded.)

Louis had Dad's Browning automatic and Gary had a classic L. C. Smith double barrel. Kenneth was reading a Superman comic book and snoozing on his bed. I had just come in from doing chores and was trying figure out what Gary and Louis were talking about. Louis was aggravating and teasing Gary about some girl Gary was trying to date. Louis hit a raw nerve with Gary and all hell broke loose. Louis bolted out the door as Gary grabbed his shotgun and chased after him yelling, "I'm going to shoot your ass off".

Kenneth and I, not knowing exactly what was going on or why, ran outside and followed the excitement. Louis made a big circle around the yard and was headed back towards the Little House. Gary was right behind him with the double barrel in his right hand; and Kenneth and I were trailing up the rear. Louis took the three steps of the concrete porch in a single bound with Gary on his heels. Louis pushed open the door and slammed it behind him in one smooth stroke. The slamming door hit the end of the shotgun barrel in Gary's hand. The unloaded gun turned out to be loaded!

The impact of the door on the gun barrel either caused Gary to pull the trigger or released the internal hammer accidentally. Regardless, the hammer hit the firing pin, which then hit the primer of the shot shell. The explosion that ensued created a deafening blast, leaving the acrid smell of burning gun-powder permeating the air. The edge of the door and the adjacent frame exploded as the magnum load of number 6 shot splintered through the air looking for a target. Gary was paralyzed with fear, not knowing what might be on the other side of that door. Kenneth and I were both surprised and stunned by the blast.

To our great relief, the next thing we saw was a white tee shirt tied to the end of a broomstick slowly protruding out of the door and a small voice from the inside meekly saying, "Okay, I give up". Louis pulled open the door and peeked outside.

The energy of the chase was instantly deflated at the sound of the blast. The events following seemed to be in slow motion. We were all dazed by the episode; there was a quiet air of stillness. We all sat down on the concrete steps with looks of relief on our faces and for a long time no one spoke a word, even though a crowd of younger siblings started buzzing around us, asking what had just happened.

The slamming door had diverted most of the force away from Louis, but he was picking splinters out of the back of his left arm for the next few days. It was a good thing Kenneth and I had joined in the chase; the walls on over half the inside were peppered with pock-marks on about six inch centers where the shot had penetrated.

We prepared ourselves for an ass chewing of cataclysmic proportions from Dad, but it never happened. It was evident that he wasn't happy about the incident. He put the shotguns up and we had to miss a few duck hunts. He gave us a stern talk on how guns and "grab-assing" around were a dangerous mix. I suspect he figured the episode itself was the biggest teacher of all.

*　　*　　*　　*　　*

I close my eyes to get some sleep, and I see Birdwell's lanky frame running circles around the platoon with his arms fully extended above his head grasping his M-14. His flushed red face is emitting a breathless chant as I fall asleep hearing, "I'm a shit bird. I'm a shit bird."

I actually enjoy target practice at the rifle range and bayonet training with pugil sticks. I cannot throw a hand grenade far enough. The back blast sprays the area above me with shrapnel. After several attempts, I am banned. I blame baseball for that. Baseball season and planting season happened at the same time each year. I was never able to play.

There are three levels of expertise in the accuracy of shooting at basic: marksman, the lowest, sharpshooter, next, and expert, the highest. In order to graduate from basic, we are required to score marksman or better. The targets are silhouettes of the human upper torso. Each firing position is about ten yards wide and three hundred and fifty yards long. The targets pop up at random, and we are graded on the number of hits we get out of a twenty round clip. On the day of qualification, I am disappointed in my sharpshooter pin.

There is no certification with pugil sticks, but I wish there were. A pugil stick is a wooden dowel, six feet long and an inch and a half in diameter, with canvas covered pads six inches in diameter on each end. The purpose of this training is so that if we ever hear that dreaded command "fix bayonets", we will have greater proficiency in their use. Two combatants with football helmets on their heads hop up onto a ten-foot long log and swat, poke, and pound on each other till one falls off the log. Being six feet four inches tall, two hundred twenty pounds, with thirty-six inch long arms and a decent sense of balance gives me a distinct advantage. We learn with the log on flat ground. Next we practice on a log that is perched over a mud hole. I never get muddy.

We train for gas warfare, too. No one likes the training for gas warfare. We have a couple of hours of classroom instruction on the different gases, and then we get a taste of practical experience. We are assembled in our squads and practice putting on our gas masks and making sure the seal is good against the skin on our faces. We look like giant insects with the masks on. After several dry runs, we don our masks and are marched into a small block building filled with CS gas (tear gas). Once in and seated on a bench, we are ordered to remove our masks. Without the mask, the gas instantly attacks my eyes, nose, and face with a vengeance. Shouts of pain fill the room, and our eyes are like waterfalls. Several of the men bolt through the door, but we are ordered to stay seated. The ten or fifteen seconds feel like an eternity, until we are told to put our masks back on and blow into them to clear the gas. The pain melts away almost as fast as it came. The men who bolted from the room get to do it again and also get KP (kitchen police) duty this weekend.

Payday is the last day of each month. It's another line I don't mind. We line up in front of the orderly room in alphabetical order. The Executive Officer and the First Sergeant are seated at a table. We are called up, given a slip of paper with our pay and deductions shown. If we agree with the amount, we sign the slip and are paid in cash and given a copy for our records. For me the crap game in the corner of the latrine that night is just a spectator sport.

After six weeks, if we don't have too many demerits, we get passes to go into town. It's Saturday afternoon.

I unfold my "class A" uniform that's neatly stacked in the bottom of my footlocker and along with the thousands of other privates that I have been penned up with prepare for a night on the town. This is a welcome break after having spent more evenings with Brasso, polishing buckles and buttons, and Shinola, spit polishing combat boots than most people do in a normal lifetime. We catch the bus to Leesville, Louisiana.

In town, there are rows of bars, shops, massage parlors and many other places just waiting to separate me from what few dollars I have. This grungy dirty place is all new to me. I have never been in a bar before. The legal drinking age in Texas is 21, but in Louisiana it's 18. I am still developing a taste for beer; what little I've tried was with a bunch of guys around a campfire on the banks of Austin Bayou.

Between the cigar that I smoke and the many cans of 3.2% beer I consume, my body is starting to reject my earlier idea of good time. As the night wears on, the music is blaring in this "Go-Go" bar. Scantily clad girls dance in elevated cages, and you'd think there must be a fire in the room, the smoke is so thick. I'm feeling more and more less good, as I head outside for some air. After I puke behind a bush in the alley, I see a few skirmishes between drunken recruits. The MP's are quick to put a lid on things and deliver them to the stockade. I take the next bus back to the base and sleep it off. I have a better understanding of why Leesville is nicknamed "Diseaseville". I vow I shall never return there.

I lied earlier. I have been in a bar before.

*   *   *   *   *

My brothers, Louis, Kenneth, Peter and I had been rabbit hunting on a Saturday night when I was twelve or so. Being the youngest, I was mostly along for the ride. The ride was in a black '53 Plymouth sedan. We were hunting in the new right of way of State Highway 2004 which when completed would connect Hitchcock to Brazosport. Peter was driving and carrying his chrome plated Colt Huntsman pistol. Louis and Kenneth shared the family's Remington automatic; both guns were 22 caliber. My job was to watch, open and close gates, and keep quiet. The area delivered plenty of rabbits as we drove down the right of way shining a spotlight, surveying the area from right to left. Once spotted, the rabbit would freeze as we quickly dispatched it with one or both guns. Peter spotted one that Kenneth was about to bag when Louis whispered, "Don't shoot!"

"Why not?" Kenneth breathed.

"Because I want to try and sneak up behind it and save a bullet."

Louis quietly eased out the window of the car and started making a wide circle around the rabbit. I was surprised at the amount of time that passed while the rabbit stayed frozen in place. Louis was stealthily coming up behind the rabbit. The closer he got, I just knew the rabbit was going to bolt. Suddenly in the blink of an eye, Louis quickly kicked the rabbit in the back of his head and broke its neck. For a moment I couldn't believe what I had just seen. We scrambled out of the car with much admiration and celebrated with the jubilant hunter.

Then we killed a nice bunch of swamp rabbits, more than we wanted to eat. We knew that if we took them home we knew we would have to eat them all.

Momma typically fried the rabbits. Then she made a large skillet of gravy and simmered the rabbit in the gravy until the meat was falling off the bone. While the rabbits were simmering, she would make plenty of biscuits or rice to go with the rabbits and gravy. We loved that meal, but we could kill rabbits almost anytime and that night Peter had an idea.

He told us that he had heard we could take the rabbits to a bar in Angleton and sell them for fifty cents apiece. We had a dozen rabbits, so that was six dollars. It sounded like a fortune to me, especially for killing rabbits, because we hunted them for fun anyway. So off we went to a place that I was pretty sure was off limits for us.

The target bar Peter located for us was on the "other side of the tracks" (colored town) in near an ice house that stayed open all night. I was elected to carry a rabbit inside and do the selling. Looking back, I'm sure my brothers knew better and that I was just plain stupid.

The bar was dimly lit, mostly by neon beer signs adorning the walls, with a bright down light over the tattered pool table. Smoke was thick as fog and it smelled of yesterday's stale beer. I wandered from table to table announcing, "Rabbits, fifty cents." A few black faces looked my way, but mostly I was ignored. I just couldn't compete with the sounds of Motown that blared from the jukebox. A couple in the corner was slow dancing to the fast music.

As I was nearing the pool table, an older man sitting at a table against the wall nursing a longneck and a cigarette waved me over. "My first sale!" I excitedly thought to myself.

I stopped in front of his table. He leaned over close to my face and said, "Son you ain't going to sell no rabbits in here. You ought to git on about your business somewheres else."

I was speechless. I nodded to indicate I understood. I turned and surveyed the bar one last time as I made my exit. The air outside was a lot better than it was inside.

As my head cleared, I realized how dumb a stunt I had just pulled. I threw the rabbit into the trunk and told the story to my brothers. They had a good laugh and we went home and cleaned the rabbits. The rabbits tasted really good the next morning with Mom's biscuits and gravy.

*   *   *   *   *

I wake up Sunday morning with a pounding head and I think, "Moderation is a virtue I need to learn."

Recycle is a dreaded word. All during basic training Sgt. Mitchell hangs the thought of it over us continually. If at any time during training you fail to achieve a minimum score or goal in a required task, you must start basic training from day one with a new training company. This threat is a big motivator to satisfactorily complete all the benchmark goals because with the passing of each week the training is more bearable and you are treated more and more as if you are actually human.

There are a few medical discharges for mental or physical problems that show up in training and several dishonorable discharges for those who are totally unable or unwilling to conform to the military, but nobody wants a double dose of basic training. This motivator keeps our boots spit shined, our aims straight, our obstacle course times short and our close order drills tight.

The last week of training includes overnight field exercises to test the skills we are now supposed to know. We eat "C" rations, patrol through mock up Vietnamese villages, crawl under barb wire in trenches with live fire being shot over our heads, and go through a large obstacle course that pushes our physical stamina to the limit. The grand finale is a five-mile forced march back to the barracks. I wave goodbye to the rest of my platoon from the back of a deuce and a half as they are forming up to leave on the march. I have been scheduled for KP duty and am transported back to base on a supply truck. I'm really going to miss that five-mile forced march.

All the new recruits get to experience KP duty about once a week during basic training. The cooks don't do the menial work. The lowly privates get to cut and slice vegetables, crack eggs and clean giant pots and pans coated with baked on grease and gunk. There is a small reward. We get to eat a little better if we do a good job and the cooks approve.

Our next duty station is "Advanced Individual Training" (AIT); almost everyone who enlists knows what his Military Occupation Specialty (MOS) is and where he will get that training. For the large portion of us who are draftees, our duty is assigned to us for the convenience of the service. A large percent of draftees are assigned to the Military Occupation Specialty of "Infantry", coded11B20 (eleven bravo) training. This Military Occupation Specialty designation extends your stay at Fort Polk in an area designated as "Tigerland". This training is a continuation of close combat skills and introduces the use of many small arms not covered in basic training.

I imagine myself with an M-60 machine gun strapped to me because I'm one of the biggest guys around. Few people actually sign up for eleven bravo. There are many MOS designations; they're necessary to keep the Army on the move. There must be cooks, mechanics, communications, medics, artillery, and many more.

All of us draftees are anxious for our orders in this last week of basic as they will tell us what kind of work we will be doing for the rest of our service. The combat units are supported by all of these Military Occupation Specialties. For example, there is a medic and an RTO (Radio Telephone Operator) assigned to each platoon. But most of us don't look forward to continuing training as eleven bravos (also referred to as "ground-pounders" or "grunts") because they take the brunt of the front line combat. The Army keeps reminding us that we are all infantry soldiers first and foremost, no matter what specialty training we receive.

When orders are posted, I am elated. I am going back to Texas. My orders are 91A10 Medical Corpsman, Fort Sam Houston, San Antonio, Texas. Several of us have been assigned to that duty, including Clarence Sasser, one of the guys I was inducted with in Houston. I wonder if not being able to hurl a hand grenade further than its blast area has anything to do with my corpsman assignment. I guess I will never know the answer to that question.

The only thing I know for sure is that I'm going to corpsman school because that's where I'm ordered to go and I'm very happy about it.

Finally, graduation day from basic training arrives. There is much pomp and ceremony; the brass bands are playing loudly and all the troops are spit-shined and polished in our dress uniforms. The parents of many of the graduates show up as spectators. It's rice harvest time and I know my folks will not be in attendance. We, along with several other graduating companies, march around the parade field performing various close order drills. As we march before the shaded reviewing stand in the hot August sun, we hear "Eyes right!" shouted out by Sgt. Mitchell. All heads react in unison and turn forty-five degrees to the right. On the stand are all the top brass who review the results of eight weeks of training that began with a bunch of individuals unable to walk and chew gum at the same time and ended with units of men who look and feel like part of a well greased machine.

After the final review, the companies are marched to their designated positions facing the reviewing stand. We assume the position of "parade rest" as ordered. The Commanding General congratulates us for the successful completion of basic training. After this short speech (surely he doesn't want any of us to pass out in front of him from the heat), we are dismissed. We all throw our headgear high into the air in celebration with lots of whooping and hollering.

I say my goodbye's to a bunch of good guys I may never see again. I know many of us will end up in Vietnam, but with around a half a million servicemen over there, the chances of our paths crossing are slim. I load up on the bus marked Fort Sam Houston and stow my duffle and my bag of civvies in the belly of the bus. I shed no tears as the bus pulls out of Fort Polk's main gate. As the air conditioned bus travels through the monotonous pine trees of East Texas, I relax and snooze. I feel pretty good about successfully completing the first leg of my time in the military. I think of my dad in another place and time.

*   *   *   *   *

He walked ahead of me following a rice field levee shouldering a round point shovel. His stride was long and deliberate; his torso, like a brick, went straight up from his hips, a little over six feet tall with a big barrel chest and as strong as an ox. He wore the same thing every day - blue denim pants, long sleeved blue poplin shirt and a wide brimmed straw hat with the front pulled down slightly. The straw hat was stained and dirty where its crown met the brim from many long hot days of exposure. Carrying a tow sack full of more tow sacks and a jug of water, my ten year old legs had to churn to keep up with his pace. It was a hot day in May and Dad and I were flushing water through a freshly planted rice field.

We came to a break in the levee and stopped to dam it up and install a small spillway. If we just dammed up the break, it would likely break again because of the pressure on the levee at that point. The addition of a spillway relieved the pressure on the whole system.

I pulled out a sack from the bag and held it up with the top open. Dad started filling it with a mixture of watery clay and mud. After filling that one and one more, Dad pulled them into place in the break. My job was to walk and stomp the top of the sacks to compact them securely in place while Dad built up the ends and water side with more dirt. Soon water was spilling over the sacks.

When we were finished, he pulled off his straw hat, revealing his tightly cropped thick dark hair with a little gray starting to invade around the edges. Mopping the sweat off his face with a faded red bandana, he sat down on the levee for a break while I puddle-ducked around in the shallow water of the bar-ditch. Cooled down, I got up and headed his way. His face and neck were leathery and weathered, but his blue eyes softened his handsome, rugged look. I sat down beside him. He offered me a drink of water from a brown glass Clorox jug that Mom had sown several layers of cotton feed sack material on to keep it cool and protected. He didn't make much small talk with us kids. He told us what to do. If we didn't get it right, he would tell us again in stronger terms.

As we sat there resting, I would get an occasional whiff of his body odor, acrid and strong but not particularly unpleasant. After he got up he turned and offered me his hand, I grabbed hold. As he pulled, I felt his power flow through my body. His rough and calloused hand reminded me of the harsh life he had endured, from the dust storms of drought stricken Kansas wheat fields and Great Depression of the 1930's, through the invasion of Normandy on D-Day plus a week with an Army medical battalion, collecting the dead and the wounded that were scattered in its wake.

We continued to walk the levy; I glimpsed a water moccasin darting away from us in the bar-ditch. Before I could utter a sound, the shovel on Dad's shoulder went from zero to a guillotined projectile in one smooth motion. The headless four foot snake lay coiling and swirling around the shovel handle. I stayed clear while Dad buried the snake's head and threw its body out into the field. This was a reminder that a snake ceases to be dangerous when its head is separated from its body and is buried.

As the orange sun lay low in the western sky, we arrived at the car. There we met up with my older brothers, Louis and Kenneth, who had walked other levees. Soon we were homeward bound.

When we arrived home, Kenneth milked the cow, Louis fed the pigs and I took care of the nurse cow and calves. Stephen and Paul had already gathered the eggs and fed the chickens. Soon we were all settled around the dining room table and Dad led us in a prayer of thanksgiving and praise to our Lord Jesus. We were as happy and contented in this warm and joy filled place as anybody could possibly be.

*   *   *   *   *

When we arrive at Fort Sam Houston, it's late afternoon. We are assigned billets that have only two people per room. I've never experienced this much privacy in my whole life.

6

COMBAT MEDICAL TRAINING

It's mid August of 1967 and San Antonio is scorching hot. We arrive at Fort Sam Houston Saturday afternoon and settle into the our assigned barracks. The accommodations are great. I share an air conditioned room with one other person and we share a bath with another room. The feel of Fort Sam is more relaxed and more like a school than at Fort Polk with its seemingly nonstop harassment. Maybe it's because upon graduation from Basic Training everyone earned a step up in rank to Private E-2. With that goes a small boost in pay from $95.70 per month to $106.20 a month. Now we are senior to all those recruits going through basic training back at Fort Polk, but still the lowest ranking GI's at this new post.

The prayer below is stapled to the bulletin board by the main door of our barracks:

The Combat Medic Prayer

Oh, Lord, I ask for the divine strength to meet the demands of my profession. Help me to be the finest medic, both technically and tactically. If I am called to the battlefield, give me the courage to conserve our fighting forces by providing medical care to all who are in need. If I am called to a mission of peace, give me the strength to lead by caring for those who need my assistance. Finally, Lord, help me to take care of my own spiritual, physical and emotional needs. Teach me to trust in your presence and never-failing love. Amen.

Every Sunday of my life I attended Mass, until I entered the Army. I could have gone during basic but opted to spend that time in a bunk. I decide to attend Mass in the morning.

Church services for the different denominations are held in the same facility at different times. The schedules allow for Catholic Mass at 08:00 and a Protestant service at 09:30. The Mass is the same as it was during the many years that I was an altar boy at St. Anthony's in Danbury. The attendance is very light and without my family and friends around, and kids climbing over, under and around the pews, the service just doesn't seem the same. I just don't feel the same connection to God that I feel in my home church.

The corpsman's course is another eight weeks. The time spent at Fort Sam is more like a job. We get to sleep in until 0600 here. We do physical training (PT) for an hour, eat breakfast, and go to classes in one hour blocks, but we are still in the Army and have time scheduled for a little marching and drilling each day to keep us tuned up.

We still sing cadence songs as we march and continue to add new verses. Rob, a guy from California, plays his guitar in a break area in front of the barracks many evenings. His melodies draw us in like bees to honey. We listen, sing and laugh at his tunes. His latest song, about a Thanksgiving dinner at home that he is imagining, starts out:

"Momma bought a chicken
And she thought it was a duck.
She put it on the table with its legs sticking up.
Sister comes in with a spoon and a glass
And started dipping gravy from its big fat ass."

Soon we forget about the Army and we are singing, roaring with laughter, and truly enjoying ourselves.

The classes include everything from basic anatomy and physiology to emergency life saving techniques and basic nursing procedures. By the end of the eight-week course we have enough basic knowledge to work as an orderly in a hospital or be called "Doc" in a combat unit.

Most of my weekends are free. On Friday I get a weekend pass. I don my dress uniform, grab my small overnight bag and head to eastbound

Interstate 10. Less than ten minutes after I stick my thumb in the air, I am heading toward Houston. Ray, the eighteen-wheeler driver tells me, "I'm turning south at Columbus. Does that help you?"

"I'm heading to Houston, then Danbury. That will get me about a third of the way", I say as I hop up into the cab of his truck.

Ray is an older man. I can tell he's been driving a long time. He looks like a statue behind the wheel. We talk about the war. He really doesn't like the idea of sending troops so far away to fight. I tell him, from the view in my catbird seat, I don't like it either. Before I know it, it's dark outside and he's pulling over to let me out.

It's about 21:00, and I've been waiting about twenty minutes. There are not a lot of cars out tonight, but finally a man pulls over. He is heading to Houston, so I load up. It's a quiet ride. A little before 23:00, he drops me at Ella Boulevard and 610 North. My brother Peter's father-in-law, Joe Hyams, lives a mile from here so I head that way. I knock on their son Mike's window, not wanting to wake up the whole house. That doesn't work too well though. I scare the hell out of Mike and he wakes up the whole house. They make me feel at home, and I'm soon settled in on the couch.

After I'm fed a big breakfast on Saturday morning, Joe takes me to work with him to his boat shop near downtown. I find hitchhiking in the city doesn't work as well as on the interstate. After walking with my thumb out for an hour, I see a taxi and wave him down. "How far will $9.00 get me towards Telephone Road?" I ask.

He tells me, "I'll take you there for that."

Heading across town, I can only think of how important my family and that little town of Danbury are in my life.

The idea of a safe place, with warm, loving, caring people never really occurred to me until now. I've always thought that life is the same everywhere and never really factored family and relationships into the mix of things. I am starting to understand that being cut off from all the things I've become so familiar with over the last eighteen years has been the source of my homesickness.

Now, after being away for three months, I'm getting a "wake-up" call on reality, that being that I'm going to have to adapt to the outside world because it surely isn't going to adapt to me.

I look up as the cabbie is pulling off the road with the meter on nine dollars. I give him a ten-dollar bill and tell him to keep the change. Riding my thumb to Danbury from here is easy. Telephone Road and State Highway 35 are the same. Danbury is just two miles off State Highway 35 and I'm only 45 miles away. It takes two rides to get there. The last one is with a farmer from Alvin, Texas; he knows my dad and takes me directly home.

It's Saturday about noon. Our rice is already harvested, but farm work never ends. I give Mom and my sister Becky a warm bear hug and head to the barn. Dad and my younger brothers, Stephen and Paul, are cleaning and servicing the combine for off-season storage. Soon I'm alongside them helping out. I'm actually enjoying the work I complained about having to do last year.

We head over to a nearby field where my cousins, known as the Peltier Sons, are harvesting their second crop. If rice is planted and harvested early, many farmers irrigate and fertilize the field so that it will produce another crop of rice. The yield is only thirty to fifty percent of the first crop, but the farmers save the cost of working the soil. Watching the combines harvesting and the auger wagons being pulled by the tractors ferrying the rice to the waiting haul trucks is a pleasing sight. After a little small talk about when I might expect my General's stars, we head home for my first home cooked meal in three months.

The smell of chicken frying as I walk in the back door is a welcome and sure sign I'm home. Soon I am sitting around our large Formica topped table with an additional homemade wood leaf in the middle to give it an extra fourteen inches in length. Dad is seated at the far end, Mom is at the end nearest the kitchen, and seven of us clamor for spots in between. When the whole family is home we have to overflow to another table. Rice and gravy, green beans, corn on the cob, and a salad fill the table, along with the chicken. Everything but the chicken is raised right here on the farm. This place has no air conditioning, only one bathroom, and when a strong north wind blows, you can't keep a candle lit in the house. But this looks like my home, feels like my home, smells like my home, and with the constant ruckus among the boys, sounds like my home.

Today there is no other place that I would rather be.

It's Saturday night and I head to Vrazel's Ballroom, all decked out in my dress uniform.

The main building used to serve as the First Baptist Church in Danbury. When First Baptist built a new building, Donat Vrazel bought the original building and moved it out to his farm. There it was remodeled into a Germanic dance hall, complete with beer, barbeque, and live bands featuring mostly polkas and waltzes. Some of the First Baptist congregation weren't too thrilled by the idea of their old church building being converted to a dance hall, but it was soon so popular that Donat added an annex next to the main building to accommodate the crowds. The annex was outfitted with a giant hardwood dance floor, encircled with rows of tables and chairs and a stage for the band.

People come from many towns and farms, near and far, to enjoy the entertainment. The place is always filled with several generations of families and could truthfully be billed to have entertainment for everyone from eight to eighty. I hear the lively sounds of a polka: "Oohm, pa pa, oohm pa pa, oohm pa pa" and my old friends welcome me and buy me a few beers, since I am only eighteen and can't buy my own.

Here I can ask a girl to dance, or I can wait for the band to play the "Paul Jones". The Paul Jones is a long polka that is interrupted by a whistle blow every few minutes. Starting off, the men form a circle on the outside of the women, and the women form a circle on the inside. Both circles move in opposite directions. At the first whistle, everyone grabs a partner from the other circle. At the next whistle, dance partners separate and start reforming the circles. The whistle blows again and everyone grabs a new partner and continues the dance. The dance may last for fifteen or twenty minutes and ten partner changes. Most of the time the second whistle blows as the circle is still forming.

Since I have been out of town for a while and have had a few beers, I decide to join in on the next Paul Jones. I spy a cute young lady that I don't recognize and start angling in her direction. The whistle blows and I'm immediately grabbed up and dancing with someone's grandmother, who is about as wide as she is tall. I feel like I'm driving a truck on a crowded freeway as I maneuver across the dance floor. (I should mention that my truck has power steering, as she is a much better dancer than me.) The whistle blows, I thank her for the dance and start forming up to find my next partner. I hear the whistle and target the same young lady. About the time I get there, she's taken by someone who might be the husband of the grandmother I just danced with, so I connect with Leslie, a girl I know from school.

"How are you liking the Army?" she asks.

"It's not what I really want to be doing, but I need to do it," I reply, as I enjoy just talking to a young person of the opposite sex for a brief time.

The whistle blows again. By the end of the Paul Jones I feel that there's been a conspiracy to keep me, the Big Bad Wolf, from meeting Little Red Riding Hood.

I sit down and have another beer with some friends and we talk about the war and my chances of going to Vietnam. I look out over the dance floor and see grandpa's dancing with granddaughters, children dancing with children, and couples of all ages dancing together. What I don't see is that cute young lady. It's just as well. It doesn't make much sense for me to try and start a relationship with a woman at this juncture in my life.

Sunday morning I get up and go to Mass with my family. I'm happy to be in the comfort of all the people of the congregation, but I don't feel the presence of God that I used to.

I get one more home cooked meal and catch the two o'clock bus from Angleton to San Antonio. I don't want to take a chance on hitchhiking back; the Army doesn't take kindly to soldiers being AWOL.

After the weekend at home, I feel energized and ready for the week of training. The classroom lecture and study time just kills me. It's not that I'm not interested; it's just that I can hardly keep my eyes open. It seems that every time I'm in a class or church when I'm not actively involved, I nod out.

(When I was in high school, Mr. McMillan, my high school algebra teacher, was always getting on to me about sleeping in his class. I was sleeping so soundly once that he took an eraser from the chalkboard, walked over to me and powdered my face with it. I woke up and smelled the chalk dust, but I didn't realize what had happened. After class as I was walking down the hall, my cousin Bobby Anne asked me if I thought I should wash the chalk dust off my face.)

One of the things we have to learn to do in corpsman training is to give injections. We have some classroom study on sterile procedures, the difference between intramuscular and subcutaneous and everything else we need to know in order to administer vaccinations and antibiotics, draw blood and so on. I've been giving shots to cows and horses for years, but this is the first time I have ever recieved any formal training. That reminds me of a time that I wished I'd had better instruction.

*   *   *   *   *

Right after school let out in 1960 a storm blew through the farm with lots of rain, thunder and lightning. Sparkle, Louis's year old filly, was spooked by the storm. She bolted into a barbed wire fence gate and got tangled in the wire. The more she struggled, the worse her injuries became. By the time Louis found her, she had worn the flesh off her left front leg to the point that the bare bone was exposed. He tried to settle her down as he cut the wire away. The veterinarian told him to "put her down", but Louis would have none of that. He worked with that horse every day, changing bandages, irrigating and debriding (removing dead tissue) the wound and administering an injection of ten cc's of penicillin intramuscularly every other day. She was recovering but had lost a lot of flexibility in her left leg.

One day Sparkle needed an injection when I was the only one around to give her the shot. She was becoming more and more wary of needles and was getting very tired of being poked and handled. Typically when administering the shot, we would come alongside her, talking low and gently, give her a pat on the butt, stab her deep into the muscle, and quickly push in the serum. Then it was over. But she was getting more nervous and anxious each day we handled her and that day she wouldn't let me close to her.

I had her head tied close to a post, and as I laid my hand on her neck, talking to her as I worked to the rear, she started kicking and stomping and snorting. I just couldn't get into position without getting kicked into next week. I decided to retreat and figure out another way to skin that cat. I knew the frontal attack wasn't going to work, so that left the rear. At twelve years old I didn't know just how bad that idea was. I let Sparkle settle down for five or ten minutes, then started sneaking up directly behind her very quietly so she couldn't see me or hear me. I thought I could give her the shot so quickly she wouldn't know what hit her and it would be done. Not all animals are dumb, just as all young boys can't be accused of being very smart. When I got within three feet of her, all I saw was her jolt, then a flash of white light inside my head as I went down.

The next thing I remember was laying on a gurney in the Angleton Community Hospital Emergency Room.

The doctor had just sewn a dozen stitches into my face and was explaining to Mother how lucky I was.

 "Another inch to the left and the blow might have shoved his nose into his brain," he told her.

That happened late in the week. The next week was the start of CCD (Catholic Christian Doctrine) classes. I looked terrible; the right side of my face was black and blue and swollen up like a volleyball. By Sunday I was feeling better but still looked pretty bad. My right eye was just a narrow slit to see thru.

 I was going stir crazy so I decided to walk out to the barn to see if Sparkle wanted to be forgiven. On the way back I walked by the old abandoned out house in the back corner of the yard and disturbed a nest of yellow jacket wasps. I was stung below my left eye. Soon my head looked like it should be attached to a very fat Chinese guy. Both my eyes were like thin slits that I had to see out of.

Monday was the first day of CCD. I could hardly stand to stay around the house another minute. I begged Mother to let me go. My face may have looked like it might make a freight train take a dirt road, but I was really feeling pretty good. She let me go with the understanding I would take it easy.

Well, I did, until recess. I had a box of Red Hots and had just popped a handful of them into my mouth. Ronnie, my best friend, and I were playing. I remember he was chasing me. I turned my head to look over my shoulder to see if he was catching up. He was, and as I turned to look back I saw a telephone pole about a foot from my face. There was that dreaded but familiar white flash in my head again. It was a glancing blow, but I knew I wasn't badly hurt.

The thought of the Red Hots melting in my mouth and oozing out like red sticky blood struck me as funny. As I drifted down to the ground in what seemed like slow motion I started laughing. Looking up, I saw a dozen concerned faces peering down at me as the Red Hot ooze that was drooling out of both corners of my mouth added a ghastly look to my already swollen and bruised face. They mistook my laughing for crying, but soon figured out I wasn't dead or dying.

I was given a good scolding by the nuns for scaring everyone half to death. I'm sure Catine, Ronnie's mother, told Mom. She must have decided I had been through enough because she didn't say anything to me about the incident. Maybe she got a chuckle out of it, too.

*   *   *   *   *

As I prepare to give my first Army injection, I carefully snap the plastic protector off the end of the hypodermic, pull the plunger back, insert the needle into the vial of serum, push the plunger forward and load the vial with air, creating pressure. Then I turn the vial upside down, placing the end of the needle in the bottom of the liquid as I draw the serum into the syringe by drawing the plunger back. At first, the plunger comes back on its own, due to the pressure inside the vial. If it weren't pressured up, it would be very hard to retrieve the serum. The more serum I remove, the more vacuum I work against. Taking a firm but gentle grip on my target with my left hand I grasp the syringe in my right like I would throw a dart. Aiming carefully I thrust the needle in to its full depth, aspirate by slightly drawing back on the plunger to make sure I am not in a blood vessel. Then I push the plunger forward ejecting the serum into the target.

The exercise is a success. The orange doesn't flinch, bleed or howl.

For our next exercise the class members practice on each other. Then we spend a half-day giving vaccinations to a large group of Vietnam bound soldiers. No one told them they were guinea pigs for a group of trainees that day.

One of the nurses shows me how to hold three syringes between my thumb and fore-finger and do three injections at once. I am a quick learner so giving shots and drawing blood becomes easy.

As we are winding up our corpsman training, we go out to Camp Bullock, which is on the outskirts of San Antonio, for maneuvers.

We are divided into groups. Some groups are designated as wounded from a firefight and other groups are assigned as medics tending the wounded. The tag on my shirt says, "Sucking chest wound", which requires immediate evacuation. I have to be loaded into a helicopter for transport. Our wounded group is laid out over a field with many different types of wounds. Soon we are receiving treatment for our wounds and being appropriately evacuated from the field. I am given first aid and a large compress is placed over my chest. Then, very gently, I am lifted and moved to a stretcher.

As we approach the Huey 14, I note that the bottom two spots on the chopper are already occupied. The third and top spot is going to be mine.

Because I am one of the biggest men in the platoon, it's a struggle for the four men carrying me to secure my stretcher in place. I'm thinking, "These guys have got to lift me into the most awkward spot on the chopper. I could get killed before the chopper gets off the ground."

I really want to offer to get off while they secure it in place and climb back in later, but that's not an option. The stretcher is strapped in place without incident, but the patients aren't. I've never liked heights and this is going to my first helicopter ride.

I'm thinking, "I need a couple more straps on me."

As soon as the medic on the chopper indicates to the pilot that we are secure, we lift off with a blast from the rotary wings. The pilot pours the coals to it, and we are moving up and out at a very fast pace as I feel my body being pushed hard into the stretcher. Both the side doors are open and the wind from the down-blast and the noise from the engine fill the air. Suddenly we go into a deep banking turn. My head is pointing towards the ground and the soles of my boots are shading my face. Both hands have a death grip on the side rails of the stretcher as terror takes over my brain and body and a new phrase enters my mind: "butt suction". I know the pilot must be having a lot of fun, but I'm not. We are up in the air for less than five minutes before we land and are unloaded. (This is, I'm sure, part of the reason I am still a "white-knuckled flier".) As I get up off the stretcher I feel an adrenaline rush just by having my feet on solid ground.

Next, it's my group's turn to be the medics and the other group to be the wounded, and I like that a lot better.

When we return to Fort Sam we find that the orders for our next duty station are posted in the orderly room. The National Guardsmen and Army Reservists go back to their hometowns. A few Regular Army men draw stateside duty for more training. I'm in the group with the majority of men. We are authorized a 30 day leave and are to report to Oakland, California, for transportation to Vietnam. We are all prepared for this; it has become evident the war is heating up and the peace talks don't seem to be going anywhere.

The graduation exercise is similar to graduating from basic training. Mom and Dad came up for the ceremony. I say goodbye to my buddies, not knowing if I'll meet up with them later or not. So far, this Army life is filled with meeting a lot of guys, bonding with a few, then reassignment and not knowing if I will ever see them again. Many of us exchange pictures for mementos of our time together. Clarence Sasser gives me a picture of him in uniform signed "See you in Vietnam."

We are all happy for a break from Army life. In addition we are promoted to Private First Class (E-3), which gives us a mosquito wing stripe on our sleeves.

Clarence and I didn't see each other in Vietnam, but in February of 1968 he was busy being the hero. He pulled several wounded soldiers to safety during a firefight. He was later awarded the Congressional Medal of Honor for his bravery. (The Congressional Medal of Honor is the most prestigious award the military offers.) Years later I had lunch with him. He was still the humble, good natured friend I remembered.

He told me, "I was just doing what I was trained to do. A metal was the last thing I was thinking about."

The ride home from San Antonio was long and quiet. Mom finally broke the silence.

"All the family is going to get together for a welcome home dinner tomorrow. What would you like me to fix?" she asked.

She really did know the way to a man's heart, and I answered, "Meatloaf, green beans, rice and do you have any dewberries left in the freezer?"

"I think so," she replied, "but I'll have to get some vanilla ice cream to go with the cobbler."

"That sounds good to me, too!" Dad chimed in.

Just the thought of a berry cobbler sent my mind back to all those times we went berry picking when we were kids.

*   *   *   *   *

A dewberry is a wild, sweet tasting, purple berry that grows in a low bramble. Its vines are reddish in color and totally covered with sharp thorns. The best place to find a dewberry patch that produces the best berries is along waterways with full sun exposure. For us that meant along a bayou, a stream bed, or the banks of a rice canal beyond the shade of branches. They grow low to the ground, unless there's a fence, brush or other type of structure for them to climb, which takes much of the bending over out of the picking.

Dewberries are in season for only couple of weeks in the spring of the year.

In those days of spring we always paid close attention to the white flowering blooms on the berry vines that were plentiful in the region of Southeast Texas where we lived. The green berries formed. When the berries turned red, then it was only a matter of days before they turned deep purple to almost black. When they were ready, there was an undeclared competition amongst us kids to see who would bring home enough berries to make the first cobbler of the year.

The whole family was involved in the harvest. Dad went by the school cafeteria and picked up about a dozen empty cans that had contained fruits and vegetables. They held a little less than a gallon. He drilled two small holes opposite each other through the tin near the top and then tied a bail on them with baling wire. Presto, we all had berry picking buckets.

We went out in groups, with Michael and David from next door or by ourselves. That was one chore that didn't feel like a chore; everyone was a winner. We girded up in blue jeans, boots, hats, and long sleeve shirts. We carried a stick and a bucket in one hand and picked with the other. We carried the stick to push the vines around so we could get to the berries with minimum exposure to the thorns. In a good spot we could get on our knees and pick with both hands. We never wore gloves because we had to feel the fruit to pick it, so our fingers and hands always were scratched up and purple with berry juice during the picking season. Our mouths and lips also always turned purple because of the berry juice.

When you had a berry in your hand that was plump and a little overripe, it was like a "test berry" and went straight to your mouth where it fell apart and exploded into your sensory glands and tasted like you needed to find another one just like it.

After we came home Mom would cut up lemons and squeeze the juice over our hands to release the purple stains.

Served raw on cereal or ice cream or in salads, the full ripe black ones were the best. If we were cooking them for pies, cobblers, jellies, jams or sauces, then we needed ten to fifteen percent dark red ones to give a little tartness to the mixture.

Once Louis, Kenneth, Michael and I were picking berries by the bayou after school. We were spread out over a fifty foot area along the bank hunched over, pushing vines around and picking in a nice patch of berries. We talked a little but mostly picked berries.

All of the sudden Michael hollered and bolted out of the patch as if he had been shot from a cannon. The rest of us dropped our buckets and ran over to him.

"S,s,s.... SNAKE!!" Mike exclaimed, pointing toward where he was picking. (Michael stuttered, especially when he was excited.)

"Did it bite you?" Louis asked excitedly.

"N,n,no! I saw its head and thought it was a berry, then it moved and it was the head of a cottonmouth water moccasin!"

"Michael, I've never seen you move so fast. You disappeared from that spot like a puff of smoke," I said. (Michael was quick and wiry and loved the outdoors.)

As soon as we knew he was all right, we all were laughing about it.

"That just goes to show that we're not the only species that likes to eat dewberries. I just saw some raccoon scat on the trail and it looked like 100% dewberry seeds," Kenneth said.

"And all the birds around here eat them, too," Louis added.

We finished topping off our buckets and went home with a prize that turned into a cobbler.

At the peak of the season Dad would gather up all the able bodied pickers, five years old and up. Even if you weren't a big producer, I believe he thought that you had to get out there at some point and get some experience. Dad always had several "honey holes" he had located while working in the fields.

On a warm Saturday in the spring of 1959, eight of us kids, Paul, Stephen, Becky, me, Kenneth, Louis, Kay, Peter, and Dad started loading up our old Plymouth cars for the trek. We took several big pots and the three gallon stainless steel milk buckets, plus all the berry buckets Dad had made up, plus a couple of one gallon water bottles. Peter and Dad drove us to the rice fields and we stopped by the main canal that provided water for the rice.

"Take all the containers and the water down to that willow tree on the side of the canal bank," Dad said, pointing at a tree a couple of hundred yards away.

We toted all the buckets, pots and water, while Dad took a pair of loppers and cut each of us a straight willow branch about thirty inches long. We laid all the containers and water in what little shade the willow had to offer.

The canal bank was about five feet high and as we went from the top of the bank to the bottom, we could suddenly see why we were there. The berries were three deep and as thick as the mosquitoes, which looked to be about the size of a thumb. The patch was bracketed by a cow trail on top of the canal bank and another cow trail at the bottom of the bank. In between, it looked like an artist's canvas painted with lush green vines underpinned with a sea of black dots and a sprinkling of red dots so thick that you couldn't touch just one.

Kay said, "I have never seen a berry patch as thick as this in my life!"

"Y'all be on the lookout for water moccasins. They are thick as thieves along the canal," Dad said as we started into the patch.

We spread out about five feet apart and started filling our buckets. When we picked out our areas, we leap-frogged in front of the line and kept picking. When our buckets were full, we went back and dumped them in one of the pots.

There were a few snakes spotted in the canal, but as a general rule when there were this many people in a small area, the wildlife evacuated the premises.

Dad had us organized into one big picking machine. It wasn't as fun as going out after school by ourselves where we experienced the joy of picking at our own pace, but there we were much more productive and experienced the *job* of picking. That was one job we really didn't mind.

After a couple of hours, all of the pots and buckets were full and we had about picked out that honey hole. In a few days the next batch of berries would be ready at this same area, but the best picking was the first picking.

We headed back to the house to process the berries. After the berries were rinsed and cleared of any loose debris that may have gone into the buckets during the picking, some went into quart freezer containers for cobblers between seasons. A few were set in the refrigerator for cereal or snacks, but most were cooked down and made into jelly.

After ten more days or so, the berries dried up and disappeared, but we still got to enjoy the remnants of them for the rest of the year from the jars and the freezer.

*   *   *   *   *

Thirty days off. I have never had a vacation in my life. As a family, we went to Huntsville State Park when I was in junior high for a weekend. There is really no place I want to go except home, so I go back and help out around the farm. There's always plenty to do there.

Football season is in full swing at Danbury High School and there is a pep rally on Friday, the last class period of the day. I head up to school a little early to walk the halls before the pep rally begins. Less than six months ago as a senior here, this was a big part of my life. Now as I move through these familiar surroundings and talk to some of the senior students and the teachers who molded this mind of mush, the realization comes to me that something in these hallways has changed, and I'm sure it was me. The thought gives me a chill. All of a sudden I want to leave. I know I don't belong here. My time here is over. That door of my life closed and can't be re-entered. I watch the pep rally as a spectator and enjoy it from that view. That night the Danbury Panthers take a terrible beating.

I turn nineteen on leave. I feel like I am just marking time. I go duck or goose hunting for a couple of hours nearly every day. I work on the old 1958 Plymouth that I bought last spring, but she doesn't respond. I just can't seem to get her to hit on all eight cylinders.

On my last Saturday night of leave, Louis is in town from Fort Hood on a weekend pass. We go to Fillip's Café and have their two dollar sirloin strip, then head out to Vazel's Ballroom. I have never been much of a whiskey drinker, but Louis brought out a bottle of Southern Comfort and I started tugging on it with some regularity. We dance, sing and reminisce. My last song is more like a groan as I am on my hands and knees behind a giant oak tree. The Southern Comfort tasted a lot better going down than it did coming up. It will be the last time I taste Southern Comfort. After that night, I start turning green at the slightest smell of it. The next morning my head is pounding like it's been placed in a fifty-five gallon drum that is being beaten by ten baseball bats.

My leave is over on Sunday. After a big family dinner I give everyone a hug. I want wise counsel from my dad. I shake his hand and he says, "You take care of yourself over there."

"I will," I replied, knowing that "being careful" may be the best advice there is as you enter a war zone.

Louis is heading back to Fort Hood and drops me off at Houston International Airport. As my first ride on a commercial airline takes to the air, I watch Houston disappear in the distance. I realize it will be a long time before I return. I know a season of my life is ending.

My mind tries to think ahead now to my next duty station. First Infantry Division, First Medical Battalion, A Company, Vietnam. It's all so far away and distant. I have no clue exactly what it means for my life and my fate.

7
GOOD MORNING, VIETNAM

For transportation to South Vietnam, I report for duty in Oakland, California, on November 19, 1967. After wading through an hour of paperwork, I fall in line for another battery of shots to prevent all kinds of tropical diseases. I wonder if they have one to prevent "lead poisoning". Right on schedule, we are loaded onto a Boeing 707 heading to points very west. I don't know how many seats are in the plane, but I do know none of them are empty. I was in hopes of seeing some of the guys from Basic or AIT, but all the faces are new to me.

The first leg of the journey lands us in Honolulu. Growing up, I had always wanted to go to this exotic place. I can't count the hours I nestled on a couch with an old girlfriend listening to Elvis's Blue Hawaii album. Now I'm here, but my visit is short lived and confined to the airport. The closest I get to the crashing waves is seeing the ocean from the observation deck of the airport, where I am also able to view block after block of tall hotels standing at attention along the shoreline.

Next stop is Clark Air Force Base in the Philippines. It's dark outside when we land so I leave with only the knowledge that I was there for a short time.

As a green PFC (Private First Class), I walk down the steps of the Boeing 707 to the tarmac at the airport in Ben Hoa, South Vietnam. A blast of hot air and the booming sound of artillery fire greet me. Is the artillery fire incoming or outgoing? I have no idea.

To help prepare us for this strange new world, we spend the next few days completing an in-country orientation at a place called Dagger University. Until now I have only heard of the M-16 rifle. All our rifle training so far has been with the heavy, clumsy and antiquated M-14. We are given a short course on the care and operation of our new weapons. I really like the way the M-16 fires and handles; it's like comparing the drive of a sports car to that of a rice truck. On the range I qualify as expert and feel absolved from the sharpshooter qualification I had received with the M-14 in basic training.

The next day a group of us who are assigned to the "Big Red One" (First Infantry Division) are loaded onto a "deuce and a half", (a two and a half ton diesel truck) and are driven south to Dian (pronounced " Zeon"), a division base camp. We have no escort and the drive appears to be as routine as going from Fort Sam Houston to Camp Bullis.

The next day a group of us who are assigned to the "Big Red One" (First Infantry Division) are loaded onto a "deuce and a half", (a two and a half ton diesel truck) and are driven south to Dian (pronounced " Zeon"), a division base camp. We have no escort and the drive appears to be as routine as going from Fort Sam Houston to Camp Bullis.

My first view of Vietnam is not the one I saw every night on the 10 o'clock news back home. The ride to Dian makes me think that my flight from San Francisco was a time machine transport from 1967 to the distant past. The farms we pass have no tractors and no implements. I see black water buffalo pulling carts and wooden plows. The fields are dotted with people hunched over planting rice in what look like black pajamas and conical headgear. I can tell the countryside is more tropical than Texas by the banana, coconut and palm trees, but the terrain is mostly flat as a pancake, just like the coastal plains where I grew up. The heat and the humidity are just as bad. I would like to have left that part behind.

As soon we arrive in Dian, I am dropped off at "A" Company, 1st Medical Battalion, which will serve as my home base for the next fourteen months.

I realize that I have a lot to learn. I have the feeling that I'm starting first grade all over again, in an entirely different kind of school.

I report to the orderly room, which consists of offices of the Commanding Officer, Executive Officer, First Sergeant, and Company Clerk. As standard operating procedure (SOP), I fill out more paperwork for duty and billet assignments. I also receive the new wardrobe required for service in Vietnam: jungle boots, jungle fatigues, a flak jacket, and a new M-16, with another serial number to memorize.

After I get all my gear together, I start settling into my spot in the hooch. The hooch is my new home. It's of wood frame construction, on a concrete foundation with a corrugated asbestos roof, louvered walls four feet off the floor, and insect screen above that, all of which make for a well ventilated tropical shelter.

Staff Sergeant Miner comes by to give me the nickel tour of the company compound. SSG Miner is black, about 6' 6", skinny as a rail, very likable, and a career soldier. He tries to make everyone feel at home in this place so far away from home. A few days after I arrived, he put together a makeshift Christmas tree out of some lights and an aluminum pole.

The first stop on the tour is the Clearing Station. The main purpose of the Clearing Station is to take in the wounded, providing them first aid and stabilizing them enough to med-evac them out to the main in-country hospital in Long Bien. The evacuations are done either by ambulance or chopper. This facility also provides other emergency aid, sick call, and field support. There is a ward of about twenty beds, an emergency room with six workstations, and a helicopter pad about 50 feet from the back door. SSG Miner also points out radiology, dental and lab facilities.

The enlisted men's latrines are just glorified outhouses. The buildings are wooden, with horizontal siding giving them a louvered effect. Inside are about 15 toilet seats in a row, screwed into what looks like a long plywood window seat. Beneath each seat is half of a steel drum to catch the excrement. This place stinks to high heaven. It is all business, not designed for contemplating, relaxing, or reading.

Vietnamese civilians are contracted to maintain the latrines. To do that, they pull the steel cans out, mix diesel in the cans, and burn the contents, stirring continuously with steel rakes. The smell of the operation would gag a maggot. I stay clear of it whenever possible. Urinals are 55-gallon steel drums half-buried in the ground, filled with water mixed with disinfectant, with an inch of diesel floating on top. They are out in the open air and screened with sheet metal about chest high around the top.

The mess hall is just around the corner from the hooches. I think that whoever said "armies travel on their stomachs" knew what he was talking about. I'm surprised to find a milk dispenser here, just like in the states. The coffee is always hot and the food is generally good and plentiful.

It isn't like Mom's, but I do remember there were times at home that the food wasn't to my liking.

*   *   *   *   *

Eating was one of the favorite pastimes of the *Herd*. We ate lots of common, everyday meals, and then there were other very memorable ones.

My godfather Eddie dropped off half a deer occasionally during deer season for us to enjoy. We all loved venison, cooked any way at all.

Once he gave us two javelina hogs. We cleaned them and Mom baked them with carrots, onions and potatoes. It sounds good, but the roasting meat sent a noxious odor throughout the house. We ate the vegetables, but not one of us liked that hog meat.

As a result, the next day Mom fried the already baked hog meat and tried serving it with mashed potatoes, green beans and cold slaw. Again the vegetables disappeared, but we didn't touch the meat. We complained about the javelina meat being too gamey and tough, and it was!

Mom was very adamant about *"waste not, want not" so* the next day we were served the javelina drowned in barbeque sauce with roasting ears and ranch style beans. That was it. Our domestic pigs got to finish their cousins.

In front of Orderly Room

Hooch Group Area

Company Barbeque

Company Barbeque

Party in Clearing Station

My Lving Area

Monsoon Rain

Mom should have known it was bad; her *Herd* generally ate anything and everything if it wasn't moving too fast.

Along the same vein, in the early years when we came in with a bunch of geese, she baked them and make a big batch of goose dressing with giblet gravy. We loved the dressing and gravy, but the meat was stringy, dry, and mostly untouched.

In later years we canned the geese. It was pretty good served over flat noodles.

We liked sandwiches, too, especially made with peanut butter, mayonnaise and tomato slices fresh from the vine. Sliced calf heart and tongue on sandwiches were good, too.

* * * * *

Right outside the mess hall is a white painted movie screen on a panel made from four sheets of plywood. SSG Miner says there are movies shown a couple of nights a week.

While this might not be the Vietnam I was expecting from the nightly news programs I had seen at home, this is definitely the one I would choose. I know that many of the men I have trained with must be attached to field units humping the boonies, so I'm not complaining.

As the newest, youngest, and lowest ranking member of my unit, I am assigned to guard duty in the motor pool, filling sandbags, and building bunkers, in addition to working in the hospital. In the hospital I give injections, draw blood, take vital signs, and help with sick call.

On the last day of each month we stand in line to collect our pay. With my new rank of PFC , I now make $128.70 a month, plus $55.00 a month in hazardous duty pay. We are paid in Military Payment Certificates (MPC) so the Vietnamese can't use our currency against us. The denominations are 5 cents, 10 cents, 25 cents, 50 cents, $1, $5's, and $10's.

They can be spent only at military establishments. I have most of my pay sent home, as there is not much to spend money on here unless you want to gamble it away. We turn the MPC's in for greenbacks when we leave the country for home or R&R (Rest and Recuperation).

(I should have saved some of the crisp ones. As of this writing, March 2015, a $1.00 MPC in good shape is selling for between $400 and $500 online.)

First Sgt. Johnson, whom we address as Top, (a typical nickname for the First Sergeant because he is the highest ranking enlisted man at the company level) is a rotund black man in his mid-forties and the Army is his life. First sergeants run operations at the company level; commissioned officers, while having command responsibilities, leave the daily routines to the discretion of the non-commissioned officers (NCO's). I like Top, but I don't know him well and he is the last person in the world whose shit list I would want to be on. He has more control of my life that anyone else, including me. He makes assignments for any requests for manpower from Division. He recommends enlisted men for promotions. He approves leave. All these things make me want to be invisible to Top.

Top sends for me after a month in-country. I report to him at the orderly room. He asks, "Private Peltier, I understand you're a farm boy from Texas. Is that right?"

"Yes, we raised rice," I reply.

(It's still hard not to say "Sir" to men older and of a higher rank. Only officers are called "Sir". If you call an enlisted man "Sir", he will likely scornfully tell you, "I work for a living; I'm not a "Sir".)

"Do you know how to drive a truck?" Top ask.

"I've delivered a lot of rice to the driers in bobtail trucks, Top."

"Good, I need you to report to the motor pool at 0600 tomorrow. You're going to be driving a deuce and a half in a convoy to Lai Khe. Do you think you can handle that?"

"Yes, I don't think that will be a problem."

"Bring your rucksack. You may be there overnight. Oh, Private Della will be riding shotgun. ("Shotgun" is an appropriate reference to the

Old West, where the guy sitting next to the stagecoach driver carried a shotgun; here he carries an M-16.)

After being dismissed, I think to myself, "That wasn't so bad. Top treated me with respect and was friendly, not like the sergeants of basic training and AIT that treated privates like dirt."

The next morning Jerr Della and I grab breakfast at the mess hall and are out by 0530. Neither one of us has been on a convoy before. It's about a fifteen-minute walk to the motor pool and we get there a few minutes early. There are about forty trucks idling in rows of ten; the rumbling sound and the smell of the diesel exhaust reminds me of waiting in a line of trucks to unload at the rice dryer back in Texas.

We enter a work barn for a short briefing on how to drive in the convoy. The briefing officer tells us to keep the spacing tight and to not run into the back of the truck in front of us. Also, he says, be aware of the young Vietnamese kids along the roads throwing rocks at the trucks because every now and then one of the rocks has a tendency to explode. That bit of information gets my attention. I *had been* looking forward to today's adventure. He also tells us that if we have a mechanical problem and can't keep up, to pull out of line and one of the escorts (MP jeeps with post mounted M-60 machine guns, interspersed among the trucks) will come and check on us. Another comforting thought. We are also instructed to "lock and load" our weapons as soon as we exit the base camp gate.

Each truck has a driver and a "shotgun" in the passenger seat. I also have my M-16; it will be riding handily in a rack between us. We are also given goggles similar to the ones snow skiers wear to keep the road dust from getting into our eyes.

As we head to our assigned vehicles, I ask the sergeant directing us, "What is our cargo?"

"This truck is carrying the detonators for the 105-millimeter artillery rounds that are being carried in the twenty trucks just behind you," he answered.

Now, I can only hope and pray that "Charlie" doesn't (a) target this convoy and (b) can't identify our load from any other one.

("Charlie" is slang for the Viet Cong; over the radio waves the call sign for the Viet Cong (VC) was "Victor Charlie", from the Army's phonetic alphabet. It was just shortened to "Charlie".)

This duty is looking less and less attractive; I had thought a break from the base-camp would be a welcome change.

Soon we are lining up and then moving out the main gate. We are somewhere near the middle of the convoy and all the trucks have the tarp enclosed beds so we all look alike. Again I'm feeling better about this assignment.

I tell Della, "It's your job to catch anything thrown at this truck and throw it back to the pitcher."

"Yeah, right," he responds.

We both get a final chuckle as we leave.

It feels good being behind the wheel of a truck again. Just moving through the gears and driving kind of frees up my mind and body. For the first few miles the MP's are moving up and down the line of trucks, tightening up the convoy to their liking. Once things are moving smoothly, the pace is picked up to between forty and fifty mph.

The dust kicked up by the trucks is so thick I can't see the road so I slow down a little. The thick dust reminds me of driving a tractor and dragging a harrow over a field's seedbed just prior to planting, with the breeze at my back. Only now, the speed has changed; I have goggles on to protect my eyes and a flak jacket and helmet to protect my body. The next thing I see is an MP in a cloud of dust about five feet to my left waving me forward to tighten up the line. I ease forward until I can make out the truck in front of me; it's about twenty feet away. When I see his brake lights, I immediately hit my brake and he pulls away from me. I gun the engine to catch up. In a short time my full concentration is on the truck in front of me. I maintain my distance, depending on the visibility of the next truck and its brake lights.

The convoy slows down as we pass through towns and villages where there isn't much of a dust problem. In the villages the road is lined with kids shouting at us with their hands out. Some of the drivers have brought bags of candy and are throwing it out to them. Jerr and I are paying close attention to the kids. We get to talk a little as we pass through towns, but while we are cruising the countryside, between the roar of the engines and the focus on driving, there are few words spoken between us.

We arrive in Lai Khe after about three hours. It feels good to dismount from the truck. I don't realize how tense and tight my body is until after the drive. It takes a few minutes to straighten up and move around.

You can call me anything as long as you call me to chow, and that is our next stop. The mess hall is close by and we are told to go get lunch and take a break while they get the trucks unloaded.

The first thing we look for is a place to wash up. Everyone on the convoy is covered with a quarter inch of fine dust. It has permeated our clothes to mix with sweat to create a muddy grime. After taking off the goggles, everyone's face has the look of a grasshopper. Della and I find a hose, strip to the waist and wash our heads and torso. We rinse out our tee shirts, wring the water out the best we can, and put them back on to dry. We shake out our fatigue shirts and leave them with the rest of our gear and head for chow. Just as in the days of farming, my body is soon rejecting the dust I have been breathing and I am blowing long streams of black snot from my nose.

After lunch we report back to the staging area to find that the convoy will be rolling back to Dian in about 20 minutes. One thing I have learned in my short Army experience is how to take a "power nap". I can put my head down almost anywhere and catch a few winks. I see an inviting tree with a few of the other drivers around it with the same thought in mind and my lights go dim.

I feel a light kick against my boot. I look up and don't recognize my surroundings; then almost immediately, I remember where I am. Della and I find our truck, give it a quick check, and get in line for the trip back.

Without a load, the trip back seems to be faster and easier. The dust is still as bad, but the truck responds more quickly. I am much more relaxed because I don't think Charlie is going to attack a convoy of mostly empty trucks. This is one of the few times I've been off base-camp since I've been in country and it's certainly the most ground I've covered, so on the way back I drink in as much of the countryside as I can. The towns seem busy with people on bicycles and Lambrettas (small tricycle-like motorbikes with a small cargo area behind the driver), and the countryside that I can see through the dust is dotted with small farms with rice fields and vegetable plots. It's a pretty soothing sight for a displaced country boy. As I drive, I reminisce about the many different driving experiences that molded my life on and off the farm.

* * * * *

My brothers and I all had to learn how to drive at an early age. I had been driving for five or six years in some capacity before I got my driver's license at 14, which was the earliest age you could get license at that time. At the ripe old age of 16, I attained a commercial license so I could drive rice trucks.

Driving was a necessity on the farm. At 8 or 9 years old we would get to drive from one part of the field to another. Generally the youngest would get to do that because the older you were, the more work you could do, and driving wasn't very hard work. Being younger that Louis and Kenneth, I got to drive in the fields a lot.

Our cars in the mid 1950's were Kaisers and Fraisers, and although they quit manufacturing them in the mid 1950's, the one I drove first was a 1948 or '49 model. After that we switched to Dodges and Plymouths. One of the reasons for the switch was that their engines, a flat head in-line six cylinder, would fit in our old Massy Harris model 21 combines. We always had several cars around. Generally one or two were running, while one or more were broken down. There were always plenty of required repairs and maintenance.

The only nearly new car we had was in 1955 when Dad bought a 1954 Kaiser demo. It was the last year they made Kaisers in the USA, and I'm sure he cut a good deal on it.

Farmstead

Crops in Fields

Rice Drying on Mats

Shocks of Rice

Working the Fields

In about 1962 after Peter washed out of Texas A & M, he bought a 1957 Plymouth Belvedere. It was about the finest car I had ever seen. It had a 318 CID V8 engine, Juke Box Drive (push button), automatic transmission, and it would haul butt. It was seldom we would get to drive that car, as Peter used it to commute to Alvin Junior College and work. After he got a room in Alvin, it was out of reach most the time. Farm to Market Road 2004 was brand new and several times we would get it out and "clean the soot out the tailpipe", like we used to say. Thinking back on those times we had that car cranked up over 100 mph and every tire on the ground was a "may-pop".

I mention only cars. That was because that was the only type of transportation my mother allowed. While most of the other farmers in the area worked out of pickup trucks, she was afraid that if we had one, one of us would fall out. We wore out many a sedan and station wagon, but never a pickup.

Most of our county road driving was just to the rice fields and back, until I was in the 6th or 7th grade. After that it was always toward Hoskins Mound, which was only three or four miles from the house.

In 1961 Hurricane Carla deposited too much salt in the fields that we leased for raising rice. As a result, in 1962 Dad rented land near Angleton and farmed there, hoping to make a better rice crop.

We had to pump water from a canal to irrigate the field. That was done with a belt about 10 inches wide and 12 to 15 foot long with one end attached to a pulley on the tractor and the other to a pulley on the top of the pump. For the clutch we backed up the tractor to tighten up the belt to engage the power to pump the water. To adjust and hold the belt tension steady we used a railroad jack under one of the steel lugs on the steel wheel of the tractor. To get the exact tension needed, we would tighten the belt by jacking up on the lug and push the whole tractor backward. To loosen the belt, we would let off on the jack a click. To start the pump, we put the tractor in neutral and engaged the hand clutch on the tractor. The pulley on the tractor rotated and the belt rotated the pump. Then the water flowed copiously from the canal to the field.

The set-up had to be checked every evening before we went to bed. We had to check the level and top off the fuel, the oil and the water, add belt dressing, and grease the pump and tractor. We had pretty strict instructions to go straight to the field to check the pump and come straight home. None of us had drivers licenses and while the roads toward Hoskins Mound were pretty desolate, the Angleton area was a lot more populous.

One night Kenneth decided on his way back from checking the pump that he would drive the longer route through Danbury and make the block several times around his girl friend's house. As I explained above, our cars weren't always in tip-top shape. That night the tail lights weren't working, a fact observed by the local police. They also noticed him going around the same block time after time. Needless to say, when Dad got the call from the policeman, he was none too happy. Ken had to work a lot of hours at a dollar an hour to pay off that ticket.

One of my earliest driving experiences was when I must have been nine or ten. I had dropped off Dad, Louis, and Kenneth on one end of a field and was going to wait for them at the other end while they checked the levees to that point. Soon it started to rain cats and dogs, so I decided I would turn the car around so it would be headed toward home. I tried backing it up and going forward several times to work the car around, but that didn't seem to be getting it done so I decided to go for broke and try to go fast enough to go in and out the edge of the ditch, hoping that my momentum would carry me through. Much to my chagrin, I ended up stuck in the ditch.

In hopes of getting someone to pull me out, I stood in the rain on the side of the road with a chain in my hands. When a car came by and stopped, I asked the driver to help me get out of the ditch. He had a new car and while I pleaded for his help, the driver was really concerned he might damage his car. He soon left me standing on the side of the road in the rain.

When Dad and my brothers showed up, I'm sure I looked like a scared, drowned rat. Dad has a temper and I feared he might administer the punishment that I likely deserved, but he just took it in stride and took steps to get us on our way. He found a fence post, positioned Louis and Kenneth to push and on his signal, Dad pried, the boys pushed, and I drove. That car just seemed to leap right out of the muddy ditch. I was amazed!

In the summer of 1966 between my junior and senior year in high school, I worked part of June, July and most of August for Vincent Heckler. He was also a rice farmer, so I was familiar with most the work he had me doing.

He had a full time hand, a colored man of about twenty five years by the name of Leon. Leon had arms as big as my thighs, was a good man, and a joy to work with. Vincent paid me the grand sum of ten dollars a day and was told to keep that under my hat because Leon was getting only eight dollars a day. That might have been considered unfair, but I thought nothing of it because Leon was also provided beef to eat and a shack to live in with his wife and kids.

So much for that, this is on driving.

During the rice harvest my main job was truck driving. Vincent had a fairly new Chevrolet truck with a small engine and a transmission that had a two-speed rear end. The truck was not easy to drive with heavy loads.

The rice dryer we loaded out to was in Alvin, about twenty miles from the field. When I arrived at the rice dryer, there were always long lines of trucks to be unloaded, so we always heaped up the rice on the truck to haul the maximum load.

There were two main problems with that truck, getting up to cruising speed and then stopping. While the truck wanted to stop when I braked and downshifted, the heavy load of rice wanted to keep going. It seemed to take forever to romance that truck up to 45 or 50 miles per hour. Then I learned that I had better think about stopping about a mile before I needed to. Shame on the guy who whipped in front of me and slammed on the brakes. There were several times that I needed to stop quickly, when my guardian angel protected me and those nearby. Amazingly, I worked the whole harvest season and wasn't killed and didn't kill anyone.

The truck didn't have a dump bed, so when I pulled into the unloading bay at the rice dryer, the front wheels landed on a platform that tilted the truck for the grain to run out the bed. The truck was weighed on the way in loaded (gross) and on the way out unloaded (tare). Vincent was paid for his crops by the net weight, the difference between gross and tare.

I never complained or said anything about the working conditions in the rice farming environment. At the age of seventeen, I was happy to have the job, and at that time and place it was the rule, not the exception, to have a job. Safety was never mentioned as part of the work plan.

I think it was a miracle that no one in my family broke a bone or had a major injury during our years growing up.

*   *   *   *   *

We arrive in Dian late in the afternoon. It feels good to be back "home" in the safety of the base-camp. Even though we had not encountered any hostilities, that possibility is present everywhere and any time in this country. After we drop the truck off and check in at the company orderly room, we head for our hooch to do battle with the grime that has penetrated our pores. I strip half way from both ends, wrap a towel around me and head to the shower, hoping for hot water.

There is cold water piped to the showers. The pressure is always low. The hot water heater is a fifty-five gallon drum mounted on the top of the shower room with a diesel burner on its bottom. The hot water gravity flows to the showers below; sometimes the water is near boiling, sometimes it's lukewarm, and sometimes it's nonexistent. You have to check the temperature before you get under the drizzle of the shower head or you could scald yourself in very hot water.

The water is plenty hot and after a thirty-minute scrub I get out feeling refreshed and clean. I take a closer look and can see my pores are still plugged with dirt by the black dots I see. In about two more days I may feel that I have expunged the grit from this carcass.

For the first time, I think of this place as home, or at least home away from home. My bed feels welcome and familiar and sleep comes easy and deep.

I am totally unprepared for the Christmas season of 1967. The weather here is hot, dry and dusty. There are no Christmas movies, no Bing Crosby singing "White Christmas", no family bustling around with the excitement and expectation of Christmas morning, and no community of saints worshipping together in a small country church. The only sounds I can depend on are the constant fire of artillery and choppers flying in and out of the airfield on the next block. SSG Miner's tree looks a little bleak and skeletal. It's a ten foot high aluminum pole with colored lights radiating to the ground around to its base on a four-foot radius, and it's the only thing that shows any semblance of the season.

A box arrives from home. It is filled with Mom's oatmeal cookies. They are my favorite, with lots of raisins and pecans. My joy fades to disappointment as I start to munch on them. They are so crumbly and stale I throw them out and, as I do, I feel like I'm discarding a part of my family. I attend church services but still feel a giant disconnect from all the things I love and care about. I think of home.

*   *   *   *   *

Christmas morning was always the biggest day of the year for me and all of my brothers and sisters. The tree stood proudly centered in a baby's playpen in the corner of the living room. It made more sense to contain the tree for its safe keeping than to try to keep the toddlers at bay – it attracted them like a magnet. It was covered with strings of different colored bright lights. Some of the lights had a stem of liquid with air bubbles rising up through them. Pretty shining silver and gold ornaments hung from the limbs, along with some other ornaments that we had made that weren't so pretty, but Mom said they made the tree special. Each of the kids were given a few slivers of silver icicles to put on the tree for the finishing touches. The tree seemed to glow with a life of its own by Christmas morning.

Mom and Dad were always up early Christmas morning. I know

they must have been tired after taking us all to Midnight Mass on Christmas Eve. On Christmas morning, we woke to the smell of baking kolaches and coffee cake filling the house. The plate of cookies that had been left on the table for Santa the night before was reduced to a few crumbs, and the glass of milk was empty.

We were not allowed into the living room with the tree and presents until Mom and Dad called us. It was all we could do to restrain ourselves at the door of the bedroom. The air was filled with shouts and pleadings.

"Are you ready yet?"

"Can we come now?"

"When can we come?"

The reply would be, "Hold your horses!"

"We're almost done."

"Just a minute."

When we were finally called, it was like a dam bursting as we scrambled for a place in the living room. Alice Mae, Aunt Esther's daughter, was always there to pass out the presents. The first thing we each got was a sock with an orange in the toe, some hard candy inside, an apple in the heel, and a small gift on top.

I vividly remember the Christmas of 1954. As we flooded into the living room our eyes were scoping out all the bright wrappings in the playpen where the tree stood. Tied to its top rail was a row of bulging socks; presents overflowed onto the floor around it. My eyes locked onto a green John Deere tricycle tractor with a big red bow around it, parked against the wall on the edge of the presents. My body reacted involuntarily at its sight; first with a word, "*Mine*!" and then the next I thing knew I was straddling the tractor sitting in its seat. I looked up beaming at Mom and Dad and they smiled back with a little nod. Then I knew it was mine. Dynamite couldn't have blown me from my perch as Alice Mae passed out presents. Each of us who were old enough got a pair of roller skates, the kind that clamped to the soles of our shoes and had steel wheels.

After all the presents were passed out, we moved to the dining room for kolaches and coffee cake. I rolled there on my new tractor and ate from its seat.

I just couldn't wait to get my tractor outside to test it out. Construction on the barn had started and the slab was poured, but nothing was on it. By the end of Christmas Day that slab was covered with black rubber marks from my tractor tires, as I raced and turned and chased the skaters all over it. We had a few crashes and falls that resulted in some scrapes and bruises and at the end of the day we were all exhausted, but I couldn't have been happier that Christmas. I got exactly what I wanted and there was nothing else that could have made me happier.

For a long time afterwards every spare minute we had was spent playing roller skate hockey with homemade sticks, pucks, and goals and, of course, I made scores of more black marks with the John Deere.

*   *   *   *   *

On this first Christmas away from my family I look around me and see other young men feeling the same as I do. My years make me still a teenager, but in my mind I feel older. Christmases in prior years were all about me and the joy from giving and receiving gifts from loved ones. This year those folks are a half world away. This day has 24 hours just like yesterday, tomorrow and any other day, and I know that I have to deal with the facts.

I hear some Christmas music from a radio in the clinic. At least someone at Armed Forces Radio thinks it's Christmas. I have to quit feeling sorry for myself and dump this "woe is me" attitude. I know I can choose to be miserable or choose to be upbeat and be part of the solution instead of part of the problem. Christmas is supposed to be a celebration of the birth of Jesus our Savior, not about how many presents are under a tree or a homesick soldier far from home. For me, it has always been a time when our family came together and celebrated His birth, but it was also a celebration of family love and unity.

*   *   *   *   *

Greg Junemann, Steve Salines, a few others who drift in and out of our hooch and I sit around in our flimsy lawn chairs as we do many nights solving the world's problems. Tonight, this is my family, and we sit around and reflect on what we might be doing if we were at home instead of here. I've been here a little over a month and these guys feel like brothers. We eat, sleep, and spend twenty-four hours a day, seven days a week together. There are many times in life you don't get to choose your circumstances. Greg, Steve, and the rest of us lean on each other to make this time in our lives bearable, even entertaining. At present it's the only home I have and I am going to make the best out of it.

January of 1968, sick call is over. Today I've been working the clinic's front desk, signing in patients and taking vital signs. I've seen the same man come in here several times in the last two months with gonorrhea, or "the clap" as it is commonly called. It takes about three days of incubation for it to show up after a sexual encounter with an infected prostitute. Then it takes about three days of antibiotics to cure it and not much time to get it again if a guy can't keep his pants zipped up. Every day we see numerous cases of clap and other venereal diseases. All the Army's preventive training films and distribution of written information don't seem to do much good.

Clark, from the orderly room, comes rushing in and says, "Peltier, Top wants to see you."

"Any idea what he wants?" I ask.

Clark just shrugs his shoulders and shakes his head.

I enter the orderly room and see Top at his desk engrossed in a pile of paper. I knock on the door, and he looks up.

"Come in, Peltier," he says as I enter the small office and stand in front of his desk.

"Peltier, headquarters is short a medic and I need you to report in front of Division Headquarters at fifteen hundred hours."

"What will I need to bring?"

"You will be going out on ambush patrol. Bring your medical bag, M-16, and anything else you think you may need."

As he spoke, the pit of my stomach started feeling a little hollow. Being assigned to a clearing station had been a real stroke of luck, and I thought I had dodged field duty with the infantry.

"Any questions?"

"Will I be reporting back here in the morning?"

"I hope so," Top laughs.

"Me, too," I reply as I force a laugh as I am leaving.

I think to myself as I walk back to the hooch to gather my gear, "Lucky me, I get the temporary assignment. I will be glad when I am not the newest, youngest, lowest ranking private in "A" Company.

I head over to Headquarters, giving myself plenty of time to get there. Here I am introduced to the lieutenant in charge. During a briefing I find out we are going out about four clicks (one click is one kilometer) from the south gate to set up a "listening post" (LP) and are to engage enemy combatants should we encounter them. It's too soon to be scared, but I'm uneasy at best. Until now, the VC have had opportunities to engage me in my movements about the country, but now I'm going out with a unit that is making an effort to engage them. I can only believe that the VC's ability to monitor our movements is much better than ours to monitor theirs. They live here; we are just visitors, welcomed by some, despised by others.

We exit the south gate an hour before dark. As soon as our squad of a dozen men clears the gate we "lock and load" our M-16's. We move out towards the designated area of the listening post in loose staggered columns with point men leading the way a short distance ahead. Everyone appears to know what to do, so I just blend in and stay close to the lieutenant and the RTO (Radio Telephone Operator), like I am told. It's been a hot day and soon sweat soaks my tee shirt, but the jungle fatigues fit loosely and allow my body to breath as we maintain a pace that is reasonably comfortable.

The terrain is mostly flat with scrub brush, weeds, and grass covering the land. Just being out makes me think of being on a rabbit hunt, only there are too many of us and we're too well armed. We are moving through the landscape quietly and attentively. I relax a little as we move, looking for anything that looks like it doesn't belong. I think to myself, "I'm the only thing here that's out of place." It's quiet; I realize that I hear no birds. I don't know if this is normal or not. I will ask someone later.

As we are moving toward the LP location, we pass several gravesites with rock-lined perimeters marking the graves. There doesn't seem to be any rhyme or reason to when or where we might encounter these gravesites. Even if there are several in one area, there is no order – one might be turned any number of degrees different from the adjacent one. It seems almost comical, too, as I figure they must bury their dead wherever they fall down and die.

In Vietnam, medics don't wear the Red Cross insignia on their helmets or armbands as mandated by the Geneva Convention to identify corpsmen for their protection. Early in the war they found that instead of offering protection, the prominent red crosses provided targets for the VC. I carry an M-16 and look like any other infantryman in the field, with the exception of the medical bag.

As we enter the designated area of operation, the sun looks like a large orange ball falling across the horizon and the coolness of evening is starting to relieve the heat of the day. The lieutenant sets up the LP in the shape of a wagon wheel. At the end of each spoke is a two-man watch armed with a combination of M-16's, M-79 grenade launchers, M-60 machine guns, hand grenades, and claymore mines laid out beyond the perimeter. No one digs a foxhole. We use natural cover, a patch of brush or weed, to conceal ourselves. The command post is the hub of the wheel; the lieutenant, RTO, and myself as the medic, occupy this area.

There are a couple of graves in the hub area. I decide that I am going to give the dead some company tonight and set up in the middle of one of the graves. I like the idea of the little rock wall perimeter offering a little cover if we make contact with the VC, and I don't think the person in the ground below me will mind me laying on top of him.

Once everyone is in position and the mines are set out, we settle into watches, one-hour on and one off. I am too wired to sleep. I munch on cold c-rations for my evening meal. The food is tasteless but offers something to do to pass the time, and for this I am grateful. My mind is imagining everything out in the darkness as Charlie working his way into our perimeter. We can't move around or talk unless necessary. The ground is hard and the space inside the grave is small. I know this night is going to be longer than any I have ever experienced.

The night is clear and the sky is filled with stars. If I weren't sure that I am half a world away from home, I would be at peace in this setting, as camping on the banks of Austin Bayou was a common activity in my youth. On those occasions someone always told a scary story to get us worked up. Tonight I'm plenty scared, as my own imagination is providing a tale of evil lurking in the darkness, complete in Technicolor and stereophonic sound. Finally, after my 0200-0300 watch, my anxiety wanes and I get a bit of fitful rest. A foggy haze has moved in and that, combined with the cool night air, makes me uncomfortably cold. I wrap up tighter in my poncho and poncho liner.

Even in Vietnam the sun rises in the east. First I notice its welcome glow, then it brings to mind the verse of a popular Cyrkle song, "and the morning sun is shining like a red rubber ball", and I am joyful. I stretch, gather my gear, get the blood flowing through my body and offer a prayer of thanksgiving for making it through the night without a personal introduction to Charlie.

This night reminds me of another night on the bayou.

*   *   *   *   *

It was a Friday night. I was a senior in high school and I had just gotten home from playing in a Danbury High School basketball game. I knew that Mike, Ronnie, Larry, and Davy were camping along Austin Bayou on a sandbar across from Uncle Bill's lakes. It was still early enough to join up with the group, so I loaded up the canoe in the back of our '56 Dodge two-door station wagon and headed for the bayou right below the lakes.

It was a beautiful cool, crisp night with nearly a full moon. I slipped the canoe into the water and started paddling up the bayou. I saw the glow of the campfire at a distance on a sandbar. I could hear them talking, laughing and having a good time. At that time I was thinking it would be fun to slip up and scare the hell out of them. Paddling carefully and quietly, I eased the bow of the canoe into the light of the fire. Just as I had thought, I did scare the hell out of them. What I didn't think about is that when we went camping, we never went unarmed. In his surprise Larry's first reaction was to shoot at whatever was coming at him as I found myself looking down the barrel of a .22 pistol.

All of the sudden "carefully quiet" became loud and alarmed as I yelled out "DON'T SHOOT!"

Larry didn't pull the trigger and I got to spend the rest of the night with them, laughing, and talking and having a good time.

*   *   *   *   *

The patrol moves out in the same formation as we did coming in yesterday. Soon I see the base-camp gate and when we reach the staging area, I am dismissed to return to my unit. I see Top as I am signing in at the orderly room. He smiles and says, "I see you made it back all right. How was your night?"

"It was quiet," I replied.

"Did you see any sign of activity?" Top asked.

"No, and I'm glad about that."

"Good. I'm sure you didn't get much sleep last night. Take a few hours and get some shut eye."

"Thanks, that sounds good to me."

By noon I am back in my hooch, cleaning my rifle, hoping that will be the last time I am assigned to that duty. I get a hot meal from the mess hall and then drop onto my bunk. I thank God for the duty station that I have drawn and then fall into a deep sleep.

Things are always changing in our lives, sometimes for better and sometimes for worse. I think when our life's routine gets too comfortable, God shakes it up with change that we always resist.

Here in the summer of 1968, circumstances take an unexpected twist.

By the time we get news from the States, it is filtered and sanitized. The Army newspaper, <u>The Stars and Stripes</u>, is our main source of outside information. I can't say I pay a lot of attention to the news anyway because here in Vietnam I feel like I'm on an island separated from home, connected by a thin lifeline with only a distant hope of returning home someday. Since the assassination of Martin Luther King in April, there have been racial riots throughout the United States. Now it is being exported from there to here.

The Clearing Station is always open, but normally after 17:00 hours there are only one or two people there, depending on how many patients are in the ward. If there is an emergency, the orderly room is called and they send for appropriate personnel who are in the compound and within a couple of hundred feet of the facility. Lately we have been staffing the ER on Friday and Saturday nights because of brawls at the enlisted men's club about a block away.

Until recently there would be an occasional drunken brawl at the enlisted men's (EM) club as a result of a friendly disagreement greased by a little too much alcohol. I'm talking about a fist-fight resulting in a minor injury that might require a butterfly bandage, aspirin, and little sleep.

I seldom go to the EM club; I have become accustom to spending my evenings sitting around the hooch with my buddies in our lawn chairs sipping beer and resolving the world's problems deep into the nights. The EM club has its regulars and is a place where the grunts getting in from field duty blow off a little steam.

It's Friday night and Mike, a very short-timer friend, is leaving tomorrow for the "World", what we commonly refer to as the States. He is having a farewell celebration at the EM club. I have ER duty, but I tell Mike to drink an extra beer for me.

Things are quiet at the ER; Glen and I are playing gin and waiting for midnight to close up shop and go to bed. About ten thirty the phone rings. I answer it, "Emergency Room."

"This is Sgt. Taylor at the EM club and there're several people who've been injured in a knife fight. Can you send an ambulance?"

"Can you tell if any of the injuries are critical?" I ask.

"I don't think so. There are some of your guys over here working on them."

"We'll be right over."

"Glen, you'd better get the doctor on call. There's been another fight at the EM club and this time they were using knives. I'm going to take the ambulance over and bring them back."

I am there in just minutes. As I pull up, I see the MP's are there taking notes. There are two men lying down with medics working makeshift bandages around an arm and a leg, and a few more men holding bloody napkins against their injured bodies. I back the ambulance up to the group. Mike comes up and I ask, "Do you need a stretcher?"

"We should transport those two on stretchers. The rest can ride or walk."

In a matter of minutes we have them loaded and are heading back to the ER. The two men are on stretchers and a few of the ambulatory men are hanging on the running boards. When we arrive, I back up to the ER door and move the two men on stretchers to work stations. Dr. Miller is already there, directing the medics and examining the two who came in on stretchers.

Glen is gathering all the pertinent information on the patients. I take one of the ambulatory men to a work station. I ask, "What is your name?"

"Roy," the PFC replies with a southern twang.

"Roy, I want you to lie down on your back on this table so I can check out your wound."

I've always pictured myself as the youngest guy around, but Roy is not a day older than me and he is outfitted in recently issued fatigues. He has a very fair complexion with freckles liberally sprinkled throughout; his red hair is cropped short, and his face is covered with a bad case of acne. His left forearm has a bloody napkin pressed over a wound.

I ask, "Is this the only place you were cut?"

"Yes," Roy replies.

I start gently working the napkin away from the cut. The bleeding has already stopped and the blood is coagulated around the wound. The wound is a clean slice, an inch and a half long and a quarter of an inch deep. As I'm irrigating and cleaning the cut, I ask Roy, "Where're you from?"

"Alabama."

"How long have you been in country?"

"About two weeks."

Captain Miller comes by, inspects the wound, and says, "Sew it up."

"Yes, Sir," I reply, trying to hide my excitement.

I have assisted in suturing many times and placed a few sutures under a specialist's supervision. This will be my first solo attempt at this operation.

Roy looks at me and says. "Have you ever done this before?"

"Yes. It's bad enough when I have to work on the battle wounded, but now we're fighting amongst ourselves."

"They started it," Roy says, nodding over to a black guy.

"The last time I checked, it takes two dogs to have a dog fight," I reply.

"This is the worst part," I tell Roy as I inject the area with lidocaine to numb the area.

He tenses up and soon the pain is gone. I glove up and get a suture set from the autoclave. Then I lay a drape around the area of the wound so that only the wound is exposed. Roy is watching nervously as I prepare, so I say to him, "Relax. The worst is over. You won't feel a thing, except a little pressure."

I grasp the half-round needle with forceps and touch the wound. "Do you feel any sharp pain?" I ask.

"No," Roy says, shaking his head.

I sponge the area and insert the needle about an eighth on an inch from the edge of the wound and rotate the needle so it comes out about an equal distance on the other side of the wound. I draw the knot together with just enough pressure to gently seat the flesh evenly together; then I give its final tie. After repeating the process a half dozen or so more times, I'm done. Captain Miller looks in as I'm finishing up and says, "Good job, Peltier. I don't think there will be much of a scar."

"Thank you, sir," I reply.

After finishing up with a bandage to protect the wound, I tell Roy, "Keep this clean and dry and have your unit medic change the dressing every day and check for infection. In a week he can take the stitches out."

"Thanks," Roy says.

"No problem," I reply and add, "There're enough problems out there dealing with the VC and we only help them when we fight amongst ourselves."

"I get your drift," he answers as he heads out the door.

By midnight we're done. We keep the two we brought in on stretchers to stay overnight, but they are going to be alright medically. The MP's will sort out what kind of disciplinary action will be taken. It's likely some of the participants will be busted down a pay grade, spend some time in the stockade, or at least pull extra duty.

When we close down for the night, I ask Mike, "What the hell happened at the EM club."

Mike kind of shrugged and said, "We congregated around a few tables in a corner and were reminiscing on my time in country. I heard some jawing back and forth by the bar between some black and white "grunts". Then it was like spontaneous combustion. There was a slugfest.

The bartender hollered at the group, 'I'm calling the MP's.'

"Then a couple of knives appeared out of nowhere. The MP's showed up in just a few minutes and shut down the fight. We went over and stopped the bleeding. The bartender called the ER and you showed up in minutes. It seemed like a blur. It was over as fast as it started."

"What a way to end your tour of duty," I reply.

"Let's get to the rack before something else happens," he says.

"I'll see you in the morning," I tell him as I head to bed.

*   *   *   *   *

In 1966, Danbury ISD integrated. I was in eleventh grade of high school. Around the nation there had been much rioting and unrest, mostly in the southern states and mostly by white people resisting the government directive. There was no real trouble in Danbury. We knew our black brethren and most of us had worked shoulder to shoulder with them in the fields, but there was still a separation. The black folks lived, worshiped and congregated in their area of town, and the white folks did the same things everywhere else.

Fillip's Café was the main eatery in Danbury. If you were black and wanted a meal at Fillip's, you ordered from the back door and ate your meal at a picnic table situated outside. It was most commonplace for farmers and ranchers to come to Fillip's at lunchtime and have lunch and have their black work hands, who were with them all day, have lunch behind the restaurant. The main differences were obvious. The hired hands sat outside in the heat and the farmers and ranchers sat inside in the air-conditioning. No one seemed to notice or even consider that there was an invisible wall placed between the blacks and whites. That was the way it was, the way it had been for generations and as long as anyone could remember. As best as I could tell, the arrangement was acceptable to all parties.

But things were rapidly changing throughout America. The words *racial prejudice* were used to condemn those practices that were commonplace in the South. The phrase *separate but equal* defended those practices that were too numerous to list but included separate restrooms, water fountains, schools, churches, colleges, break rooms at work, and so on.

So, as a junior in high school, I was elbow to elbow with black kids. No, that wasn't totally true. We were at the same school, going to the same classes, but there wasn't a lot of hugging and kissing or close friendships across racial lines. The black kids generally grouped together, as did the whites.

Football started to change that for me. At least I got to know a black kid better than I had before. His name was Woodrow Wilson Woodward III; his nickname was Bully. I had known him for years, not well, but we had worked cows and in the rice fields at times, and he was on the same bus route as I. His nickname, Bully, was not given to him because he liked to push other people around, but because he was a heavyweight built like a bull. We both played tackle, offensively and defensively, on the high school football team. The number of students at Danbury was so small that nearly all the players had to play both ways.

Towards the end of the season after a particularly hard hot workout, we were in the locker room dressing. I asked Bully, "How about having a soda with me to cool off?"

"Sounds like a plan," Bully replied.

We headed over to Fillip's and sat at the bar together. Mr. Fillip came over said, "Can I help you?"

I said, "I want two scoops of vanilla ice cream in a glass and a Sprite, and give Bully whatever he wants."

"I'll have the same," Bully said.

We sat there making small talk and slurping the tasty foam off the top of the glass, as the Sprite reacted to the ice cream making a foamy mixture that rushed to the top. When we were done, I laid two quarters on the bar. The drinks were a dime apiece. The ice cream was a nickel a scoop, and that left a nickel tip each.

After we left, Bully said to me, "Did you notice the people in Fillip's looking at us?"

"I didn't notice anything. Bully, I think your imagination is working overtime."

A few days later I went into Fillip's and sat at the bar. Mr. Fillip came over to me and asked, "What did you do that for?"

I was surprised and asked, "What are you talking about?"

"Bringing Bully in here the other day. You know our rules about serving blacks."

I was stunned, "I just thought that with changes in the school and with all the integration rules that it was all right," I answered with respect.

"I will let you know when it changes," he replied. Then he asked, "What can I get you today?"

"I'll have a Sprite and two scoops of ice cream in a glass."

As I sat there, I thought about what Bully told me as we left the other day. He had noticed the racial prejudice while I was oblivious to the whole thing. Mr. Fillip was a very nice man and I don't know if he was prejudiced, if he was protecting his business or if he was just opposed to change. I certainly didn't bring Bully there for the purpose of making a big political statement. I was just trying to be friendly with a new friend and an old acquaintance.

*   *   *   *   *

The racial issues seem to continue. It doesn't take much to flame the coals from either side. There is more than one war going on over here, and I'm not sure how we're faring on either front.

8

WINNING HEARTS AND MINDS

Mid January 1968 rolls around and my duty changes a little.

Until now my job has been filling in wherever the powers that
be need a warm body. Off and on over the last month I have been
filling a slot in the MEDCAP (Medical Civil Action Program) operation
and I like it. Spending several days a week in the field working and
doing humanitarian aid gives me a feeling that I'm doing something of
value in this war zone. The first of MEDCAP'S objectives is to
provide outpatient care for Vietnamese civilians living in rural area.
The program started in 1963 and by 1968 is treating nearly 200,000
civilians a month.[1]   Overall, the goal is to win the hearts and minds of
the civilians.

Our group is made up of several doctors, half a dozen enlisted
men and three civilian translators. We go out into villages within
driving distance of Dian and pull sick call on the local population.
Typically we leave the base-camp with two jeeps and a trailer for
personnel and supplies, a three-quarter ton truck outfitted as a rolling
pharmacy, an ambulance and an escort of Military Police (MP)
consisting of three men and a jeep outfitted with a M-60 machine gun

---

[1] Vietnam Studies- Medical Support 1965-1970: Medical Assistance
to Vietnamese Civilians,
http//amedd.army.mil.booksdoc/Vietnam/chpt13.htm

and a radio. Occasionally we load our jeeps and pharmacy into large two-prop Chinook helicopters and provide service in more remote locations.

In the military the definition of "*shamming*" is doing nothing, but looking busy. Well, while I am shamming, talking with Greg in the medical lab, while he is busy counting white and red blood cells as he looks through a microscope, Clark comes in and announces, "Peltier, Top wants to see you."

"Any idea what he wants?" I ask.

Clark shrugs his shoulders and shakes his head as he walks off.

I say to Greg as I am leaving, "I wonder what kind of crappy duty I've been chosen for this time?"

He looks up, smiles and says, "Ours is not to reason why, ours is but to do or die."

Standing in front of his desk, Top says, "Captain Walker's driver for MEDCAP, Olsen, is cycling back to the States next week and he has requested you for that job. What do you think?"

"I think I'd like that," I answer.

My mind starts whirling as fast as a chopper blade on takeoff. This, I think, is duty from heaven. It is relatively safe because we are giving medical aid to the mothers, fathers, brothers and sisters of the VC and because there are several doctors on each outing, there is a high level of security. Finally I will have a regular assignment and maybe I won't feel like a ping-pong ball being bounced all over the place. Plus, it will also insulate me from some of the temporary duties handed down by Division.

"I'll let Captain Walker know and put you on the MEDCAP duty roster," Top replies as he looks down examining some paperwork on his desk, signifying I am done.

Truck Driving

Medivac

Refugee Pottery

Tops' Monkey

Mat Weaving Material

Pottery Kiln

Bricks Drying

Brick Press

I can hardly contain my excitement. I go back to the lab and see Greg still bent over the microscope counting blood cells with a counter clicking in his right hand.

"Greg, you won't believe it. I'm the newest member of the MEDCAP team."

Greg looks up and says, "Yeah, that's great, if that is what you want."

"It will be nice not bouncing from one duty to the next. Now at least I'll have a regular duty and still all the other duty that comes up," I reply.

He doesn't share my enthusiasm. All Greg wants to do is go home. When he graduated from college, he was immediately drafted into the Army, as he lost his student exemption status. He likes working in the lab and has no yearning to leave the base camp except to return to Minnesota.

Steve Saline sticks his head in and says, "What's up, guys?"

"Captain Walker requested that I take Olsen's spot on the MEDCAP team," I say excitedly.

"That's great. It will be good to have you out there as a regular," Steve replies.

Steve is a dental assistant and he and the dentist, Captain Miller, go out on many of the MEDCAP operations.

I tell them both that I'm going to put a few beers on ice and that they'll be on me so they can celebrate with me; then I head out to do just that.

MEDCAP's are scheduled three or four days each week. Wherever we go, the areas are secured by US or ARVN (Army of the Republic of Vietnam) forces; civilians are given notice of our coming. We set up in the center of villages at schools, pavilions, town halls, orphanages and refugee camps. From time to time we bring tents and set-up in them.

Moving Out

Patrol Dog

Patrol

MEDCAP Security Armor

This duty fits me well for a multitude of reasons because there are always new places to see and I get a feel of the people and the country. There is no comparison to this duty and working around the aid station day in and day out. We rotate through the different villages periodically and get to see many of the same faces at different times. Security is a concern, but the VC leave us alone because we are actually caring for their families.

Our civilian interpreters, two young women named Thuy Van and Kim and Papa-son, a man in his forties, love their South Vietnamese people and they show it clearly in their interactions with the people.

Patients are plentiful, the lines are long, and the days are hot and humid. One interpreter works with an enlisted man in front of the line handling triage. One is with the doctors and specialists in treatment, and Papa-son is stationed in the rolling pharmacy dispensing medicine. Much of the treatment is tetracycline injections to combat infection. We also clean and protect wounds and sores and give immunizations. The largest patient groups are the very young and the very old. There are cases of children with shrapnel wounds from land mines, grenades, booby traps and other war related injuries. We treat them all without question. The people always seem happy to see us and extend us every courtesy. We, in return, strive to show our respect and to provide them with quality care.

Things are changing here as fast as the weather changes in Texas, where you can go from a drought to a hurricane in an afternoon.

On the night of January 31, 1968, the base camp is attacked with barrages of mortar fire and rockets from several points around our perimeter. This is the Chinese New Year or Tet, as it is commonly referred to, and there is supposed to be a cease-fire in place. The alarm sounds that sends everyone to the bunkers for protection; I head to my assigned bunker.

Travelling to Medcap Locations   Patients

Small Town Traffic   Lots of Injections

Kim Checking in Patients

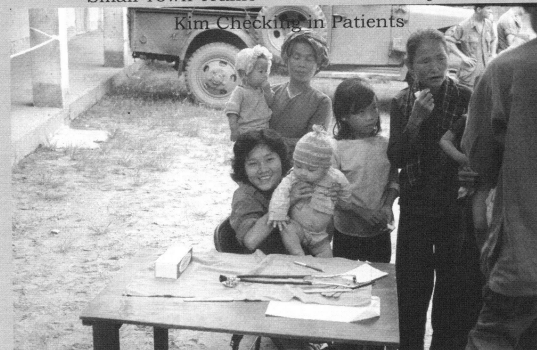

Every night, beyond the base camp perimeter, there are orange illumination flares floating in the sky on parachutes to light the terrain below. They are deployed by being dropped from aircraft or fired in artillery rounds. As I head to the bunker it is apparent that there are a lot more flares out than normal. In the western sky the activity is also heightened. I can see rockets flashing through the black sky and streams of tracer rounds erupting from helicopter gunships attacking VC positions a mile or so beyond our perimeter. The tracer rounds look continuous, and it's hard to conceive that there are four rounds of ball ammunition between each tracer round.

It sounds like the artillery firebase is working overtime by the amount of shellfire I am hearing. Observing the engagement from here is a lot like watching a thunderstorm rolling in across the Texas prairie, but much more serious. I can see the flashes of the rockets, the streaming tracer rounds, and the steady light of the flares, but the sounds of battle are just a rumble in the distance. I thank God that I am experiencing the battle from my present position and not in the ground action just below those flares and gunships.

I enter the bunker, which is just a glorified trench with a three-foot thick layer of sand bags protecting the top. I can hear the exploding mortars walking in closer to the south of us. I don't think we are in any immediate danger. Everyone inside is a little bleary eyed. We stand there quietly waiting for the "all clear" to sound. After ten minutes it sounds and I head to the ER, my emergency post.

When I arrive at the ER we are preparing to take on casualties. We get a few shrapnel wounds from the mortar rounds but nothing critical. I hang around to be of help and to clean up. This is the biggest sustained attack I've seen since arriving in Dian. Most previous attacks consisted of the VC lobbing in three or four mortars or rockets over the perimeter, but they would be retreating by the time the last shell hits the ground.

The next morning news is drifting in that we are not the only base camp that has been attacked. It sounds like there have been attacks in all the major camps and cities throughout the country. This is soon to be known as the "Tet Offensive", the battle that turned the tide of the war.

Drying Fish

Farm with two cantilever water well dippers in front

I've just started being a regular with the MEDCAP operation, but, as of this morning, the operation has been suspended until further notice.

Other things we have grown accustomed to have are also suspended. There will be no more "hooch maids" to clean our quarters and to do our laundry. The civilian workers who keep the outhouses and urinals clean and do the other unskilled routine work are gone. The enlisted men will now enjoy these tasks and the lower the rank and time in grade the more "enjoyment" they will get to become accustomed to. After Tet, security is elevated and all civilians are being more closely screened and monitored.

After a few weeks of tightened security, the MEDCAP operation is resumed. I am glad to be out in the field again and working with the team.

One of the first sites we visit is an orphanage in Saigon. The orphanage is housed in a large building that may have been a school in its first life. All the walls are painted with a beige glossy paint and the whole place looks and smells clean. In one room are rows of cribs filled with infants.

Next to it are the toddlers. There are also rows of beds for them. The beds are the type with partitions of wooden spindles on four-inch centers that raise and lower to keep them from crawling out. Next to the rows of beds is a common area filled with toys. I watch the rambunctious toddlers playing in the common area; if the decibel level is any indicator of fun, they are having a good time. The next large room is a dormitory with rows of bunk beds for the older kids. It reminds me of the barracks we lived in during basic training. A large dining hall that seats about two hundred is next door and that is where we set up.

Having never been to an orphanage before, I had no idea what to expect. Here I experience a side of the war I had never considered. Most, or maybe all, of the children here appear to be offspring of American soldiers, or *Amerasians* as they are called.

Nuns Shading the Way   Girls' School

Class Room   Checking Out the GI's
Kids Waiting Patiently

None of us get to choose our parents or relatives and my heart goes out to these kids; it's obvious they didn't get to choose theirs. As a group they seem to be burdened with an excess of birth defects and abnormalities like cleft lips, double joints, and Down Syndrome. Their physical appearances are also very "abnormal" compared to the general Vietnamese population. It makes me think their genes have been put through a blender. There are albino twins, Asian looking children with black kinky hair, black children with slanted eyes, and many other mixed ethnic combinations. They all have one common trait. Because of their mixed blood, they all are outcast by the Vietnamese and unwanted and unknown by their American fathers.

At first these spoils of war horrify me, but as I work with these innocent victims, I find they are children who need the same love, care and nurturing as I did as a child.

The ladies who work here are wonderful. I can tell theirs is a labor of love. The whole place is like a family unit, with the older children helping out with the younger ones.

We administer childhood immunizations and the doctors do what they can to treat specific maladies. When we finish seeing the patients we pack up all of our equipment and then take about thirty minutes to play with the children. This place is special and I will try to

be a part of making it more so on future visits.

The town centers in the many small towns and villages within a half hour drive are always a welcome spot to set up a MEDCAP. Many times market day coincide with our visits. On one occasion at the end of a busy day, we were packing up all the equipment, tables and chairs and had a small delay in leaving. A couple of us walked through the marketplace aisles. I was surprised by a four hundred pound sow pig walking through the butcher shop area of the market.

I laughed out loud as I thought of the time a pig ruled the roost one day on our farm.

*   *   *   *   *

We always had a couple of pigs around just for the pork in our diet. Louis showed pigs for FFA projects a couple of years.

One time we were feeding out a couple of pigs and steers at the same time in adjacent pens. I can tell you that the pigs and the calves were not always friendly to each other.

Cattle have always had the "grass is greener in the other pasture" syndrome. Driving down the road where cattle are grazing, I would often see several cows pushing their heads through the fence to graze on the other side. Generally, on a barb wire fence, they can take their time, work their heads in and out and not get into too much trouble.

One day one of the steer calves we were feeding out was not so lucky. He had decided to steal some of the pigs' feed. The pigs' feed trough was right on the other side of the wooden corral fence, so he pushed and turned his head between the boards. It was a tight fit, but he reached his mouth into the trough and was able to chow down on the pig's feed. One of the pigs wasn't too enamored by that, so he started chowing down on the steer's right ear. The steer couldn't pull his head straight back thru the board fence because he was pinned in and he was too excited to remember that he had to turn his head to pull it back to free himself.

Later that day Aunt Margret came by to visit Mom. She heard the calf bawling in the barn and went over to check on it. The calf's right ear was gone. The pig ate it smooth off the side of its head and blood was squirting out like a sprinkler hose. She came into the house and frantically told us about that pig chewing on the calf's ear. We scrambled out there as quickly as we could and twisted the calf's head free; it was a bloody mess. If we hadn't separated them, the calf may have gone from a earless calf to a dead headless one. As it turned out, there was no permanent damage. The calf healed and fed out just fine.

After we had the calf butchered, we cooked it up and it was as tender as you please, so we got to eat our share of the pig's leftovers.

*   *   *   *   *

Child at Market

Pig Walking through Butcher Shop

Busy Market Day

Town Market

Sidewalk Vendor

Another place we regularly visit is a refugee camp which holds several hundred people displaced by the war. There are rows and rows of small wooden houses. The administrator of the camp is an Australian nurse and she is like an angel the way she cares for these displaced people. When I was back in the States and read or saw news coverage of the war, I never considered so many of the things here that have to be dealt with. Until I saw the numbers of refugees, I didn't know that problem existed at all.

As on most of our MEDCAP sites, the biggest problem is infection. It can be from a sore, scratch or whatever. The people can't or don't keep the areas clean and dressed. We always have a workstation for cleaning wounds with an antibacterial cleanser called Phisohex. After that, we apply a clean dressing and then administer a shot of tetracycline antibiotic.

On one occasion Thuy Van and I were sitting at a table screening patients. A teenage boy was next in line. The whole left side of his face was red and swollen with an angry looking abscess. I reached up to touch it to feel how tender the skin and how hard the abscess was. With just my slightest touch the abscess erupted and puss leapt from his cheek, covering my face and drenching the front of my fatigues. I yelled at a green uniform behind me, "Get me a f*#$%ing towel!"

The man responded quickly and helped me get cleaned up. Only then did I realize that the man I had yelled at was Major Stewart and not one of the enlisted men. I apologized to the major for talking to him like a sailor. He was very gracious and said that the extreme condition demanded speedy and direct action.

After I cleaned up, I checked on the boy. The doctor had lanced and cleaned the wound, then packed and bandaged it up. The doctor ordered a double dose of tetracycline. As I gave him a shot in each cheek of his buttocks, he smiled and thanked me.

He was there on our next trip to the site and almost totally healed.

MEDCAP to Remote Village.

Second trip, landing zone marked by yellow smoke

Loading Jeep and Trailer   View from the Inside

Lift Off

Landing View

Tape recorders are also a popular way to send correspondence back and forth. I buy two, three-inch reel-to-reel tape recorders and send one home. They are easy and simple to use, but having a conversation with a box is almost as hard as writing a letter, except they are easier to understand. My original plan is to send a tape home, have the family overwrite the same tape and send it back. This doesn't eliminate the chore of writing because I found out that for this to work my family back home had to talk into a box to respond. What ended up happening is I would send a tape and get letters in return. That was an acceptable arrangement for me.

As a side note, these tape boxes serve many of the potheads serving in Vietnam well. They could send as much mail home as they wanted for free. Marijuana is cheap and plentiful, and its use is unchallenged over here. Serious users box the stuff in tape boxes or ones of a similar size and mail them home, addressed to themselves.

I receive a letter from my brother Peter shortly after Tet. It's a long letter with the details of his moving from Texas to Tennessee during one of his transfers.

Louis had taken leave from Fort Hood to help him move. Peter said that Louis was driving his car and that he was following in a rented pickup and that they had both vehicles tightly packed. Early in the morning after driving all night, Louis fell asleep and careened off the road, totaling Peter's car and breaking his jaw.

I stop reading for a moment and take a breath thinking, "I'm in a war zone and it may be safer place than home."

He went on to say that Louis had surgery on his jaw and that his mouth was wired totally shut. For the next six weeks Louis would be getting all of his food through a straw, but, other than that, he would recover completely.

The letter also included a picture of my first niece, Lisa Marie Peltier, who was born shortly after they arrived in Tennessee. He also included a picture of a skinny, broken faced Louis. Peter was so proud and happy to be a father. The letter was electrified with his happiness.

The next problem Peter addressed in the letter was that Louis's accident put him in the position of not having a car to get to work in. He asked if I could spare a few hundred dollars so he could buy a clunker to get around in.

Sending him the money is an easy decision. There is nothing here I want or need to spend money on. The times have changed a lot since we were growing up in Danbury. He is in the Navy in Pennsylvania with a new baby. Louis is at Fort Hood, Texas, with a broken jaw. Kenneth is at Stephen F. Austin University pledging a fraternity, chasing girls, and I'm here, homesick, wishing I were somewhere else.

It isn't uncommon to encounter U.S. and ARVN troops in the field as we travel to and from MEDCAP sites. In March of 1968 we come upon a U.S. infantry company that had been involved in a firefight a short time before we arrived. It is apparent there was a firefight because there are about a dozen VC bodies laid out in a row. Our little convoy halts and Captain Parker offers assistance to the commander of the infantry company.

While the Captain is with the infantry commander, the rest of us get out and check out the situation. The area appears to be secure because the infantry company's men are relaxed, sitting around in groups talking. I go over and take a look at the dead VC. They are all dressed in what looked like black silk pajamas and look like small boys younger that myself. The pile of captured AK-47 rifles and grenades look as if they could kill a man just as dead as those boys who carried them.

This is my first sight of death first hand. I know this war is about killing the enemy as they try to kill us. Those boys were living and breathing an hour ago and it just seems to be a waste. Now their bodies lay over there motionless, mangled and bloody and all we have is the assurance that they won't be a threat to us anymore.

The wounded GI's have already been dusted off to the hospital in Long Binh. We are rounded up and head back to the base camp. The captain passes the word that no GI's were killed and four were wounded in the firefight. As I drive back to the base camp my mind is going over and over the sight of those dead boys. I had been out of the habit of praying and going to church, but that night I prayed for those dead men and I had a long one-way talk with God about this war.

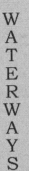

Saigon River   Muddy Tributary

Taxi   River's Edge

Washing, Bathing, Carrying Water, Transportation

WATERWAYS

Commerce on the Water

Living Near the Water   Living on the Water

Within a month of seeing the dead VC, one of the doctors I work with regularly on MEDCAP's asked me to drive him to Long Bien and assist him with filling out death certificates. I can only guess that they rotate this duty to all the doctors in the area because it is about a thirty minute drive to Long Bien and it is the site of one of the largest military hospitals in the country.

We enter the Graves Registration Building, a large cold air-conditioned room. Two enlisted men, eating sandwiches, are talking and sitting at a desk by the door. There is a musty smell of death in the air. There are three lines of ten gurneys each with a heavy gray rubber body bag laid on top of each one, zipped up tight.

An enlisted man hands me a clipboard of death certificates with names, serial numbers and unit information filled out. The certificates lack cause of death and need a doctor's signature to be complete. They show us how to match them up with each bag and then they go back to their lunch.

As we start this gruesome task, I unzip the first bag. The doctor writes down a brief description of how it appears the soldier died. I zip it up and we go to the next one. It is impossible to tell how some of these men died. When in doubt, he writes "*gunshot wound to the chest*". One thing is for sure and that is that they are all dead and a day earlier they had been alive. The men all looked to be in their late teens or early twenties. It seems to me that their lives were over before they had a chance to pursue the happiness that we all dream of.

We finish our task in about an hour and a half. I am happy to leave that place and get back on the road to Dian.

*   *   *   *   *

I was raised in the Roman Catholic Church and received the sacraments of Baptism, First Communion, and Confirmation as part of my religious education. I was an altar boy and assisted the priest in the sacrifice of the Mass. I had committed my life to Christ and accepted him as my Lord and Savior when I was thirteen. I attended church every Sunday and Holy Days, but none of that prepared me for this.

Nighty Flares around Basecamp Perimeter

Recorded Tapes in Lieu of Letters

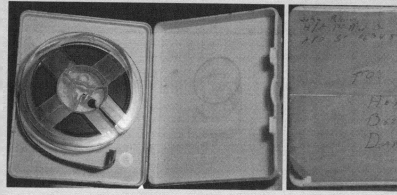

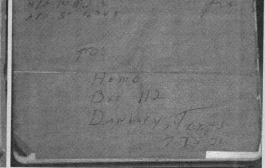

C-Rations Postcards

Accessories

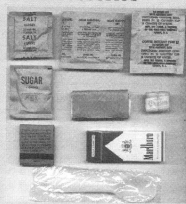

MEAL, COMBAT, INDIVIDUAL
Spaghetti W/Ground Meat
B-2 UNIT

MEAL, COMBAT, INDIVIDUAL
Ham and Eggs, Chopped
B-1A UNIT

Being raised in the Roman Catholic Church, every Sunday without fail we heard the Mass in Latin from the priest and didn't understand a word. Peter and Kay were older and could stay still during Mass. Louis, Kenneth and I started that way, but soon one of us would slide down under the pew, playing with the kneeler, being generally disruptive. Corralling us was like keeping fishing worms in a coffee can. Some are always trying to crawl out over the lip.

Every summer after public school let out we had to attend Catholic Christian Doctrine (CCD) classes for one week of half days in the mornings. We still did our normal chores, but we got a break from work in the rice field. We surely liked that part. There were always lots of fun games and the snacks were really a treat. The church shipped in nuns to teach us, but they always seemed bold, cold, old, and a little scary to me.

In the summer after finishing the first grade we prepared to receive First Communion. We learned about Jesus and how he died and suffered for our sins and how to confess those sins through the priest and all would be well. I may not have understood all that I was being taught, but I was astute enough to get the facts sufficient to join the rest of the children. The girls dressed in their frilly white dresses and we boys wore snappy miniature coats and sharp clip-on ties as we received our first Holy Communion.

Every Wednesday after school during the school year, we went to Catechism classes to further our spiritual education. The real highlight of the class was that on the walk from school to the church, we were allowed to charge a nickel each for a treat at Griffin's Store, which served both as the local post office and the local grocery store. Now days that doesn't sound like much, but then it was a big deal. The choices were a bottle of pop, which we had to drink there because the deposit on the bottle was two cents, a hand dipped scoop of ice cream, a candy bar or a handful of hard candy. I remember going in one time and asking for a coke. Mrs. Griffin opened, and handed me a bottle of Coca Cola. I looked at her, kind of dismayed, and said, "No, I want a Grapette Coke."

As my spiritual education continued I learned that a penance of three "Our Father's" and ten "Hail Mary's" covered most of the sins I confessed to the priest. I started training as an altar boy with Ronnie Peltier, the son of my godparents, Catine and Eddie. Ronnie was my best friend in those early years. We had to learn all the Latin responses to the priest during the Mass. It took us some time and we learned them, but we still didn't know what they meant. (It wasn't until the early 1960's that the Mass was said in the language of the population.) We also learned how to prepare the wine and water for the Mass. Ronnie and I learned about the taste of wine from experience.

The Church was steeped in tradition and ceremony. We participated in weddings, funerals, holy days, and Sunday Mass. Occasionally someone would slip us a few dollars for our service. That part I could get used to.

In my early teens I started preparing for the sacrament of Confirmation. In the Catholic Church, the sacrament of Confirmation is a sacrament given to those who are already baptized. It is the Church's belief that when someone is confirmed, that person receives the gifts of the Holy Ghost, enabling him to be a stronger Christian and a soldier of Jesus Christ.

My spiritual life until that time had been mostly social and just going along to get along. A series of events at that time occurred that transformed my spiritual life.

During the time I was recuperating from Sparkle's kick in the face, I became more serious in my studies of God and how He interacts with us mortal beings. The thought that my life could have been ended or greatly impaired by the slight difference of the trajectory of the flying horse's hoof haunted me. Was it just fate or did God have a hand in it?

Conservative by nature, I chose God.

Theresa, a young lady (18-19) helping with our Confirmation instruction at that time, took an interest in me and my plight. She came to our home several times while I was recovering from my injuries. Through those meetings, her explanations and instruction, I saw God's love through her.

It became clear that God's love wasn't about me, or her, or feelings. It was about trusting and actions and a personal relationship with a god I couldn't see, I couldn't hear, but whom I knew was there. I'm sure Theresa had no idea how she was an instrument that changed my life. God really entered my life. He was as real to me as the scar on my right cheek, and I knew that He would be with me wherever I might roam.

*   *   *   *   *

Ever since we came upon those dead VC lying on the ground and then today seeing the bodies of our young soldiers, I have been trying to reconcile this war with my faith.

That night I prayed for these men and their loved ones back home. I asked God how he could allow these young men to be snuffed out like candles in the wind.

I continued to talk to God, but I'm sure he didn't like my tone or what I had to say. There was no praise in my thoughts, only cursing and shouting and lamentation. I laid the blame for all these circumstances directly at His feet.

There are times when I lose most of whatever soft or gentle nature I had when I arrived. When I consider the death, destruction and chaos that is all around, I feel like I'm living within the shadow of darkness.

Then I hide and gird myself up in an armor of drugs and alcohol and try to escape from all the things that my 19 year old mind and body are experiencing, but not understanding. I can't leave this country and the war, but I try to take my mind on mini-vacations from time to time.

My transformation is not the exception but the rule for most of the soldiers during their time in Vietnam. A popular and appropriate axiom embroidered on the back of silk shirts available in local markets is *"Yea Thou I Walk Through the Shadow of the Valley of Death I Fear No Evil, Because I am the Evilest Son of a Bitch in the Valley"*.

Survival is our main goal, to get home in one piece. There are no front lines in this war. Being creatures of habit, we fall into place for weeks or months; then a booby trap, a satchel charge, or a land mine disrupts, changes, or ends unsuspecting lives. We are never prepared for those incidents, but we are never really surprised by them either. The best we can do is to put up a hardened shell around us that doesn't let a lot of things in or out of our lives.

Note: Twenty years after my return from Vietnam and after fifteen years of marriage, three children, twelve years in my own business and God only knows how much prayer and encouragement from my wife and others, I returned once again to the peace and comfort of a personal relationship with Jesus Christ.

In a nutshell, the answer came to me as I was in a Bible study of Romans and the passage in 6:23- "For the wages of sin is death, but the gift of God is eternal life through Jesus Christ our Lord."

We are all sinners, including all those men who died in Vietnam, World Wars One and Two, and everyone else living and dead. That is our death warrant. Jesus is our salvation, like a "get out of jail free card" because He was pure and sinless, died for our sins before we loved Him and is our conduit to heaven.

I had experienced success in business, a wonderful wife and family, including all the trappings that went with them. With all those things, I still had a big hole in my life. When I recommitted myself to Jesus, all the parts of my life came together and I was made whole again. I found the inner peace that I had lost long ago in Vietnam.

Vietnam is hot and humid and that never seems to change much. It isn't a great deal different than the Texas Gulf Coast. I guess the main difference is how we cool off. During the monsoon season the rain cools us down nearly every day. In the hooches we have fans that are continuously humming during the day when the power is generating. The evenings cool down to a comfortable level. It reminds me of the way we dealt with heat in Texas.

*   *   *   *   *

Water was the secret of staying cool during the hot summers of Texas. Most of us learned to swim in a reservoir that stored water for irrigating the rice fields. There was a gradual slope into the water and no current. Peter and my cousin Ralph taught me how to swim, which meant to tread water and dog paddle. As soon as they figured I was good enough not to drown myself, I graduated to swimming in the bayou.

Austin Bayou was about a quarter of a mile northwest of our house on Hoskins Mound Road. It was our favorite swimming hole. Sometime earlier our cousins had taken a tractor and stretched a three quarter inch cable across the bayou at a fork just east of the bayou bridge. We fashioned a trolley from an old pulley off a combine, some flat steel and a ten-foot length of thick rope. When we would come in from the fields we headed to the bayou for a swim. We wore ourselves the rest of the way out by taking a running start in front of the oak tree, grabbing the rope as high as we could reach as we cleared the bank and glided on the cable to the middle of the bayou, making a big splash as we dropped off. We built a little pier out of fence posts and some scraps of wood and constructed a raft by strapping together four thirty gallon barrels under an eight foot square deck. Uncle Pete gave us the barrels. Over the years we always added ways to make our water park more fun.

The drainage district dredged a sharp turn out of the bayou, creating an island out of what was a peninsula. It was only about fifty foot square, but it served as a fort and a nice playground. It rose about five feet out of the water and was made up of a reddish-yellow hard clay. We worked a slide into the clay bank and kept it slick with buckets of water. It was hard on our cutoffs and shorts but a lot of fun. We never took towels to the bayou. Mom was afraid they wouldn't make it back to the house, so after our last dip in the water for the day, we would shake off the water like dogs and drip dry on the walk home.

Another way to beat the Texas heat was ice cream. Having milk cows there was always plenty of milk.

I remember one hot August day in 1958. At six o'clock in the afternoon Dad pulled up in our 1954 gray Kaiser. Louis, Kenneth and I were playing football in the yard.

Dad broke up the game saying, "You boys unload the feed bags from the trunk and take care of the block of ice."

That could only mean one thing. We were going to have ice cream for dessert that night.

Louis drove the car up to the barn and he and Kenneth

unloaded the bags of feed. They had to be careful not to rip the bags. They were made from a heavy cotton cloth with a blue and brown paisley design. In a few days those bags would be emptied of feed and would contain us in the form of new clothes.

I put the fifty pound block of ice in a gunny sack and took it down by the garage to break. I took an ice pick and chipped it into two halves. I put one half in the freezer on the back porch. Mom was busy mixing up the recipe for the ice cream mixer. The aroma of pineapple pies baking in the oven was fighting with the smell of Sloppy Joes Dad was frying up for dinner, and they all had my mouth watering in anticipation.

I went back out and started banging with a sledge hammer on the rest of the ice inside the sack. When the ice it was down to fist-sized pieces, I picked up the gunny sack and swung it like an ax against the concrete slab to finish crushing the ice so it was in pieces small enough to fit into the ice cream maker.

As I was finishing up, Peter and Kay brought out two ice cream makers filled with Mom's not yet "ice" cream. Peter carefully poured my chipped ice, alternated with salt, all around the containers inside the ice cream makers. When they were filled up to the top, he covered each with a beach towel. Becky, Stephen and Paul then took turns sitting on the towels to steady the makers while Louis, Kenneth and I took turns cranking.

After about twenty minutes of steady cranking, our arms were tired. The younger kids complained of cold butts, as the cranks were getting hard to turn. That meant the recipe that started with the consistency of milk was becoming thick and creamy. Dad pulled the top on one of the mixers, took a taste with the end of his finger, smiled and said, "It's ready."

We took the crank mechanisms off and set the buckets in the kitchen sinks. The ice cream cans sat immersed in the ice and salt water bath inside the buckets. They appeared to be almost hiding under the drapes of the colorful beach towels. Our ice cream matched up nicely with the four pies sitting on their cooling racks in the pass-through window to the back porch.

All of us sat down around the table.

Dad looked around at us until we were all quiet and still. Then, starting with the Sign of the Cross, we all recited together: *"In the name of the Father and of the Son and of the Holy Ghost. Amen. Bless us, Oh Lord, and these Thy gifts, which we are about to receive from thy bounty, through Christ our Lord. Amen. In the name of the Father and of the Son and of the Holy Ghost. Amen* (as we all made the Sign of the Cross again). "

We eyed the ice cream cans in the sink as we ate our Sloppy Joe's. Soon we all completed the prerequisite of eating the main course. Only after we had all finished our supper did Dad finally go over to the sink and uncover the ice cream makers. We were all eyes as he carefully removed the cover of the containers protecting the ice cream from the salt water and ice. Then, taking a rubber spatula in one hand and with his other hand pulling out the dasher, he pushed the ice cream back into the can as the dasher came out.

Mom said, "Kay, you and Becky start serving up the pie. Peter, stay and help your dad take the ice cream outside after he gets the dashers stripped out of the cans. The rest of you kids go outside; it's hot as Hades in here."

Soon Becky and Kay came out carrying trays of beige Melmac bowls filled with pieces of warm pineapple pie. They spread them all out on the picnic table. Dad stood at the end of the table with a long handled stainless steel spoon ready to scoop out portions of ice cream into our bowls. We formed a line; each took a bowl and held it out in front of Dad as he served us ice cream to go on top of our pie.

All of us really enjoyed homemade ice cream, but in our exuberance many of us were sometimes ended up moaning and holding our heads in pain because we'd eaten so much so fast. We knew ice cream needed to be consumed with a little more moderation and that in order to enjoy it we had to pace ourselves a little; otherwise we'd be holding our heads in pain. Not all of us ever fully learned that lesson, but we surely did love our ice cream!

After the dishes were done, we went outside and played "Murder in the Dark". Then we chased the lightning bugs that filled the night air like sparks from a fire. We caught them between our palms and then peaked at them through a gap in our thumbs. A lightning bug was like a one-man show on the stage inside our palms, doing both the acting and providing the light.

*　　*　　*　　*　　*

Now as I sit on the bunker, half a world away from those nights of the enchantment of the fire flies and night games, I see flares floating down and lighting up the landscape outside the perimeter of the base camp. Instead of fireflies, I see streams of machine gun fire streaming out of a helicopter gunship tearing into the area, destroying everything in its paths.

I want to return to those carefree days of my youth, but somehow I think those days are forever past. I have entered another season of my life.

9
MORE THAN YOU EVER WANTED TO KNOW ABOUT CATTLE

You can take the boy out of the country, but you can't take the country out of the boy.

Being part of the MEDCAP program allows me to be out into the Vietnamese countryside frequently. I really enjoy the rural backdrop. I feel at home seeing the cattle, pigs, and chickens, as well as the crops growing in the fields. The scale of the operations are much different than that which I am accustomed to. Here a herd of cows might be five; where I grew up, it might be fifty to several hundred.

Seeing the cattle here reminds me of the Houston Livestock Show and Rodeo Calf Scramble I had the good fortune to participate in during my last life.

*   *   *   *   *

My brother Peter ran in the Calf Scramble in1957 at the Houston Fat Stock Show and Rodeo.

The rules for the Calf Scramble were simple. There were 20 contestants and 10 calves. Each contestant would try to catch one of the 10 calves. The contestants lined up at one end of the rodeo arena, each armed with a halter rope and an overwhelming desire to capture a calf. Ten calves were let out at the other end of the arena. The scramble began when an official on the Calf Scramble committee waved a flag to start the race. In order to win a certificate of $200 to buy a calf to show the following year, the contestant had to catch one of the ten calves, halter it, and then drag it into a large marked square in the middle of the arena. If the contestant happened to catch a calf inside the square, then he would have to pull it outside the square, turn it around and take it back into the square.

Another rule was that once a contestant had his hands on a calf, no other contestant could touch the calf, except to help the first contestant. Once any contestant got a calf into the square, an official let him know he'd been successful and a committeeman would help with the calf. With his purchased calf, he had to train the calf and take it back to the Livestock Show the next year and show it.

Peter successfully caught a calf and was given a $200 certificate to purchase a heifer and raise it to compete in the Fat Stock Show the following year. He bought a Guernsey heifer he named Patches because of the large white splotches that mingled with her reddish colored hair. He halter broke her, fed and groomed her and made her ready for the show barn. He showed her in competition in several youth fairs, the Brazoria County Fair and finally the Houston Fat Stock Show. At that time, I was eight or nine and got to help out with her training.

We were sad when Patches died giving birth to her first calf.

From Peter's experience, I knew that when I was old enough, I wanted to run in the Scramble and get a calf, too.

When I reached junior high, I became a member of the Four H Club. The Four H pledge was: *My head to clearer thinking,*

> *My heart to greater loyalty,*

> *My hands to larger service, and*

> *My health to better living,*

> *For my club, my community, and my country.*

It was my first club experience outside of church and school. The main draw of Four H for me was that each year the club was allowed several slots in the Houston Livestock Show and Rodeo Calf Scramble event. (In 1961 the name was changed to Houston Livestock, rather than "Fat Stock," because the people of this country were starting to think "lean" as far as their beef was concerned.)

The Future Farmers of America (also known as FFA) were also offered slots for the Calf Scramble, but I couldn't join them until I was in high school.

Finally, when I was in the eighth grade, I became old enough to participate in Four H. One part of the requirements for eligibility for the drawing for one of the slots was that we had to write an essay giving the reasons we wanted to participate. My writing skills were shaky at best. In my heart I knew a thousand reasons why I should be chosen, but getting them down on paper, communicating them in the written word was another story, a very difficult task for me. But I finally got the essay complete and sent in.

The weeks of waiting after that were real torture for me.

Finally, one day I received a envelope in the mail with the Livestock Show logo and return address in the corner!   I was so nervous, I could hardly breath. Louis and Kenneth were standing beside me at the time, yelling, "Open it! Open it!"

I wanted to rip the envelope open, but I was afraid it might contain bad news and dash all my hopes.

But I did borrow Louis's pocket knife and got the envelope open. About halfway down the page, I saw the good news!

I leapt in the air, screaming, "Yaa hoo!!"

I was selected to run in the 1963 Houston Livestock Show and Rodeo Calf Scramble event. A long awaited wish came true.

There was not much I could think of to do to prepare for the Scramble, other than be in good shape.   Playing on the basketball team pretty much took care of that.

The day of the event finally arrived.

I had a large group of well wishers cheering me on. The Livestock Show and Rodeo was held then in downtown Houston at the Coliseum.   The meeting room where the contestants gathered was full. The committeeman explained the rules to us one more time. The rules were the same as when Peter was a contestant. Then we were given a tee shirt with a number on it. We changed into the tee shirts and a roll call was taken to be sure everyone had his or her right number. Then we were herded out into a bank of seats at one end of the arena to watch the rodeo until it was time for the Calf Scramble to begin.

I felt like a gladiator as I was waiting to perform. I was ready and confident. I could still count. There were only ten calves and twenty contestants and I knew half of us would leave empty handed. It seemed like only minutes had passed before we were winding through the gates and pens behind the chutes, getting into position to go out. The roar of the crowd and smells of the animals as we walked added to the excitement.

I heard over the loudspeakers, "And the next event will be the world's largest calf scramble."

We took our positions across one end of the arena. A large group of committeemen, sponsors and photographers formed a funnel to direct the calves toward us. The calves were two to three hundred pound Angus. To me, they looked like black boxes with legs, not at all like the tall lanky Brahma crossbreeds that we raised.

With his flag raised, the official watched the calves as they approached us. Then he dropped the flag. As all twenty of us charged the herd, the calves scattered like a covey of quail. I was no match for the smaller kids when it came to running, so my strategy was to trap a calf in a corner of the arena. After a few minutes, I could tell that about half the calves were in the process of getting haltered. Soon the rest of us contestants were running out of gas. Fortunately, the calves were starting to slow down, too.

By that time, I still hadn't touched a calf, but I saw one coming my way. I angled in to cut him off and leaped for his neck. All of a sudden I had my hands full of calf, but that calf was not at all happy and proceeded to drag me around like a rag doll. I couldn't stand up to get control, so I had to hang tight onto the calf's neck until he stopped. When he finally did, he was standing on top of me. I knew I was doomed and would have to let go. There were four or five other contestants circling me and that calf, like vultures on prey. The calf dug a hoof into my abdomen, my arms fell away from its neck, and it was gone.

As I lay there for a minute catching my breath, a committeeman came up to see if I was okay. I told him I was fine. My tee shirt had a gaping hole in the front. I felt like I had been run over by a small truck, plus I was calf-less. Finally, I got up and moved toward the winners square and helped another contestant get his calf across the finish line.

The sympathy I received from my family and friends was nice and they said that I had put on a good show, but I was still disappointed. The calf's hoof laid back my skin about an inch wide by two inches long and it took a long time to heal because any large movement I made would reopen the wound again.

I was in high school the next year and joined the FFA. I just couldn't wait to buy an FFA jacket, with my name on the front and the giant FFA insignia on the back. It was the in thing. Gene Bigbie was our ag instructor and when the time came to apply for a slot in the Calf Scramble he encouraged me to do it. I knew there were a lot of guys who wanted to participate, but the fact that I already had prior experience gave me little hope. I put together a half-hearted essay and submitted it. My best friend and cousin Ronnie Peltier did the same.

The notice came and I wasn't selected as a contestant, but as an alternate. That left me with a glimmer of hope but not much, even though I didn't know how far down the alternate list I was. Ronnie was selected.

Lo and behold, a few weeks before the show I got another notice. I was in! I was so happy I could hear the alleluia chorus playing loudly in my head.

In late January as we were putting out hay to about twenty cows and calves in the pasture behind the house, I called Ronnie up told him, "Why don't you come on out and let's practice for the scramble on the calves out back?"

He thought that was a good idea.

About twenty minutes later he showed up in his dad's truck. We grabbed two pieces of rope for halters and tucked them under our belts, just like we would carry them in the scramble. We approached the herd as quietly as we could. They were used to us because we fed them every day, but I figured that in the open pasture we still might have trouble getting close enough to a calf to grab it and I knew that we couldn't trap them.

Ronnie suggested that I go first.

It was my idea, so I just nodded and eased in close to a black heifer about the right size whose mother was grazing about twenty feet away. Like a lightning bolt, I rushed in, grabbed the calf and threw it to the ground. Like another lightning bolt, the mother charged in, pushing me off the calf and into the dirt. As soon as the calf was a safe distance away, the cow snorted and moved away, too. Ronnie was laughing so hard that I thought he was going to split his gut.

I told him, "Thanks for keeping that cow off me."

He just laughed harder.

I was glad about Dad's policy to dehorn all of our cows.

Ronnie decided not to try for a calf that day, but had great fun telling that story to my brothers and the whole school.

Ronnie's scramble was a few nights before mine was scheduled. I told him everything I knew about what not to do in the arena, like don't use all your energy the first few minutes and work the calves against the walls or corners and not the open areas. I sat with his family on the night he ran and was happy to watch him successfully catch a calf and win a certificate.

After that, the heat was on me. Most of my family, along with Ronnie and his family, came to watch. Not like the cool calm guy I was the year before, I had a bad case of butterflies. I was determined to give it my all anyway.

When the flag dropped, I followed my own advice and hung back. Soon there was a group of four or five calves coming my way being chase by six or so contestants. I headed them toward the corner where I was able to grab the closest calf by his front leg. This time, when the calf jumped, I kept my feet under me, grabbed a hoof and lifted up hard. That took his other legs off the ground and I landed on top of him like I was supposed to do. I worked the halter over his head, making sure it was aligned and snug. I was taking no chances this time. With my left hand, I grabbed the halter close to the calf's chin and grabbed its tail in my right hand. I rose up, pulling the calf with me. Together we headed for the square in the middle of the arena. I was so relieved when the official took my name and number and told me I could relax.

Until then, I hadn't heard the noise of the announcer, the crowd or the band. After my success, that was all I could hear.

Ronnie and I both received certificates of $200 to purchase a dairy calf. My sponsor was the Houston Press Club of Houston. We went to Alvin to the Knape Dairy and purchased our two Holstein heifers.

I named my calf Daisy. Over the next year I fed, groomed, and halter broke her. Ronnie and I both showed our calves in youth fairs throughout the area, though with lackluster success. The biggest show was the Brazoria County Fair in October where I got a white ribbon. The Houston Livestock Show was coming up in February of the next year (1965). I had a feeling that I was going to make a poor showing, but I knew that I had to go anyway.

The time arrived and Ronnie and I, with our calves, were delivered at the Coliseum in downtown Houston. Our parents helped us get checked in. We were in adjoining stalls. Each stall was just a slot about eight feet wide on a long aisle. We centered our show boxes in front of our stalls and stacked our hay between them. I had built my show box in woodshop and had designed it to hold all the gear I would need to groom, feed, and care for Daisy and myself while showing her.

The best part of the Houston show was that it lasted all week, which meant I got to stay all week; it was too far from Danbury to drive back and forth each day. No school! Ronnie's parents let Ronnie stay only on show days so I took care of his calf while he was gone.

Accommodations were sparse. For fifty cents a night I could stay in the dormitory on an army cot, but I decided to sleep on the hay with Daisy and save some of the five dollars Dad had given me to last the week. The first night, I rolled out my bedroll about eleven o'clock. I didn't know that the lights would never be turned off. About midnight the cleaning crew showed up and worked till about four a.m. I was pretty miserable the next day. Ronnie didn't know what he was missing.

The next day, a man showed up from The Press Club of Houston and invited me to have dinner with them on Monday. The invitation was totally unexpected. I could count on one hand how many times I had eaten in a restaurant. I knew Ronnie was going to be around, so I asked if I could bring a friend. The man said that would be okay.

The Press Club was on the top floor of a tall skyscraper. Ronnie and I walked over from the show and were a little intimidated as we entered the dining room. We could smell the cigar smoke and see men sitting around in deep conversations. It was a big fancy room with walnut block paneled walls, thick velvet drapes on the windows, and crystal light fixtures. The tables were set with at least twice as much glass and silverware than I thought we needed. A waiter sat us down at our table in oversized leather chairs and offered us menus. Then he took a chance and told us to order anything we wanted!

Ronnie and I looked at each other, wondering what we were doing there in our western shirts and jeans, looking and probably smelling like we had just cleaned the stalls, which we had.

Ronnie smiled and whispered, "What the hell, I'm having a steak."

"That's exactly what I was thinking," I replied.

We both ordered large ribeyes, with all the trimmings. When we finished that, we each polished off a couple of pieces of hot apple pie a la mode. When we were finished, a few of the members came over to inquire about my project. I felt pretty sorry after having the finest meal I had ever eaten to let them know that Daisy was more than likely not going to take a blue ribbon. They didn't appear to be overly concerned. As we were about to go, one of the members pulled an envelope from the inside of his jacket and handed it to me. I hoped it wasn't a bill for the meal because I had only a couple of dollars on me. Furthermore, I knew from the prices on the menu the cost of the meal we'd just eaten was more money than I had ever made in a week.

I opened the envelope. Neatly tucked inside were twenty five dollars, along with a note wishing me good luck with my calf. I didn't know how to thank them, but I tried every way I knew how.

Ronnie and I both showed our calves the next day. The judges lined us up in descending order. Ronnie and I stood side by side. I was at the end of the line, dead last.

Ronnie went back home that night and I stayed with the calves. I had all I could stand of trying to sleep with the lights on, so I started looking for another place to bed down.

After the rodeo was over that night and everyone had left the Coliseum, I did a little scouting around. I found up in the very corner, behind the highest seats, a small triangular concrete floor space with about five feet of headroom. I got my bedroll and made myself a little nest up there. The concrete was hard and rats ran through from time to time, but it was dark and I finally got some sleep.

The rest of the week was mine to do as I pleased. I tried to sleep late, but I couldn't. I fed, watered, and walked the calves and then cleaned the stalls, but that only took an hour. Afterwards, I walked the streets of Houston and discovered the Rivoli Art Cinema. My eyes bulged at the pictures of scantily clad girls on the posters outside. I tried to buy a ticket to see a show, but the man in the ticket booth told me to get lost and not to hang around there.

A couple of the afternoons I rode the bus over to West 34th Street to visit my cousins Johnny, Phyllis and Pat Fischer. It took me several tries to get there and conferences with different bus drivers. Pat told me to get on the route that was posted on the front of the bus and I did, but never saw the stop.

The driver pulled over and told me, "This is the end of the line," as he started turning a crank in the front of the bus.

"What are you doing?" I asked.

"I'm changing the route on the front of the bus."

I felt betrayed. He was changing the route without taking me where I needed to go.

"I was told to get off at 34th Street, but this bus never stopped there," I said disappointedly.

"This bus is the express bus and doesn't stop at all the stops that the regular route does," he informed me.

Then he went on to tell me how to get to where I needed to go.

My education about this big city continued. By the end of the week I could get around on Houston's public transportation like a veteran.

Friday came and it was time to leave. I had seen and learned a lot, but life on a farm didn't have large blocks of time with nothing to do and I realized that I would rather be busy.

Bored and broke, I was happy to leave the big city lights and get home to Danbury.

*   *   *   *   *

Compared to the Vietnamese people, the way we raised and produced cattle was like night and day. In Vietnam their cattle almost lived in the house with their owners. I cannot help but compare their way to how we operated our place in Texas.

*   *   *   *   *

The cattle part of the family farm was a very important part of our lives.

The cattle provided milk, butter, cottage cheese and beef for our family diet, as well as much needed income. At the start of school each fall, Dad sold a few steers and bought us all new shoes, shirts and blue jeans. He also provided a steer to the school cafeteria in return for our lunches. But none of that just showed up on the table, in the closet or in the bank. There was always a process.

Our herd was made up of Brahman crossbred cattle. In order to survive the harsh summers, insects, and enormous swings in humidity and temperature, the cattle needed to be one quarter to one half Brahman. The Brahman breed coped better with parasites like ticks and horn flies, too. They also did better with the heat and humidity in our area of Texas. So cross breeding Brahman cattle with Angus, Hereford, Charolais, Limousin, and other great meat producers worked well for us. The term for crossbreeding animals of different species to maximize their best traits to produce the best animals for a specific purpose or climate is called "heterosis". The crossbreeding had to be done in specific ratios for best results.

My first memory of working cattle was when I about seven years old. It was in the spring and Homer Prunty, a family friend and cowboy, was driving us in his pickup to the corral where some neighbors had gathered their herd. My cousin Ronnie and I were there as passengers, jumping and pushing each other around in the cab.

"You boys quit playing and sit down, or I'm going to hog tie you both," Homer warned us.

We didn't quit the roughhousing, and sure enough, he stopped the truck in the middle of that salt grass prairie, tied our wrists to our ankles behind our backs and put us in the back of the truck on top of some loose hay. When we arrived at the corrals in about ten minutes, he untied us and told us to stay out of the way, and that was that.

I don't think those cows had seen a person all winter. They were chasing each other and running around, wild eyed just trying to hurt someone. Ronnie and I watched through the fence at the cowboys herding the cows into a catch pen. One of the cows broke away and ran straight toward us, butted the board fence, and let out a loud snort. We both screamed and bolted to the truck for safety. We kept a low profile for the rest of the day. Dad and the other men tried to get us to tackle the baby calves for branding. We looked at them. We both weighed about fifty pounds. Those calves weighed at least twice that much, so we decided to do what Homer told us earlier and stay out of the way.

*   *   *   *   *

All summer we checked on the cattle as regularly as we did the rice fields.

The herd was in one of the pastures next to the rice fields, enabling us to always be looking for circling buzzards or a cow separated from the herd or anything else that looked out of order.

In my early years, one of the things we looked for was screwworms. The worms were placed on a cow by flies depositing their eggs on the edge of an open wound of warm blooded animals. When the eggs hatched, the resulting larvae crawled into the wound and fed on the living flesh. Unchecked, the animal would die in five to ten days. Various other types of flies also laid eggs in the same way, but their larvae ate only dead flesh. That was not so fatal.

We always had a jar of Smear 66 in the car. Smear 66 was a black petroleum based antiseptic paste that would kill the larvae. We applied it to the cattle with a thick brush or a small wooden paddle. The hard part was that the animal had to be immobilized to administer the paste. Sometimes the animal was down and already immobilized or almost dead. Other times we had to round up the horses and rope a cow to treat it. Screwworms were ugly. If we came upon an animal with screwworms the wound would be boiling with the little worms. At times the animal would be walking and some of the larvae would fall off as it moved. Cattlemen before the 1960's lost around ten percent of their herds each year to screwworms.

Someone figured that if sterile screwworm male flies were introduced

181

into the female screwworm fly population, their eggs would not reproduce. That program was initiated in Texas in 1962. As a result, in 1964 Texas was declared free of the epidemic proportions of classified screwworm population. That not only gave the cattle business a boost, but the life expectancy of deer and all other warm blooded animals also increased.

We had an old broken down set of corrals located between the two sloughs in the northeast quadrant of the leased land near where the cattle and the rice fields were located. Running through those abandoned structures was a concrete vat about 30 feet long, 3 feet wide and 6 feet deep.

One day when we were working in that area, I asked Dad what the vat and pens had been used for.

He told me that at one time all the cattle in the area were driven to that vat and had to swim through an arsenic compound bath to kill ticks that caused something they called "Texas fever".

I looked it up later and discovered that the State of Texas had passed a statewide dipping law in 1918; all of the southern states worked together with the federal government to eradicate the tick that caused "Texas fever". The program started in 1906 when many areas in those states had to quarantine their herds for a time before shipping them out. By July of 1922, Texas alone had nearly 10,000 dipping vats. By 1943 most of the quarantines were lifted. In Texas it took a little longer because the whitetail deer were also host animals for the ticks. All of that was before my time, but just seeing that old relic of a vat out in the middle of nowhere was very interesting.

The farming and cattle operations, like everything else, were joined at the hip. Many times on horseback we would check the rice fields for breaks in the levees. We rode carrying shovels much like Sir Lancelot carried his battle ax. We became pretty good at killing snakes by throwing the shovels off our shoulders like arrows or spears. At 10 to 15 feet we were deadly and could pretty cleanly chop the head of a snake off in one motion.

While we were out there in the rice fields, we also rode through the cattle herd and checked on them.

The mosquitoes were so bad at times I had to wear a bandana over my mouth and nose to keep from inhaling them. So many times I recall looking back at my horse Tony's rump to see it covered with mosquitoes so thick that his red coat of hair disappeared under a solid dark gray cover alive with mosquitoes, hunkered down and penetrating his hide. He was constantly swishing his tail to remove them, but his tail just didn't cover enough area to do him any good. I would take my hand, slap his rump and kill hundreds of mosquitoes. Doing so left an impression of my hand in his hair and his back dripping with blood. I would watch that spot and within a minute or so the impression would be gone and blackened again by the hungry mob.

Sometimes we would run the horses just to get away from the mosquitoes. That never worked very well; they still seemed to be everywhere. We protected ourselves with long sleeved shirts and wide brimmed hats, but when the mosquitoes were bad, we were eaten alive.

*   *   *   *   *

Once in the early 1960's when I was fourteen or fifteen, we were rounding up the herd at the field to move them to the house pasture. It was a cool fall day and a calf separated from the herd. Generally a separated calf is easily gathered back up. With a little encouragement from a horse and rider, it would rejoin the herd. This calf would have none of that and was running wild and crazy in every direction but toward the herd. I was on Paint and Louis was on Sparkle. Louis ran behind it and I flanked to its left. I was frustrated with the calf and without giving it much thought, closed in on it. When I was close, I decided to tackle it and end the chase. I jumped from the horse, grabbed the calf around the neck, and bulldogged it. The calf and I went tumbling to a halt. Glancing up during the tumble all I could see was Sparkle's hooves and the underside of her airborne body.

Louis rode back to me and hollered, "Are you trying to commit suicide?"

I just shrugged and told him, "I was just tired of chasing that crazy calf!"

He threw me the loop of his rope. I fashioned a halter out of it, put it on the calf and Louis dragged it back to the herd.

*   *   *   *   *

Once the cattle were moved to the house pastures, there was always a fall roundup.

The first thing we did was clean up the pens. Then we tested for weak spots in the board fence of the corral and repaired it as required. We picked up all the wood, trash, and anything that would burn and piled it all up for a fire adjacent to the corral, using the fire to heat up the branding irons.

Dad registered our family brand at the Brazoria County Court House as "Bar Bar A", or Barbara, which was my mother's name. It looked something like this — ‾ A. All the farmers and ranchers for miles in any direction knew our brand, as we knew theirs. There were always cows jumping fences or maybe just walking through a poorly kept one. The roundup was prime time to get stray cattle back to their owners.

The first thing we always did was to separate the calves from their mothers by pushing the cows into the next pen. One man worked the gate and two worked in the pen with cattle prods trying to separate and push the cows out. The gate man had to be fast to let the cows in without letting the calves follow into the other pen. The two in the pen with the cows and calves needed eyes behind their heads because the cows might take to being separated from their calves personally and try to run down the perpetrators. Once separated, those "momma cows" stared fiercely at us through the fence, bellowing loudly as we started working their calves.

It was easier to brand and castrate small calves of 100 - 200 pounds than large calves of 250 - 450 pound range. We didn't have a calving season. The bull stayed with the herd all the time, so calves came year round. When we worked calves it was better to be so close to them that we were touching or farther away, totally out of the range of their hind legs. Anywhere in between was dangerous.

One person could "throw" a small calf by catching it loose in a pen or as it ran out of the chute. To do so, we would grab a front hoof. When the calf jumped trying to get away, we would jerk up on the hoof. That took the other three legs out from under it. As it hit the ground, we would land on it with one of our knees on its neck and the other on its flank. We could also grab an ear and the tail and then move it to the work pen.

John, Louis and Peter

Neighbor, Ken, Billy Michael

Nieghbor, Kenneth, Billy, and Mike

Then we would reach over its back and grab its front leg with one hand and the skin of his flank with the other hand. In one motion we lifted it and pushed its feet out from under it with a knee and land on it the same way. Another one of us would quickly tail it by grabbing the back leg that was on top and pushing the bottom leg of the calf forward with one of our feet in its hock and stretching the top leg backwards while sitting on the ground. Then a third person would brand, vaccinate, castrate (if it was a bull) and earmark the calf. We would then release it in reverse order.

The third person got out of the way; the person tailing the calf got clear and the catcher released. It sounds like an intricate dance, and it was. If anyone of us got out of step, it was likely he would get the fire kicked out of him.

The large calves had to be roped. The roper worked a wrap around what we called the "snubbing post" in the middle of the pen. It took two of us to throw a large calf. Once it was snubbed up close to the post, two of us would attack one side of the calf. We both would reach over the back of the calf. The one in front grabbed the loose skin on the calf's neck and behind its front leg, while the one in the back grabbed its rear flank. Both then yanked and lifted on a signal. The calf would then fall and we would land on it with our knees similar to the way we did small calves. The one in back worked into tailing position and pulled and pushed on the calf's back legs. Once the calf was secure, the roper loosened the rope and the calf would be treated and released with the same routine as we did on the small calves.

That operation was always accompanied by lots of loud sound effects, various smells and the occasional sharp pain of a piercing hoof when the calf squirmed free during the operation.

One time, I waded in among the calves and grabbed the front ankle of one of the smaller bull calves and started backing out toward the gate that Louis had opened wide enough to let me into the adjacent work pen. The little bull calf jumped, trying to free himself. I yanked its leg up towards the sky and pounced upon him as he hit the ground with a thud. With both hands on his front leg, now folded next to his body, I rolled him back so that both of its rear legs were flailing, trying to find traction of the ground, but it only found air. Ken stepped in behind close to the rear of the bull and snatched its top ankle and hoof and slid to the ground, planting his right foot on the hock of the calf's other leg. The calf was then immobilized.

Louis, Unknown, David Peltier and Joe Peltier 1972
Arthur and John 1972

Dad then vaccinated it while Louis pulled out his knife, notched its right ear, and went to work on the castration. The bull calf, who was soon to be a steer, was bawling as Louis sliced off the bottom of his scrotum. Louis pulled out the first testicle and tossed it off toward the nearest dog; the testicle never hit the ground. In dog cuisine, it doesn't get much better than that. Louis threw the second testicle into the air toward another mongrel for the same net effect. With bloody hands, Louis brushed over the wound with an antiseptic paste. The new steer strained to get loose, probably hoping that the end of the painful ordeal was over, but it wasn't yet. Louis dipped the knife in a Lysol solution and called for the branding iron. Paul, keeping the fire going and the irons hot, handed Stephen the "A" iron, glowing pink from the heat of the fire.

Louis said to Ken and me, "Hang on, boys. This is going to hurt!"

We tightened our grips as Louis carefully lowered the branding iron onto the calf's right hip. The hair flamed up all around the "A" iron as the calf tensed up and tried to move, but we pulled and stretched the calf out as he bawled wildly for his mother. Our lungs were filled with smoke and the acrid smell of burning hair and hide. That was the smell of work and progress that we repeated many times before the sun set.

Next, Stephen took the "A" iron from Louis and handed him the "bar" iron as he headed back to Paul so that Paul could reheat the "A". Louis quickly administered two horizontal offset bars to complete the brand. Then he handed the " bar" iron to Stephen, who returned it to Paul and the fire. The brands usually looked good, not so light as to disappear when they healed and not so cooked and heavy that the "A" would resemble a glob more than an "A".

Louis smeared disinfectant paste on the brand. Ken released the calf's hind legs and quickly got out of the way. I pulled on its leg lightly, slapped it on the side and said, "Up you go, buddy. You're done!" as I stood and backed off.

That was repeated until the last calf was done. We changed jobs to give each other breaks, while Dad did most of the vaccinating and branding. After learning the process, we also learned to step in where we were needed to keep things going smoothly.

During those roundups, we ran all the cows through the chute to vaccinate, dehorn, drench, cull, and do anything else that needed our attention.

Richard and Lloyd Allen 1971

Pug Harvey, Paul and John 1971

Pug   Paul   John

For the best results the chute needed to be packed as full as possible so the cattle had minimum mobility.

Vaccinations of large cows were easier to administer. There were walkways on each side of the chute raising us up so the cows' backs were about waist high, giving us easy access for shots in the rump or neck.

Drenching for worms and liver flukes was another story. We had to get the cow's head up and shove a drench gun, a giant metal syringe with an inch and a half diameter barrel, eight inches long with a nozzle six inches long and three eighths inch in diameter. The syringe held about ten ounces of thick green or gray medicine. We slid the syringe down one side of the cow's mouth to dispense the drench into its throat. If we didn't get it all the way down its throat, it would spit most of it out. We treated the cattle with two kinds of drench, so we had to do that twice.

Getting the heads of the animals up during this process was a challenge. We had nose tongs, but getting a 1,000 to 1,500 pound animal's head up so tongs could be clamped onto its nose was not always easy. Sometimes we would use our thumb and forefinger to act as a temporary nose tong just to get the head up. If we thought we could control the animal, we would try to drench it without the use of the tongs. If not, another person would put a rope around its snout until the tongs were secure. We would reach down and grab the animal's lower lip and bottom jaw bone and lift the head up. That worked well, too.

The older wily cattle that had experience with the tongs were hardest to get because they put their noses right next to the ground. We would try fishing a rope around their snouts to lift the snouts up enough to get the tongs attached. Once the tongs were in place, the animals would give up the fight.

The nastiest job was dehorning the cattle. The good thing about dehorning was that it only needed to be done once in the life of each animal. With the nose tongs still in place, one of us would pull the head to one side, trying to turn the horn upward toward the sky. Then another one of us, on the opposite side of the chute, would take the dehorner and place the blade over the horn as close as we could to the animal's head, pulling the handles together as fast and hard as possible to shear the horn completely off. The dehorner looked like a heavy duty limb pruner, only it was much heavier duty. On some older animals with large horns, we sometimes had to use saws to cut off the horns.

After the first horn was done we handed the dehorning tool and the nose tongs to the person on the opposite side of the chute and the second horn got sheared. Blood would go everywhere as we doctored the wounds with the same paste we used for all the other wounds.

Before a horn hit the ground the wound would sometimes spray blood like an artesian well in several directions as much as five to eight feet away. Interestingly, the blood squirted out at the same pace as the animal's heart was beating.

By the time all the drenching and chute work was over, we were all about spent, but not done for the day. We still had to put weaning calves in a separate pen and put the rest of the calves with the cows.

Often we had to get a 700 pound steer in the trailer for Dad to take to be butchered. On those occasions, Dad had to back the trailer up to the chute to load the steer.

I'll never forget the time we had to load a particularly wild eyed steer. Louis, Kenneth and I started pushing the steer toward the crowd pen at the entrance of the chute opposite the trailer. The steer got close, then turned and broke through our line, attacking at least one of us as we clamored up a fence or hopped out of reach onto the chute walkway. He had blood in his wild eyes and was so mad and frustrated with us alien creatures that he just wanted to try and hurt us and do the opposite of anything we had in mind. After a third try we were really tired, aggravated, and out of cuss words.

Suddenly Louis took off his straw hat, hollering some kind of war yell as he ran towards the steer, looping around in front of it, waving his silly hat and slapping the steer on its foaming nose. Immediately that steer took the bait and went after him like a greedy dog chasing a chicken. As Louis turned the corner into the crowd pen, it looked like his butt was trying to outrun his head! The steer was right on him as he leaped out of the far end of the chute with a little lift from the steer's snout. The steer kept running and finished his run into the trailer as Dad closed the gate behind him.

Relieved and happy, the rest of us gave out a load cheer for Louis, even though we thought he was out of his mind for pulling a stunt like that. If that steer had pushed him down and trampled him, it would not have been a pretty picture.

*   *   *   *   *

Milk Cows. Sometimes Dad bought a Jersey crossbreed that had just had a heifer calf because in a couple of years the heifer would grow up and also be a milk cow. Other times he would be watching for certain cows out of our herd with some "dairy" in their bloodline so that when they calved, they could serve as milk cows.

Milk cows got first class treatment. They would come running when we hollered "Su.. Boss" towards the woods. Before each milking, the cow would receive a ration of sweet feed, have her teats washed before milking, and her bag massaged to get it to drop the milk.

One year Dad chose a big brown Jersey crossbred cow from our herd in the field. She was wilder than a March hare, but we put a rope on her and drug her into the trailer, then caught her calf and put it beside her.

"She'll settle down once we start milking her," Dad told us.

After we unloaded her in the pen, we had to snub her up to a post and tie her body to the fence to get close enough to milk her. After placing a bucket of sweet feed under her nose, we waited for her to settle down, but she just stared at the bucket.   Instead of sitting on a stool to milk, Ken leaned over and pushed his head into her flank, put hobbles on her, and started trying to milk her colostrum onto the ground. (Hobbles are kick restraining devices that attach to both hocks on the back legs, held together with chains). That's when the rodeo started. She started kicking and jumping around even though she was tied at both ends and hobbled.

Twice a day, Louis, Kenneth and I worked together trying to milk her, all the while knowing that we needed her to eat and settle down.

We called her Browne because of her color. If I could have named her, it wouldn't have been printable in this story. We didn't let her out of the pen for two weeks. She had plenty of water, hay, and sweet feed.

Finally we were able to milk her without a daily rodeo, but she seemed to always have a surly look in her eyes.

After the milking she was let out to pasture and she would come back in when she was called, but I think she came in to see her calf in the pen next to the milking pen. We were getting all of her milk, so her calf and the calf of the nurse cow dined next door on the nurse cow.

One time about a month after that, right after a thunder storm, I called Browne from the pasture to be milked. As I was walking away from her to close the gate, she came at me and butted me hard in the middle of my back. I fell face first in the mud. I got up, furious and covered with mud. I grabbed a fence post that was handy and stomped toward her. She turned and charged me with her head down. I swung that post like a baseball bat as hard as I could and hit her on the top of her head, right between her eyes. She was stunned. I put a rope on her and snubbed her up to the post with a feed bucket under her nose and milked her. Then I left her in the pen over night and warned Kenneth because he had to milk her the next morning. I never turned my back on her again.

Browne was by far our least favorite milk cow, but Dad was right, she did settle down.

*   *   *   *   *

On another occasion we attempted another milk cow capture from our range herd. It was on a Saturday when Dad had picked a milk cow out of the herd. We parked the homemade pipe trailer on the FM 2004 right-of-way that had been cleared but no construction had begun. Dad had built the trailer out of water well drill stem; it had a drop pin hitch.

Our cows on the range saw us from time to time when we checked on them, but it wasn't like we knew them like the few animals we had around the house. Out on the range we were just intruders who came out, occasionally observed, spot treated them when required, and left.

That day we were armed with ropes, with Louis and Kenneth on the two horses they rode. I stayed with the car and trailer to move in after they had a rope on our new milk cow. Louis lassoed the cow. Kenneth pushed it with his mount and Louis drug it toward me as I drove closer to them.

I drove within about fifty feet, stopped the car, and opened up the trailer gate. All was going according to the plan until the cow saw me and the trailer. Usually we could direct a cow to the trailer, jump her into it, and drive off. This cow would have none of that. Instead of her jumping into the trailer, we had to use a horse to drag her into it. Even then, she jumped, twisted, and butted at us through the trailer pipe. Her eyes were red and wild. She wanted her freedom more that life itself and seemed to uncoil like a spring. Since the trailer had no top, we were afraid she would jump out, so we tied her head short to the front of the trailer. She fought even harder.

Her calf had followed her to the trailer but kept her distance. Louis put a rope on the calf. Ken and I "hog-tied" (tied one front leg to both hind legs) it. Then we slipped its body into a gunny sack so that only its head stuck out, tightened the sack around its neck, and laid it in the back of the station wagon.

With three ropes on the milk cow to be, we started to drive out of the pasture. The drop pin hitch on the trailer had about three inches of play up and down. The cow was jumping around like a jack rabbit, bouncing the car

193

up and down with the trailer. By the time we pulled into the driveway the cow seemed to have settled down, but then we discovered that the cow was down in a crumpled mess in the bottom of the trailer. She had broken her neck and died.

It took us a few minutes to work up enough nerve to go in the house and tell Dad what had happened. All he said was, "Well…it looks like we'll have meat instead of milk." Boy, were we relieved.

Dad thought that it was no big deal. He called Benny Heiman, who owned the local butcher shop and meat locker. The plan was to simply deliver her to him so he could take it from there, but as it turned out, after Dad talked to Benny he looked at us with more bad news. It was Saturday, so Benny's shop was closed. It was opening weekend for deer season; all his men were hunting, and Benny was sick. Benny said that if we would dress and quarter the cow, he would meet us at the shop and hang it in the walk-in cooler.

At that point, Dad told us, "Take it down to the woods and butcher it."

We looked at him bewildered; we had never cleaned anything larger that a goose and had never hunted deer.

Kenneth looked at him and said, "We've never cleaned anything that big!"

Dad smiled and said, "It's like cleaning a rabbit... just a little bit bigger, and don't throw out the heart, liver or tongue. "

We shrugged our shoulders and looked at each other as Louis said, "OK, let's get started."

After we put the calf in with the nurse cow, we started trying to figure out what we needed to get together to butcher the dead cow.

We started a list: a piece of cable to hang the carcass, a clean ice chest for the organs, tongue, and meat stripped off the neck, backbone and ribs, all our hunting knives, a few sharp knifes from the kitchen, a piece of pipe and wire to mount across the top of the trailer to hang the meat and a five gallon cooler of water. Dad brought out a few old sheets to wrap the meat in after it was hanging. We loaded up the car.

"We had better get going if we're going to finish before dark!" I yelled. Then I hopped up onto the Case 930 tractor and headed towards the woods. Louis, Kenneth, Stephen and Paul followed in the car with the trailer in tow. I think Dad stayed at the house just to see what would happen.

We found an oak tree with a big branch ten feet off the ground. Louis backed the trailer under the tree. We decided to lift the cow by the head to gut it. Kenneth tossed the cable over the limb and tied the end of it off on the front of the Case, while Louis put a snatch chain around the cow's neck and hooked it to the other end of the cable. I started backing the tractor away from the tree as the cow started rising up and out of the trailer. Kenneth pulled the trailer forward out of the way. Louis waved me forward a little to get the cow to the right height.

Louis had the most experience at this kind of thing, but all of us had seen snippets of this when we dropped off calves at Heiman's Butcher Shop. Stephen and Paul held the carcass still while Louis started cutting the skin back right down the middle of its rib cage all the way down. Kenneth and I started doing the same inside each of the front legs.

When the skin was pulled back, the stomach was bulging and trying to burst out through the thin membrane that was left.

"Stand back!" Louis said. Then he took his knife and slit that membrane all the way up to the sternum.

Out came all the intestines. Louis was the only one who thought to wear rubber boots; the rest of us backed up a bit. Louis then released the kidneys and handed the liver to me to put in the cooler. Then he started working on removing the heart and lungs. Soon the cavity looked clean and empty. The smell was unpleasant, but it didn't stink nearly as bad as I had expected.

With all that mess at our feet Louis said, "John, pull the tractor forward I'm going unhook the cow's neck and connect to the back legs. Reposition the tractor another ten feet away from the gut pile."

Soon the cow was hanging by her back legs as we started to work the skin down its hind quarters, then the torso.

As soon as its head was off the ground, we removed it as close to the neck as we could so it could finish bleeding out. Kenneth started working on cutting the tongue loose. Louis and I took off the two front quarters, which came off pretty easily.

Dad was right. It was just like a rabbit, but just the tenderloins and the back straps alone made a rabbit look like a mouse. We took off the neck roasts and then started trimming all the red meat for hamburger. Finally, Louis the surgeon started cutting loose one hind quarter; he was surprised at how easily it came off.

The sun was setting with a golden glow in the western sky when we arrived at the house with four bloody sheets hanging across the inside of the trailer. We were five tired and proud boys who had succeeded in accomplishing a task that we thought was impossible. I'm sure we made plenty of missed cuts and gouges and that we ruined the hide, but we got it done.

Dad came out, took a look at our work, smiled and said, "I knew you boys would figure it out."

Kenneth went off to milk the cow. Stephen and Paul did the rest of the chores, and Louis and I went with Dad to hang the meat in Heiman's cooler.

Life was good!

10

HURRICANE CARLA: HOWLING WINDS

Tonight in Vietnam there are no stars, only a dark sky, with grumbling in the northwest accompanied by flashes of lightning, and it's rolling this way. This storm was of natural origin and not created by man like the ones we see and hear so many nights in Vietnam. This is my last pit stop for the day, and it's literally a "pit". I head back to the hooch for some shut-eye. Not long after I get horizontal, I hear the wind picking up and the pelting rain starting to drum on the roof. I am reminded of another place and another time when a bigger storm was coming.

*　　*　　*　　*　　*

My mind went back to Saturday, September 9, 1961. I was twelve, armed with a grain scoop and working as fast as I could to level out the rice in the back of the haul truck.

My brother Louis, who had just turned fifteen, hollered at me, "Watch that side. It's getting too high! Get a move on. I can see rice in the hoppers of Joe's and Dad's combines."

He was operating the tractor pulling one of the auger carts that collected the rice from the combines.

I hollered back, "I'm shoveling as fast as I can; cut it off till I get caught up!"

Louis released the clutch and the rice stopped flowing. Then he pulled ahead a few feet and augured more rice into the truck, while I was working in the spot he'd just heaped up.

Shoveling rice was a nasty job anyway, but that day was one of those hot, humid, muggy days when the dust from the rice permeated every pore of my body. I was in my usual attire - no shirt, no hat, and no shoes, just cutoffs. To look at me, I could be mistaken for someone from a different country or even a different planet as a thick covering of dirt and grime covered me. I cleared my head from time to time, blowing long streams of black snot over the sideboards of the truck.

I saw that Dad had pulled out of the cutting line of combines. His combine had slugged up and he was clearing the straw from the cylinder, the part of the combine that threshed the grain from the stalks. Combines were so named because they *combine* what used to be many separate operations into one. In front was a "table" about sixteen feet wide with a cutter blade on its leading edge. Above the table was a circular reel that pulled the grain stalks into the cutter. Behind the cutter was a large spiral auger that drew the cut stalks to the center from each end. The stalks were then taken into the machine through its "throat" with a chain conveyor into the threshing area where the cylinder was housed.

Once Dad got the straw cleared he returned to the harvesting line.

After the grain was separated, it was then sifted and the chaff was blown away. It finally fell to the bottom where it was taken with smaller augers and elevators up to the hopper, where enough grain was stored to cover thirty or so minutes of harvesting.

Meanwhile "straw walkers" sent the straw to the rear where it was slung out over the field, while the chaff was also blown and shaken out the rear. Another auger in the bottom of the hopper transferred the grain into auger carts or trucks. Auger carts were similar to hoppers, only larger, with three times more capacity to transfer the grain from the combines in the field to trucks that transported it to the dryers.

Peter was nineteen and the oldest. He was laying out the tarp to cover the rice and keep it from blowing out of the truck on its way to the rice dryer in Danbury.

A hurricane named Carla was brewing in the Gulf of Mexico, and if she didn't change course, would be coming right down our throats. Every combine in Brazoria County was working somewhere to save as much of the crop as possible before she arrived. We were in the field of our cousins, the Peltier Sons, racing to get as much grain as possible into storage. Carla would obliterate any field left in her path. Our own fields were still too green to harvest, so we could only hope Carla turned east or west.

The "amber waves of grain" were as beautiful in the fields as they are in the song. My gaze followed Louis as he made another round. The levees snaked through the field, dividing it into odd shaped "cuts". Levees, while they appeared to be randomly laid, followed the contour of the ground in two to three inch increments of elevation. Rice was irrigated by flooding and levees were just long small dams that made managing the irrigation water possible.

That day there were twice as many combines in the field as usual. They looked like giant insects gobbling up the golden stalks in their mouths, slinging the spent straw back to the ground as they crept along. I laughed to myself because it looked like the combines were giving the field a crew cut.

The combines had been fighting the dampness all day. To separate the grain from the straw, the stems and kernels needed to be dry and brittle because the moisture caused the combines to "slug up". The muggy mist was turning into light rain as the combines started pulling out of the field.

The combines and auger carts deposited any rice left in their hoppers into the waiting trucks. Everyone was a little gloomy and concerned about Carla and the wrath she might deliver.

We said our goodbye's and good luck's as Dad told Louis and me, "Hop up on the combine. We're going to park it in the barn tonight."

We climbed aboard and rode up in the hopper that was right behind the operator cockpit. I glanced down at Dad. He was looking straight ahead, focused intently, but I didn't think he was focused on the road. I think he was concerned for us and planning a strategy to ride this storm out.

We lived two miles from the field on about 100 acres. Our northeast property line was Austin Bayou for about a half mile; our house was a quarter mile south of the bayou. Hoskins Mound Road, built from oyster shell, ran in front of our house and was four miles south of Danbury. In about fifteen minutes, we pulled the combine into the rear of the barn. Louis and I pushed the two sliding doors together and bolted them closed.

The barn was sixty feet long and thirty feet wide and had a half round shape that we hoped would do a good job of holding back the wind. Along the full length of the west side was a lean-to that was about twenty feet wide. The corral was adjacent to the lean-to and consisted of six working pens with a crowd chute between the middle two pens.

The lean-to was about half full of hay and had three pens partitioned off. We didn't normally keep pigs because Mom didn't like the smell, but at that time we had several pigs that Kenneth and Louis had for FFA projects. We also had a milk cow, a nurse cow and their calves. The cows grazed in the pasture all day and we called them up every morning and evening for milking.

*   *   *   *   *

I could only imagine what Mom and Dad discussed about what to do in the face of the big oncoming storm.

Mom: *"What do you think we should do?*

Dad: *"The way I see it we don't have a lot of choice. We have one car, ten children here, plus the two of us. We would have to ride three deep and wouldn't even get ten miles before there would be a murder to report."*

Mom: *"I guess it's a good thing Kay's away at school. Do you think this house will withstand the storm? I understand Carla is just sitting offshore gaining strength."*

Dad: *"Yeah, it's funny that it is Kay's first weekend living away from home. At least she's going to be safer in Houston. All the old-timers say that the five-foot hill we built the barn on puts it above any known high water mark. If the house starts to get shaky, our backup plan will be to move to the barn."*

Mom: *"Okay, we'll stay, but I can't say I really like the idea."*

Kenneth, thirteen, was working for another cousin in another field. Dad, Louis and I got home at about the same time Kenneth did. Peter was still in line at the rice dryer waiting to be unloaded and would be home a little later.

Dad lined us out, boarding up windows and securing anything that would float off or blow away. We had already rolled the hay trailer into the barn, too, just in case we needed a camping area off the floor.

While we were working the fields, Mom had been stocking up on groceries, candles, and emergency items. Becky, eleven, had spent the day helping Mom corral the rest of the "thundering herd," as Mom affectionately referred to her clan. Stephen, eight, and Paul, seven, were ferrying jars of water, extra blankets and clothes up to the barn, just in case we had to move to higher ground. Arthur, five, and Richard, four, (born eleven months apart and twins for one month each year) were just being Becky's handful. She was also taking care of Mary Carol, who was aptly named, as she was Mom's Christmas present last year, born less than an hour into December 26th. She was dubbed Molly from the get-go.

Peter arrived home just as the milking was done, the hogs and calves were fed, and the family was nearly intact.

We all sat down to a hot meal of roast beef, rice, gravy, and green beans, all grown on the place. We said grace in unison as we did before every meal, but the imminent storm was on everyone's mind.

Mom informed us, "The news reports are warning of high tides and high winds. They think the storm will probably make landfall sometime tomorrow between Port Lavaca and Beaumont."

Peter responded, "We're just about right in the middle of that, sitting at eight feet above sea level and six miles from the Gulf. It sounds like we could be in for a bruiser."

Dad added, "Hurricanes are totally unpredictable. No one knows where it will hit. It could miss us completely. We rode out Debra in '58; she didn't ruffle our feathers too badly. We have the barn, which is above any known level of flooding. We'll be okay."

The rest of us just listened, not really concerned. We just assumed everything would be okay because we knew we were in good hands.

After dinner, Kenneth and Becky had their turn at doing dishes. The rest of us crammed into the living room, glued to the tube. By ten o'clock the beds started filling up.

Peter, Louis, Kenneth and I (the older boys) headed out to the Little House. It'd been a long day and we were exhausted. There would be no grab assing tonight.

About three in the morning, the phone rang.

Dad fumbled his way into the kitchen to answer it.

It was the county judge, saying, "Wilburn, this is Judge Arnold."

(When Mom came to Danbury in 1940 for her first teaching job, Judge Arnold was the superintendent of the Danbury schools and was later elected county judge.)

Dad replied, "Hello, Judge, what's going on this time of night?"

The judge informed him, "I'm here at the Civil Defense Command Center in Angleton. We are issuing an evacuation request to everyone south of Austin Bayou."

Dad answered, "I'll get with Barbara and see what we can work out."

Dad went back to the bedroom where Mom was sitting up in bed.

When Mom asked him who it was, he told her that the judge said that they should evacuate. Mom questioned him about why we should leave and asked him what he thought. He suggested that she take the younger kids with her into town and stay with our relatives Catine and Eddie Peltier.

Mom told him emphatically, "No, I'm sure of one thing. We will all stay together no matter what."

So we did.

*   *   *   *   *

Sunday morning came and it was time to go to church. We only had one car so we went in shifts. Mom and we older boys went to 7:00 Mass. Our day of rest didn't start until a little later; the milking and feeding had to be done twice a day every day, Sabbath or not. The weather was starting to turn; the rain and wind were intensifying. Dad and the rest of the kids went to the 9:00 Mass, while Mom baked a huge ham and fixed new potatoes for lunch. At around 10:30, Dad returned. The wind was gusting violently and rain was pouring down. He said he had to take it easy on the way home. It wasn't dangerous. The bayou was rising but still in its banks. He had borrowed a transistor radio from Eddie in case we lost power.

We spent the afternoon inside; moon dominoes occupied us older boys. Our friendly game cost a dime a point and a dime a hickey; each of us had a can of change we kept for poker and domino games. We played any time we could get a group together. I imagine by the end of a year of games, we were within a few dollars of each other in the win/loss column. Some of the kids were playing cards or reading and Arthur and Richard were running around like wild Indians. Mom and Dad were watching TV and keeping up with Carla's progress.

Dad interrupted the moon game at about one-thirty and told Peter to bring the car around to the front. I guessed that after watching the news their decision to "ride out the storm" sounded less and less like a good idea. The rest of us started gathering a few things for an overnight trip. That evacuation attempt was short lived, as Peter returned and told us that water had already risen over the car's engine. The old garage where the car was sat at the lowest point around the house, due to years of adding shell to the county road. Building the access road to the raised area of the barn had raised everything around it. All of us were surprised by the speed and stealth with which the water came up.

The bayou's main purpose was generally to drain the runoff created by the rain upstream to the Gulf. Today the opposite was true. The bayou was bringing Carla's storm surge directly to our front door. So there we sat, with all the inland rain coming down the bayou and the storm surge from the Gulf coming up the bayou. We were trapped somewhere in the middle.

The dial tone was still working on the telephone. Peter called everyone he could think of to let them know we didn't evacuate. No one answered. We were starting to feel a little alone. The games continued, but our moods were all sinking a little, like when you closed a gate after the horse had already gotten out.

The tiring sound of the wind steadily increased. It was relentlessly pounding, with threatening blasts.

I wondered where all of the wind came from and how it found a place to go that held it all.

The news reports indicated bumper-to-bumper traffic trying to escape Carla's path. Complete evacuation of low-lying areas, which would include us, was strongly suggested.

Meanwhile, Carla was still churning and building strength out in the Gulf of Mexico with no definite indication of when or where it would hit landfall. By then we were pretty sure we were going to get a piece of her or that just maybe she was going to get a piece of us.

That night after everyone bathed, we filled the bathtub and as many jars, pots and cans with water that we could find. We ran out of water just before we ran out of containers. Then the lights went off, as did the water well. Mom told Peter, Louis, Kenneth and me that we had to stay in the house and sleep on the floor that night so we would all be together. We didn't mind. There was safety in numbers.

Monday morning Mom mixed up a batch of bread. Dad organized us older boys to ferry supplies to the barn. We took all the containers of water, canned fruit, anything we could eat without cooking, canned milk for the baby, bread, crackers, and more clothes and blankets out there.

The bread went into the oven by mid morning. Not long after that, the water started to lap through at the floors. We scrambled to put everything that wasn't waterproof up higher on the table and beds, thinking they might be safe. Water had never gotten that high before.

Mom checked the bread. The oven had gone off. Peter looked out the back porch windows and saw the butane tank floating. The water had lodged it against a tallow tree near the back door. There was a large chunk of icy butane where the broken line was spewing. Dad sent Peter and Louis out to turn the gas off and secure the tank.

The wind continued to rage, as the water churned dirty gray brown about two feet deep, with whitecaps more violent than any I had ever seen at the beach. We watched Peter and Louis barely able to stand as they worked to secure the tank.

Mom dumped the bread dough into a bowl. Kenneth grabbed a cast iron skillet and a gallon of Wesson oil. Dad directed the evacuation to the barn. Paul was outfitted in his new yellow slicker with its spring-loaded catches to hold it closed. He was happy because it was the first time he got to wear it. Mom told Louis to wrap Molly up to protect her on the way to the barn. Paul quickly took off his slicker and gave it to Louis to cover her. He beamed knowing that he was playing a part in protecting his little sister.

We lined up single file on the back porch and headed toward the barn about a hundred feet away. If we weren't carrying something or someone, we were hand in hand, older interspersed with younger, out into the storm. Going against that howling wind and pelting rain was like being hurled full force against a moving wall. Louis promptly lost his balance and Molly went into the drink. He quickly scooped her up and moved on to the barn. I was with Arthur, Richard, Stephen and Paul. As they were dragged along, Arthur and Richard kept wanting to squat down in the water and pretend they were swimming. A vision of a piece of the metal roof flying through the air at any moment and cutting me half weighed heavily on my mind.

The move to higher ground happened so fast that the reality of the experience never really soaked in. We were in the barn in less than ten minutes after we discovered the runaway butane tank.

We proceeded to set up house in the barn. Becky took care of Molly, who was ga-ga happy and thought the whole operation was being produced for her personal benefit. Stephen and Paul were helping as much as they could, while Arthur and Richard were wandering through the barn. The older boys moved the hay trailer adjacent to the combine so its cockpit ladder was more easily accessible.

Dad told us that we needed to block the trailer up higher. We found four empty fifty-five gallon drums and, using a fence post for a lever, pried the trailer up while we shoved a barrel under each corner.

Dad and Mom started preparing lunch. Dad rolled the cutting torch to the table, removed the cutting head and attached a "rosebud" head, which was for heating metal and not cutting. He then proceeded to use the "rosebud" head to heat the Wesson oil in the skillet. When it was hot enough, he dropped chunks of the salvaged bread dough into the oil, like he was frying doughnuts. The chunks resembled little men. We had a lunch of "fried men" and leftover ham.

By the time lunch was over, we were all standing ankle deep in water. I could tell Dad was really surprised and concerned about how rapidly the water was rising. We covered the steel deck of the trailer with a thick layer of burlap bags. (There was always a large quantity of those around. We filled them with dirt and used them to repair levees and create spillways in levees to control the water in the rice fields.) Over the burlap bags, we laid a heavy canvas tarp. On one end we set up a collapsible army cot and a couple of lawn chairs.

Provisions were placed all around the combine into any open space available. The combine reel, which drew the rice stalks into the cutter blade, turned out to be our clothes dryer and storage for lawn chairs when the trailer deck was needed. The hopper, which stored the grain on the combine, was a designated sleeping area. All the rest of the burlap bags we could rustle up were stuffed into the bottom to level it and protect us from the sharp edges of the auger in the bottom. Flashlights, matches, candles, band-aids, aspirin, can opener, knives and spoons went into the toolbox. A baby bed stored in the rafters served as a good shelf for food.

The barn became our home, at least for the duration of this new girl by the name of Carla, blowing into our lives.

The howling winds and pounding waves were constant reminders of our newfound circumstances. The incessant drumming of the wind, waves, and rain on the thin metal sheathing separating us from the storm's fury was also deafening. We communicated by waving our hands, by tapping someone to get their attention and then yelling at them at the top of our lungs at close range.

Carla's sheer volume seemed to have an isolating affect on us. Even as members of a large family in a small tight place, we each felt alone and detached.

Everyone got up on the trailer except for us older boys. The water was already up to our knees and we were moving things up onto the workbench. A can of old oil spilled out over the water. We caught as much as we could with gunny sacks and put the sacks in a bucket, but there was still a thin film of oil floating on the water's surface. We looked for any other open oil cans and put them in high places. A large amount of oil floating in the barn would have really made the situation worse.

At one point, Kenneth was in front of the barn by the overhead sectional door. He waved and yelled to the rest of us that the bottom section was giving way. The constant pounding of the waves had damaged the door and it appeared that the bottom sheet of the metal skin of the barn was loosening. Peter, Louis and I went over there with baling wire, nails, a hammer and lumber and worked for an hour bracing the door. The tin sheathing could only be fixed from the outside, which was impossible at that point. It was very important not to lose the integrity of the barn, and that was our first weak spot.

There was a hole in the tin about the size of a dime about four feet off the floor on the wall facing the house. We looked out from time to time to get a blurred view of how the house was holding up. By then it was about five o'clock and it appeared the water was up to the windows, but the roof was still on, with the house still standing steady on her blocks. I tasted the water. It was salty. We were then on an island surrounded by the Gulf of Mexico.

By then the water was getting dangerously close to the deck of the trailer. We found some wooden blocks to raise it up another foot or so. We tried to use the lever to raise the trailer but the bottom of the barrel tried to kick out and float, so we stopped the lifting operation and started a barrel filling operation. Manning all four corners, Peter, Louis, Kenneth, Becky, Stephen, Paul and I all took turns dipping water to fill the barrels to keep them from floating. We worked for nearly an hour. Blocking the trailer up was the easy part. We were really going to have to scrounge if we had to do it again. We had used all the blocks we could find.

Mom called us to gather for dinner. We had another meal of "fried men" and the last of the ham. For dessert Mom used one spoon; we sat in a circle around her and she went around the circle spooning applesauce into our mouths, like a mother bird feeding her chicks. She said there was no way to wash the spoons and wanted to save the clean ones for the next meals. She said that if she had to wash anything with valuable fresh water, it would be baby bottles.

The milk cow bellowed over the noise of the storm from the lean-to side of the tin wall. I didn't know what made her more uncomfortable, the tightness of her bag or the wailing of the storm. There would be no milking that night. The animals were on their own until the storm gave up some of its punch. It was evident a skunk living in the hay had gotten a little excited by the storm or else its space was being invaded by other critters seeking higher ground. Fortunately, the high winds were strong enough to dissipate the skunk's smell.

We didn't know what was on the other side of the west wall. We could only hope that our cows, pigs and horses had found adequate shelter.

Soon after, everyone was out of the water and in dry clothes. We had to continually yell in order to be heard over the loud droning of Carla. Mom led us in the Rosary several times during the evening. She also kept candles burning stuck in the top of an old brown Clorox bottle. When one went out, she started another, setting it into the warm wax of the last one. The barn was holding up well; the candle flames continued to stand straight up with seldom a flicker. Dad told us to be alert for snakes, rats and other varmints looking for higher ground. Each of us older boys kept a club ready to discourage any unwelcome guest.

Dad monitored the radio against his ear until the batteries went dead at about 8:00 p.m. The last thing he heard was that the northern part of Carla's eye was touching Matagorda Island. At least we knew she was moving inland south of us.

I didn't know if it was the rain or the waves, but it sounded as if water was blowing over the top of the barn.

It was dark, we were tired, and it was time to sleep. Peter took Arthur, Richard, Stephen and Paul and bedded them down in the hopper. I didn't know how they managed it; all sides of the hopper sloped to the bottom so they were stacked in like cordwood. Soon Richard came down, complaining he couldn't get comfortable and was given a pad on the trailer. Peter and the rest of them didn't object to his leaving. Mom sent Becky with Molly up to join Peter in the hopper. She was afraid Molly might fall off the trailer during the night. No one complained. Dad slept on the cot and the rest of us looked for a soft spot on the trailer. The last thing I noticed was Mom and Dad sitting on the cot trying to talk.

I woke up in the middle of the night. There was a small barrel or something floating under the steel deck. It was clanging and grinding, but I was not about to crawl off into the water and pull it out.

The candle now had about an inch of wax left. The wind seemed to be easing a bit and changing directions. The waves were pounding the big sliding doors in the rear of the barn now. After a wave struck, a spit of water would come through the narrow slot where the doors came together. Dad had been keeping a record of the depth of the water on the side of the welding table beside the trailer. It appeared the level had receded an inch or so.

Dawn came in just as it does every day. Life on the trailer was starting to yawn its way out of slumber. It was noticeably calmer outside. The winds were still gusting, and the waves were still beating on us, but their sounds were down to a minimum roar. Breakfast was peanut butter sandwiches, water and canned pineapple. I would have loved a glass of cold milk about then.

Peter, Louis, Kenneth and I eased off into the water, which was continuing to recede from its high point of thirty-nine inches. The bracing we put on the front door the day before had failed during the night and the bottom two sections were mostly gone. A bale of hay had acted as a battering ram in the water and was halfway in the barn.

Surveying the area outside through the windows in the front of the barn, we could see that the hay shed and the chicken coop were off their blocks and that the tool shed had disappeared. The "Little House" was off its blocks; the roof was badly damaged and it would require a major face-lift. We couldn't see the main house without going outside, but looking through the peephole we can tell she was level on her blocks. The back screen door was barely hanging on and the water was up to her waist, but everything looked okay otherwise.

We rejoined the rest of the family on the trailer. Dad and Mom didn't want us to go outside until the weather had settled down a little more. Mom led us again in praying the Rosary. We thanked God for bringing us through the storm safely. We played games and read. Stephen, Paul, Arthur and Richard were climbing all over the combine, using it for a jungle gym. Molly was the center of attention on the trailer and loving it.

We heard the sounds of airplanes and helicopters flying over. We boys, of course, wanted to go out and see them, but Dad and Mom made us stay put a while longer.

About noon, we older boys went back into the water, which was now down to our knees. We unbolted and shoved open one of the sliding panels of the back door. There was a large cottonmouth water moccasin coiled up on the top of a fence post by the barn. Before it had a chance to flee, Peter and Louis dispatched it quickly with a shovel and a garden hoe.

That was our first look toward the bayou since fleeing the house. All we could see was water and the tops of the giant oaks, snaking across the horizon along the path of the bayou.

The cows, as well as the calves and pigs, had scrambled up into the hay, they didn't seem to mind each other's company for a change. Tony and Paint, two of our horses, were trapped against the corral fence by floating bales of hay. After working a few of the bales loose, we eased them out from under the lean-to. They appeared to be unharmed and started swimming out to sea towards the bayou. Soon they returned to high ground. The milk cow, nurse cow and the calves had gotten together, and we just let the calves take care of the milking until we could figure out our next move.

All we knew to do then was wait. The weather was clearing up fast. The sun was shining and the wind had diminished to just a gentle breeze.

About two in the afternoon we heard a shout, "Is anyone home?"

Our hearts leaped with joy. We knew we were being rescued. We hopped off the trailer and headed for the back door. We saw two men coming up in a flat bottom aluminum air powered boat. It was Joe and Eddie Peltier, part of the Peltier Sons farming partnership. I couldn't remember ever being so glad to see someone before in my life. They had actually come out to check on their equipment, but not knowing where we had ended up, they decided to check on us, too, while they were out.

It took three trips for them to ferry us out. We had only the clothes on our backs, but that was enough.

We spent the next week or so with Catine and Eddie. Dad and all the older boys went home the next day by boat. Water was still up but was below the floor of the house; we gauged the high water mark to be at fifty-eight inches.

We went to work salvaging and drying out what we could. All the beds were ruined. Chairs, couches, and tables were mostly unsalvageable. We piled all the ruined stuff outside so we could get to the floors for cleaning. While we were working, a helicopter came flying over. We started waving our arms, and it started coming in. We were all excited, but Dad waved it off at the last minute. I guessed my first helicopter ride would have to wait.

Most of the pictures and negatives were in the bottom drawers of the secretary. With nearly five feet of water in the house during the flood, there weren't very many things left unaffected. All the food in both freezers and the refrigerator was spoiled. We emptied them out on the slope by the barn and the pigs devoured every bit of the spoiled food, including the wrappers. Everyone was happy about the way those pigs disposed of the garbage.

We returned to the house daily. On the third day we were finally able to drive in and out. The smell was indescribably horrible. There was a muddy scum on everything, especially on all the floors and other flat surfaces. We attacked the floors with mops, brooms and squeegees. At first, while the floodwater was still up, we stood on the front porch and dipped five gallon buckets into the water, pouring it on the floors in front of the broom and squeegee crew. We pulled all the pots and pans out of the lower cabinets and cleaned them all.

The floodwaters quickly turned from salty to fresh water. The storm surge receded as the heavy upstream rains pushed it out to sea.

As soon as the road was passable, we lowered the hay trailer from its perch and parked it in front of the house. Stephen, Paul and Becky spent a whole day rinsing towels, linens, clothes, and everything else that needed to be washed in the fresh floodwater and loaded it all on the trailer. The trailer was heaped up over three feet in the middle and groaned under the heavy load. Peter pulled the trailer slowly into town so nothing would fall off and parked it in front of the local laundromat.

While the rest of us worked on getting the big house habitable, Mom and Becky, with the help of some generous neighbors, spent several days and a bucket of quarters, washing and drying that sopping mess on the trailer and separating it into boxes of wearable and usable items. Along with the laundry, they also took care of Arthur, Richard, and Molly. Once the laundry was finished and boxed, it filled Catine and Eddie's garage. They stored it for us until we could return home.

As soon as power was restored, the water well was checked out and chlorinated. Dad bought several box fans to start airing the house out. Then as soon as we had fresh well water, we washed everything again with Lysol. EVERYTHING had to be cleaned - the oven, the hot water heater, the clothes washer and dryer. We discovered many things ruined.

Kay missed the excitement during Carla but didn't miss out on all the hard work. She came on weekends to help with the clean up.

Things finally started coming back together. The big house was getting clean and in the process of drying out.

Next, we started working on the "Little House". Word of our plight had gotten out. Soon friends, neighbors and people we didn't even know were dropping off clothes, chairs, appliances and anything else we might need.

H. R. Hester, a friend and neighbor from Shadow Bend, a weekender subdivision near us on the bayou, gave us his house, which had floated off its blocks during Hurricane Carla; he rebuilt a new house on stilts. (H. R. had coon dogs and we had spent many a night running coons with him behind his dogs.)

Dad had the Hester house moved in and connected to our existing house. Within a year, the living space in the big house nearly doubled. Still we only had one bathroom because we never got around to reworking the one in the new addition. The "Little House" was redone with a new roof, windows and door. We older boys still kept using it for a bunk house.

The rice crop was mostly gone, having been blown flat by the wind and pounded into the ground by the rain. There was no way to get it to stand and dry for a reasonable harvest, but Dad went out and harvested what he could.

A month or so after Carla, a lady from the government paid us a visit. She came to try to convince Mom to take advantage of some hurricane assistance program. I was being nosy, standing around trying to figure out was going on when I heard the government lady tell Mom, in an exasperated voice, "Mrs. Peltier, the only thing keeping you from taking this help is your pride."

I remember hearing Mom, with a solemn look on her face, telling that lady, "You know, that's about all we have left, and, if you don't mind, I think we'll just keep it."

Hearing my mother say that was a defining moment in my life.

I was aware, since an early age, that we didn't possess many of the niceties of life, but I was then sure we had been given everything that we needed.

*   *   *   *   *

Here in the middle of this war in Vietnam, I wake up to another muggy and warm day. The storm has passed through, leaving everything wet and sticky.

11
Short-timer

The Army has a heart. During my tour of duty in Vietnam I'm authorized to take a one week out-of-country break from the war for rest and recuperation, commonly referred to as R & R. The Army will fly me there and back if I choose one of the destinations on their list. Among the exotic places I can go are Sidney, Tokyo, Honolulu, Bangkok, Taipei, and Hong Kong.

Many of the married men meet their wives in Hawaii to recharge their batteries, but early on, I decided to put in for Sydney for two main reasons. First, I wanted to go someplace where English was the primary language. Second, Sidney was the only place on the list that was populated with European immigrants, much like the United States. Also, I imagine it's the only opportunity I will likely ever have in my life to visit there.

I tried to get Steve or Greg to go with me, but that didn't work out. I put my name on the list and in July received orders stating that I will be leaving the last week in August. Included with the orders is a packet with a list of things to do and places to stay. A buddy of mine recommended the Whitehall Hotel, so I made a reservation there. I also signed up for a horseback ride and a steak cookout.

I went to the Post Exchange (called the PX) to buy my first suit. They took all my measurements and I picked out a color and fabric from the samples they recommended. I surely didn't have a clue what would work otherwise. I also bought a set of Samsonite luggage. Except when I bought my camera, that was the first time I'd spent any significant of amount money since arriving in country.

Just anticipating the destination of my first vacation is a treat. I have a folder bulging with information I've picked up from people who have gone already and from the R&R office.

The day finally arrives and I'm on my way. I am dressed in jungle fatigues as I climb up the stairs of the Quanta's 727 aircraft. Inside, the first thing I notice is a cute, sweet smelling, stewardess wearing an "Aussie" hat, with one side pinned straight up. Her eyes are bright, brown, and round. I can see why they ride herd on everyone going on R&R and why there are always AWOL problems on the return trip.

My arrival at Whitehall goes without a hitch. The first thing I do is ditch my uniform. Then I take a hot shower, put on some civvies and go for a long walk. The hotel faces the harbor and overlooks a park where kids play soccer. I end up at the Sydney Opera House, which is under construction. There is a viewing area with a scale model of the structure that looks like several giant seashells set up on end facing the harbor. Across the way is the Sydney Harbor Bridge, which is the longest single span bridge in the world. I am soaking up the freedom of just walking around without being concerned about something exploding. Except for the accents I'm hearing and the fish and chips, I could be in America.

That evening I stop in a nightclub named Martin's Place. I had heard that it was a good spot to mix in with the locals. I also heard that Australian men didn't appreciate American men on R&R hustling their women. Martin's Place has a telephone on each table and a small pole in the middle of the table that resembles a small street light with a number on it. If a patron wants to contact someone at another table, all he has to do is to pick up the phone and call its number. After a beer or two, I start surveying the place to see what's available. Meanwhile, to my great surprise, the phone on my table rings.

"Hello," I say, a little surprised.

"Are you a Yank?" asks a feminine voice, in proper English on the other end.

"No, ma'am, I'm from Texas," I reply.

The call was from Table Sixteen and I was invited to join them. I find the table and meet two young ladies, Donna and Brenda, who are teachers from Melbourne also on holiday. We dance, laugh, and have a wonderful evening. They invite me join them for a ride into the outback tomorrow. They are planning to drive through an African safari type ranch about fifty miles away.

I gladly accept the offer. They are to pick me up at 9:00 a.m.

The next morning I'm ready to go when they pick me up at nine sharp. We stop and pick up some drinks and fish and chips for later.

I had never seen anything like this "to go" method. They dumped the fish out of the deep fryer onto a piece of newspaper, then wrapped it up in four or five more sheets and then did the same with the fried potatoes. We head out for the safari and sure enough, we drive through pastures with lions, elephants, giraffes, and various other animals.

We fill the day talking about everything under the sun, but mainly my home in Texas and theirs in Australia. I am so happy and relaxed conversing with someone of the opposite sex and their accents are like exotic music to my ears. They drop me off that evening and are heading back to Melbourne the next morning. Donna and I promise to write each other, but our correspondence only lasts for only a few letters. It was like my correspondence with my family and friends back home. If I don't write letters, I don't receive letters.

The next few days I explore more of Sydney. I go to the zoo and see the koala bears, wallabies and kangaroos. The shopping mall is a treat; it has a playground for the children on one end, complete with miniature trains and a Ferris wheel. The busses downtown are the double-decker kind like the ones from London that I'd seen on television.

The horseback ride in the outback is like being on a dude ranch; most of the people there don't know a stirrup from a bridle. We spend an hour walking a trail. The English saddle is different from the western saddles I have always used. It is nice being out in the country, and getting to see kangaroos is a real treat.

Their barbeque is not the standard fare I'm used to, smoked and slow-cooked as we do in Texas. They use a hot fire covered with a grate. The cook slings a piece of meat onto the grate, leaves it there for ten to fifteen seconds, flips it over, and serves it. It's not even warm in the middle. Everyone here seems to be enjoying the meat, but I just nibble at mine and throw most of it away. I like my beef medium rare, but not raw. The fries are good, so I get plenty.

The week has been a blur and the last night I treat myself to a dinner at the historic Argyle Tavern. I learned that the Argyle Tavern was part of a 19th century prison used to house prisoners when they arrived from England. The rings in the walls that restrained the prisoners were still in place. The waiter knew after my first word that I was an American and asked me where I was from back in the States.

I smile proudly and tell him, "Texas".

Sydney Australia R&R August 1968

Sydney Opera House Under Construction

First Suit and First Hotel Room

Beach a block away

Macquarie Lighthouse
Constructed 1818

Left: Kings Cross Fountain

The Gap, a Popular Place
to End it All.

Kangaroos

Sydney Harbor Bridge,Worlds Longest Single Span Bridge.

"I hope to get there someday," he says.

I tell him that he'll be very welcomed in Texas and ask him what he recommends on the menu. He recommends the lobster.

I look over the menu, but follow his recommendation and order the lobster. Having never eaten lobster before, I didn't know what to expect. I am surprised that it's served cold, but it is very tasty.

All during the evening we are entertained by a man singing historic ballads and songs from Australia. Many of the customers join in the singing because the words are printed on all of the bibs they've given us. About halfway through my meal, I hear the singer stop and announce, "We have a guest here tonight from the States. Would you help me welcome him with this song?"

The next thing I hear is:

The stars at night are big and bright
Deep in the heart of Texas.
The prairie skies are high and wide,
Deep in the heart of Texas.

My heart is in my throat as tears stream down my face. I am overwhelmed as everyone in the place continues to belt out more verses of that song so familiar to me. I am easy to pick out and everyone smiles and waves at me as they belt out the tunes. Humbled by the warmth of this reception, I am reminded that Texas does not have a corner on the hospitality market.

Traveling alone and having no one to share these Australian experiences with, I feel a little like I'm viewing them through a pane of glass. I'm here, but not totally connected.

All too soon, my time in Sydney comes to an end and I'm in uniform again, heading back to Vietnam, rested and recuperated.

*   *   *   *   *

I've always had a sweet tooth, but there isn't an abundance of sweets coming out of the mess hall. The cooks come up with cakes, cobblers and pies that are good but, of course, they don't really compare to Mom's.

I have discovered a candy here called Hershey's Tropical Chocolate. The first time I bit into a bar, I expected it to taste like sweet soft chocolate, but I was surprised to find the bar hard, like a bar of paraffin. When the flavor hit my taste buds, I spit it out. It tasted somewhere between semisweet and bittersweet chocolate, not at all to my liking.

Tropical Chocolate was developed during World War II as an energy bar for hot climates because it stayed in a solid state to about 140 degrees. There are boxes of the candy everywhere. No one will eat it. Even the Vietnamese kids throw it away. One day I was craving something sweet. At the time I was sipping on a Coke when I unwrapped a bar of Tropical Chocolate and started gnawing on its corner. I thought to myself, "This is good." The Coke was sweet enough for the chocolate and the combination was actually good.

The hospital receives blood in thick Styrofoam coolers that they use only once. I commandeer one and keep it under my bunk. Beer and Coke are a dime each when I purchase them by the case at the PX; I can get a small block of ice at the mess hall. With that setup, I can have a cold beer or Coke anytime I want. Together with a cigar and Tropical Chocolate, I think I have a pretty good thing going, but when I share my idea with my buddies, they think I'm crazy. I think I am dumb like a fox.

As I travel around the countryside, except for birds, I never see any wildlife. I don't know if it is the war or over the years the wild animals have been killed off to protect the domestic ones. It makes me think of the many times we encountered wildlife when I grew up.

*   *   *   *   *

Growing up on the South Texas coast, wildlife was prevalent and we were always experiencing exciting interaction of some kind with animals.

When I was about ten years old Peter, Louis, Kenneth and I were working in the rice fields with Dad. It was the end of the day and Dad sent Kenneth to pick up a sack of gunny sacks that was hanging on the barbed wire fence about a hundred feet away. Dad was watching him and pointed to indicate we should watch him, too. Kenneth grabbed the bag off the fence and threw it over his shoulder, thinking it was a sack of sacks. After Kenneth took about three steps, we knew something was wrong by the startled look on his face.

He dropped the bag and started screaming, "There's a snake in the bag!!" as he came running towards us. Dad was laughing; then Peter, Louis and I started laughing, too, but we didn't know why.

Dad walked over, picked up the bag and brought it over to us. Then he untied the string holding it shut and opened it. In the bottom of the bag were three baby coons, squirming around. We picked them up and played with them. They were little furry balls that acted like kittens but looked like coons. We begged Dad to let us take them home, and he did.

The next day we built a cage out of 2x4's and chicken wire. It was about 6 feet high, 6 feet long and 4 feet wide. In the far end of the cage we put the remnants of an old dog-house to keep them out of the rain. There were always plenty of baby bottles around the house, so we filled one with milk; it didn't take the little coons long to figure out what they were and they took to those bottles like ducks to water. They grew fast and were soon eating table scraps. In fact, they would eat nearly anything we put in front of them. We also kept a basin of water in the coon cage. They liked to wash their food before they ate it. That worked well with things like pieces of fruit, but many other things they ate would dissolve as they washed them and made a mess.

We played with the coons and let them crawl all over us like we were trees. We learned that coons had no manners and would crap on us at any time with no warning. As boys we took such occurrences in stride; it was easy to clean up and it didn't happen often. They were tough; we tossed them around and played hard with them.

They really liked climbing. When we took them out of the cage, they would chase each other up a tree. They would also climb up the wire walls of the cage and shake it violently. We decided to wire a couple of tree limbs inside the cage for their enjoyment. They loved it and played tag, scampering and chasing each other up, down, and all around the inside of the cage.

As they grew bigger and bigger, they played harder and meaner. We finally started leaving the door open because they could take care of themselves and didn't depend on us as much. We learned to be careful with them because their teeth and claws were getting sharper and with their developing muscles, they became strong enough to hurt us. As time went on, they weaned themselves from us. At night they would leave and the next morning they would come back. Not long after that, all we had was an empty cage and no more coons.

Marsha Hackathorn 1969   Linda Hackathorn 1969

PET COONS   Kenneth 1966

John

Peter

Over the years, though, we had several other sets of baby coons grow up in the coon cage and we always had a lot of fun with them. We had many friends and cousins who loved to come out and play with our coons.

Two sisters from Angleton, Linda and Marsha Hackathorn, thought the coons were just wonderful, cuddly, and fun. They wanted to take them home and show them to their family. We told them that they would be welcome to do that. The pair of coons we had at the time was about two-thirds grown, an optimum age for playing.

No one had ever asked to borrow them before so we had never had any reason to take them riding in a car. Therefore, we didn't think anything of the girls taking them. The girls loaded them into the back seat and left for home. About twenty minutes later, the girls were back, crying and screaming. The coons had escaped, but not before they shredded the interior of the car and crapped all over everything. We spent the rest of the afternoon helping them clean the car. We never saw the coons again, but the girls came back.

Skunks were another species of wildlife we had exciting and interesting experiences with.

Every summer we filled the barn and the lean-to with square bales of hay to feed the cows during the winter. During the interim, skunks took up residence among the hay bales and raised their families there. By the end of November one year some combination of Louis, Kenneth and I were feeding about twenty bales each day to the cows. We were seeing skunks in among the bales of hay all the time, but as long as we didn't bother them they kept their scent to themselves. Occasionally they would cut loose on a dog if he got too close. If they happened to get a direct hit of spray on the dog, it would take a week before the dog wore that terrible smell off.

Our cousins told us that skunks couldn't spray unless their front feet were on the ground. They were very convincing, so we nailed an old piece of plywood on the outside fence of the lean-to and decided to test the theory.

It wasn't uncommon to pick up a bale of hay and have a skunk scurry away and disappear into the tunnels they had developed throughout the rest of the hay bales. Because Louis volunteered and because he always seemed to have a way with animals, our plan was for him to pick up a skunk by the tail the next time we found a skunk under a bale of hay. Then, when Louis was ready, he would let the skunk go by tossing it on the other side of the plywood, shielding himself from the spray.

A few days after we had decided and made preparations to snatch a skunk, an opportunity availed itself.

We were all loading up the hay to feed the cows when Kenneth yelled out, "I've got a skunk under this bale!"

Louis went over beside Kenneth, bent over the hay bale and instructed him, "Lift the bale quickly towards you in a smooth motion and I'll get the skunk."

I was standing by the hay trailer watching so I could make a quick get-away if I needed to. Kenneth pulled up the bale. The skunk was hunkered down, but before he had a chance to move, Louis snatched him by the tail. He held the skunk hanging head down. The skunk was not paralyzed, but not jerking and fighting either. After scrutinizing the skunk for a few minutes, Louis gently tossed the skunk to the other side of the plywood barrier; it sprayed. We were amazed that the phenomenon was actually true. They can't spray if their front feet were not touching something.

We were in great spirits after that and proud of our new knowledge. Ken and I were now looking forward to picking up a skunk also.

Over the haying season, which lasted until early March, all of us gained the expertise of handling skunks any time there was one under the hay bales.

The next year, the routine was the same. About a month into the season, Louis and I were loading up the day's hay ration. I lifted up a bale, quickly and gently put it down and whispered to Louis, "There're three skunks under this bale."

He quickly came over and instructed me, "Lift the bale up. I'll pick up two of the skunks, and you get the last one."

"OK," I replied, knowing this was going to be a little risky.

As I pulled the bale aside, Louis grabbed a tail in each hand and I quickly grabbed the third one. We stood there beaming, knowing that this must be some kind of record. Not wanting to end this episode quickly, I said, "Louis, this is unbelievable! Let's go show Mom what we've done."

Louis agreed and we headed towards the house with our catches. We entered the back porch, which had a screen door to keep out bugs and a solid door for weather protection. The screen door was kept closed by a spring and the solid door was open to keep the house cool. Because I had a free hand, I pulled open the screen door and Louis went in first, with me close behind.

"Mom, come and see what we've got!" Louis yelled.

Mom walked in from the living room and we could tell immediately she wasn't as proud of us as we were.

"Get those damn skunks out of this house," Mom yelled hurriedly.

I knew Mom was excited. Excited, too, Louis and I immediately started backing out of the house. I could only assume that the skunks must also have been excited, with all the hub-bub going on. With my free hand I opened the screen door and went out. Louis put his back to the screen door and was easing sideways outside. I was down the steps watching Louis. As he cleared the screen door, it was starting to close when the skunk in his right hand grabbed the screen with his front paws. The rest was history. Louis took a direct hit.

We burned the clothes he was wearing, and he spent nearly an hour in a hot bath with lots of soap and a bristle scrub brush. He came out a little smelly, with his right arm looking red and raw from all the cleaning.

After that episode, we still snatched skunks up by their tails as the opportunities presented, but we never took wild animals into the house again.

Years later, in 2006, I was with Louis when he was selling some square bales out of his barn and found a skunk under a bale. Right there in front of his customers, much to their amazement, he snatched the skunk up, carried it outside and sat it down around a corner. We all were amazed that it didn't go off.

So he still had the touch, and those people who bought his hay had an experience I'm sure they will never see again.

Armadillos were another pest we had plenty of and we played with them, too. Some of the interesting things about armadillos are that they are one of the few animals that can contract leprosy. Also, they can't swim. If they have to cross a body of water, they walk across the bottom.

We chased armadillos for sport, but they would always run into a burrow, leaving their tails exposed. We would pull and tug on their tails, but they would lock themselves in with all four clawed feet. We never succeeded in pulling one. After much pulling and tugging, we did discover though, that if we pushed on the tail the armadillo would back out of the burrow on his own volition.

*　　*　　*　　*　　*

There may not be much game or many wild animals in Vietnam, but there are plenty of things to be on the alert for, and they are mostly two legged carrying an AK-47.

Riley is a trim guy who I think is a perfectionist; his mustache is always neatly trimmed; his hair is tight and precision groomed; his dress and everything in his space is always neat, clean and organized. He's a Yankee from New Jersey and has an Archie Bunker accent, but when he talks it is very precise. His body is a canvas for artwork. An eagle spreads its wings beautifully across his chest. His arms above his elbows are decorated with hearts, snakes and flowers. I am not generally a fan of tattoos, but whoever did his work was a true artist and Riley's tattoos fit him to perfection. My favorite tattoo on his legs. As he walks around in the hooch in his boxers, I see a squirrel running up his right leg; next thing I notice is the squirrel going down his left leg with a nut in its mouth.

Riley is older, maybe twenty-two, and much more worldly than I am. We are friends, but not close buddies. He gets orders and has to leave the country on short notice because of a family emergency. As he is leaving the compound getting ready to leave, he comes up to me, hands me a plastic bag and says, " Hey, Peltier, take this."

I glance at the bag and see that it's half full of loose marijuana, a couple of rolled joints and a packet of Zig Zag papers. I ask him what he wants me to do with it.

"I don't care. I just can't take it with me," he tells me.

I never saw him again.

This is the first time in my life to be in possession of anything illegal. Here in Vietnam marijuana is illegal, but enforcement is very lax as a general rule.

In the evenings around the compound there is always a group getting together outside for a smoke. The glow of the joints could be those of cigarettes, but the distinctive smell of "Mary Jane" tells the tale of what's going on. Grunts I see in the field wear joints in their helmet band right beside the graffiti that expresses their attitudes and opinions about their present situation. In my previous life I had never seen or smelled marijuana and had grown up too straight-laced to get involved anyway. Now I'm in another world, nineteen, curious and faced with an opportunity.

To date there has never been an inspection of any kind inside the hooch, so I stash the bag of marijuana in my locker. It takes me a week to figure out what to do with it. I decide to take one of the joints that is rolled up out to the urinal after all the lights are out. I take the twisted paper end and put it between my lips. I fumble with the book of matches and finally get it lit. The smell is the same that I've smelled many times around the compound. I take a short drag and suck it into my lungs. Not being a smoker, I cough it out. I inhale another dose and it mostly stays down. I stay and smoke the whole thing. I head back in toward my hooch, thinking to myself, "What's the big deal?"

The next day after things settled down after sick call, I wander into the lab where Greg is working.

"Have you ever smoked marijuana?" I ask him.

"No, and I haven't figured out why I should," he answers, looking up at me quizzically.

"When Riley left country he handed me a bag of it and told me to get rid of it because he couldn't take it with him."

"What did you do with it?"

"Last night I went out to the latrine and smoked a joint."

Greg stopped what he was doing, turned with a serious look on his face and said, "…and?"

"I went to the urinal thinking that the nasty diesel-antiseptic-urine smell would camouflage the marijuana smell. When I was done, my first thought was this is nothing. Then when I went back in the hooch and laid down for the night, my bunk suddenly came alive. I had a sensation that my bunk was starting to turn like the rotor on a helicopter. Slowly at first… whop… whop…whop, then faster whop whop whop. I gripped my hands to both sides of the bed frame tightly and hung on for the ride. I was totally out of control, and I knew this was one ride I couldn't get off of until it was done. It wasn't fun. It was weird and released a few monsters and spooks in my mind."

"Oh, really, what kind of spooks and monsters?"

"It's really hard to explain. Bright swirling colors, people and animals looked like they were filmed with infrared film."

"Did it scare you?"

"Not really scared, but uncomfortable and unsure, not being in control of what was going on around me. I wondered why anyone would smoke that stuff. I woke up this morning famished and had a big breakfast."

"Are you going to try it again?" Greg asks.

"It's not part of my plan," I answer.

Since the TET offensive, the bars and brothels in Thu Duc have been off limits. I am on a detail hauling garbage to the dump a few hundred yards off base. The dump was just a pit gouged out of the earth with bulldozers about 20 feet wide and 150 feet long. There are local women and children busily going through everything we discard.

By the dump, there are a couple of huts made of discarded pallets, wood, cardboard boxes and plastic sheathing. The smell in the air is not exactly pleasant and the locals there are dressed in tattered dirty clothes. They all look like they could use a bath.

One of the women waves to one of the regulars on the detail. He walks over to her and goes into one of the huts. I think it's odd and, pointing to the hut, ask one of the guys, "What's going on?"

He says, "Since they shut down the trucks to town, some of the women have set up shop here at the dump."

"You mean that shelter that barely has walls and a roof is a cat house?" I ask, flabbergasted.

"Yep," he replies.

I now know I've lived a sheltered life. It's not the things I know that surprise me, but it's the things I don't even suspect that do.

In just a few minutes, the man returns with a smile on his face. The guys who know him give him a ribbing. All I want is a ride back to the base to get back to my unit.

Sunday afternoons are mostly slow, with no duty for many of us.

Steve Salines has a buddy in ordinance and they are going out to the north entrance to do some target practice. He invites me to tag along. Being bored, busy doing nothing, and liking the smell of exploding gunpowder, I jump at the opportunity.

We get our M-16's and meet the other guys at the motor pool. We load up in the back of a duce and a half and head to the range. From the looks of all the ammo riding with us in the back of the truck, we must be going to war. The range is just a couple of acres with all the brush and vegetation scraped off. On the far end are some pallets braced up on their ends with targets attached. The targets are generally paper plates and a couple of junk vehicles.

We start off plinking at the vehicles. Then we put up some paper plates with an x-y axis marked on them. We shoot for a dollar a round, at which point I realize why I was invited. After donating five dollars, I bow out of the competition and go back to shooting the vehicles. An M-16 has a selector switch for semi-automatic, which shoots one round with each pull of the trigger, and for fully automatic, which shoots continuously when the trigger is pulled. During training we were given demonstrations of shooting in fully automatic but never allowed to fire in that mode. I load up a 20 round clip, flip the selector to "fully", and blast away. I can't believe how fast those twenty rounds are expended. We have plenty of ammo and I run a few more clips through the weapon just for fun.

When the rest of the group is finished with their gaming, they pull out the M-79 grenade launcher, or "thump gun" as it is more commonly called. It looks similar to a single shot shotgun with a break-over barrel that is only about 18 inches long and 40 millimeters (a little larger than 1 ½ inches) in diameter. It has a range of a little over 400 yards. It's designed to lob grenades similar to a mortar and is fired from the shoulder.

Soon we were taking turns trying to completely destroy the vehicles on the other end of the range. It is called a thump gun because when it's fired it makes a noise like a deep thump and then you get a thump on your shoulder. I really like this weapon. I flip up the sight and start walking the rounds toward the junked armored personnel carrier (APC) and finally nail it. It also fires a round loaded with buckshot for close combat, but we don't have any of those to test.

Next they pull out the big gun, an M-60 machine gun. Again, I have never fired one of these play pretties, but now I have a chance. After watching several of the guys rip apart and destroy several five-gallon buckets filled with water, I get a turn. I take the strap and hang the M-60 from my right shoulder, take a belt of ammunition, lock it into place and then chamber the first round. It's ready to fire. After flipping the selector lever, I pull the trigger. The M-60 comes alive and leaps into action with a deafening roar, leaving me engulfed in the smell of burning powder and a haze of smoke. "Wow" is all that fills my mind, and that was just a short burst. I fire away, moving the barrel slowly and watching the bullets kick up dust and dirt as I walk the shots in on a five-gallon bucket of water that explodes with water going everywhere as it's hit by the 7.62 mm bullets. By the time we finish with the M-60, its barrel is so hot it would burn you badly if you were to touch it.

We finish off the afternoon plinking again, this time with a couple of 45 caliber automatic pistols. After everyone has had his fill of shooting, we head back into the base-camp and I learn how to clean some of these weapons that before today I had never fired. Soon we're at the EM Club, having a few beers and reliving the day's shooting experience.

For the last thirty days of a tour of duty a guy is considered a short-timer. I have three *X*'s marking out the days on my short-timer calendar.

My last day in Vietnam is scheduled to be November 19, 1968. I've been considering an "early out" program that the Army offers to get out about five months before my mid-June of 1969 normal discharge date. The way the program works is that if you have 150 days or less left in the service when you reach stateside after leaving Vietnam, you may elect to leave the service at that time at the convenience of the service.

If I do that, it would require that I extend my time in Vietnam for fifty-six days.

I work up a plan and go see Top to try and work out a deal. When I'm standing in front of his desk, Top asks me, "What can I do for you today, Specialist Peltier?"

"Top, I have been thinking about extending my tour of duty to take advantage of the early out program," I reply.

"That would be certainly fine with me," Top says.

Nervously, I ask, "Would it possible, if I decided to extend, to limit my duty to the base camp and be on outdoor work details?"

Top thinks for a moment and replies, "We can work that out, but it seems to me you'll be working a lot harder than you are now."

"I know that, but I want to get in better physical shape and lessen my risk while I'm in country."

"You've got a deal, Peltier."

"Top, there's just one other thing. I want to take a week's leave to Japan around Christmas."

Top looks up, smiles and says, "Peltier, I wish everyone was as easy to please as you. You come in here and volunteer for duty nobody else wants and then ask to take leave that you're already entitled to. We've got us a deal."

Filling sandbags and rebuilding bunkers is a perpetual job around the company compound. I have a couple of privates working with me and we do that and any other maintenance that needs doing. Around the compound we can work without shirts or hats. I have my hair buzzed as short as my first Army haircut. The sun beats down on us as we work, and I get more sun than I need at the onset of the work detail. The next day my skin starts flaking and peeling off my back and arms. I reach up and scratch my itching head. Skin is peeling off my scalp in pieces the size of a quarter. In my exuberance to get tanned and in shape, I decide the need for moderation is in order.

The USO is bringing Bob Hope to Long Binh, and I'm finally not the lowest ranking, newest soldier in Alpha Company. A group of us get to go with some of the ambulatory patients in the ward.

The show is staged in a huge amphitheater carved out of the side of a hill. Most of the seating is rows of sandbags, but there are several hundred chairs set up in front of the stage for hospital patients. We are there about an hour early to get the patients comfortably situated. The stadium is filling up and the show is due to start mid-afternoon. Everyone is straining and looking towards the middle of the amphitheater. I follow their eyes to see General Abrams, the commander of all the Armed Forces in Vietnam. To my surprise, he is sitting about the same level I am, about a third of the way back from the stage.

Bob Hope Show 1968

My Favorite Ann Margret

Bob Hope

Roosevelt Greer

The Golddiggers

My View

Penelope
Plummer
Miss Universe
1968

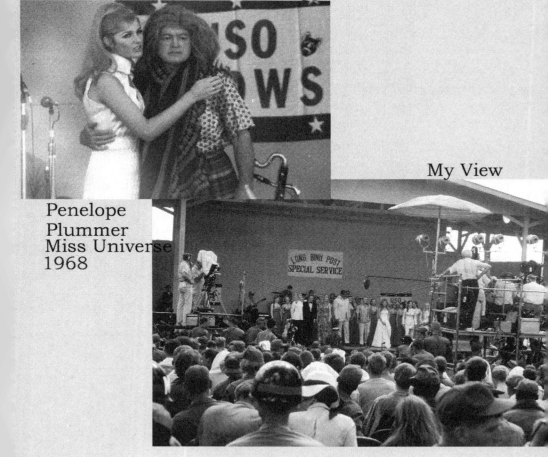

Emptying Out

Packed House
Estimated 25,000

Patients, the Last to Leave

I think the show is put on for the folks back home as much as for us GI's in Vietnam because our view is partially blocked by lights and cameras on both sides and a section of scaffolding right in the middle about halfway between me and the stage. Bob Hope has been entertaining the troops since World War II. Over the years I have watched many re-runs of his USO shows on television, but now I feel like a part of history being able to see one of them in person.

Les Brown and his Band of Renown warm up. Then the announcer introduces Bob Hope. With the exception of seeing Elvis Presley and Roy Rodgers at the Coliseum during the Houston Livestock Show and Rodeo, this is the first time I've been to a live event with world class entertainment. Bob Hope comes out and immediately connects with us soldiers with hilarious one-liners pertaining to our plight in Vietnam; he has everyone falling off their sandbag seats. He and Ann Margaret do several song and dance routines and she wins a permanent place in my heart.

(Years later, in 1974, my wife Janie and I were in Las Vegas when Ann Margaret was the entertainment at one of the casinos. "Let's try and get tickets to see Ann Margaret tonight," I told her.

She replied, "You just want to get a glimpse of her beautiful body."

"She took time off from being a movie star to support and entertain us troops in Vietnam and you're right, she is beautiful, but I'm a fan of hers and know she will put on a phenomenal show."

We did get tickets and, as I predicted, she put so much energy into her act that I was exhausted for her by the end of it.)

Next in the USO show, Roosevelt Greer, a former member of the "Fearsome Foursome" of NFL Los Angeles Rams' fame, comes out. All 350 pounds of him are dressed to the hilt in a bright yellow suit as he sings to us.

In this land where the vast majority is male, they bring us the Gold Diggers, a popular dance group dressed in scanty pink outfits, just to remind us what is waiting for us back home. Miss World of 1968, Penelope Plummer, who is from Australia, does a skit with Bob that is very funny, but most of our eyes are locked on her as she shines like a diamond in the afternoon sun.

After about two hours of continuous entertainment, all of the players come back on stage and reluctantly tell us goodbye. They made us all feel appreciated for serving our country in this far away place. In our daily routines we just want to survive our time here and get home. Most of us are not here for glory and don't have a burning desire to change the world. We are patriots who love our country and have the same sense of duty our fathers had before us. We go where we are sent and do what we are ordered. Most of all, though, after our time here is up we all just want to get back home to continue our "pursuit of happiness".

After the show we linger around as the place empties, waiting to collect our patients. It seems odd how just a short while ago this place was surging with vibrant energy, alive with thousands of green fatigues, and now it is silent and sedate. There are a few people breaking down the lighting and scaffolding, but the sandbags are empty as we load our patients into the ambulance and head back to Dian.

I spend Christmas of 1968 in Tokyo. I've been away from my family for over a year and grown accustomed to being on my own. I still miss them, but unless my luck turns very bad, I am going to be home in less than 30 days.

I find Tokyo a very interesting place. In the Ginza district of downtown, everything looks so clean and new. There are giant neon signs flashing everywhere and a round glass building that reaches fifteen to twenty stories up to the sky. I walk out of a store at closing time two days before Christmas and there is a familiar looking Santa ringing a bell next to a red pot hanging from a tripod. This Santa has string holding a fake beard that totally misses his chin and is lying on his chest with no mustache and his bare chin sticking out. I smile and walk on toward the street.

There is a big open square in the Ginza District in front of me, and today I don't think one more person could be packed into it. I am standing there at least a foot taller than any person around and, as I gaze out looking back and forth around the square, I unexpectedly find myself laughing out loud. What I'm looking at is like a sea of black mops on heads moving up, down, back and forth and what I see is not a host of individuals but more like an ocean that has come alive and has a body movement of its own. I'm sure anyone who sees and hears me thinks I am crazy, but for this fleeting moment, they are my entertainment.

Other than just getting a break from the Army and a war zone, my reason for coming here is the fact that Japan is well known for its quality sound and camera equipment at unbeatable prices.

When I arrived in Vietnam, I carried a Kodak Instamatic over with me. After several months in country, I bought a Yashica Electro 35. It was a 35-millimeter viewfinder camera and eons ahead of the Instamatic. It had features like automatic exposure to light and a time delay feature, and it took excellent pictures.

235

Now as I am looking forward to going home, it's time for me to get another upgrade. I plan to purchase a Minolta SLR 101. It is a 35-millimeter, single lens reflex camera, with several interchangeable lenses. I find all the camera equipment and a leather case to carry it in and make the purchase.

I had gotten a letter from my sister Kay saying she wanted to go in with me and buy Mom a set of good China while I am in Japan. In order to have enough place settings for family and a few friends, we decided we needed to get two sets of twelve place settings. She said in her letter that I would have to pick it out because she had no idea what brand or types would be available. After looking at many different place settings, with blue being my favorite color, and having not a clue what I was doing (because almost everything I saw was very nice), I make a selection. I chose one with large plates and bowls; Mom's thundering herd is not very petite. The design was off white with light blue trim inside a gold rim with a yellow flower in the middle. After adding two sets of matching serving bowls, a butter plate, a sugar bowl, a creamer and a large platter, I have it all shipped home to Texas. I hope it will be there before me.

So far my time in Tokyo has been taking advantage of purchasing opportunities that I might never again have. One of the guys at the USO Club recommended that I get a massage during my stay. Until now no stranger has ever touched me in a way more personal than getting a haircut, but I'd seen massages given in the movies and it looked relaxing. I decide to give it a try.

Walking into the massage parlor is a little embarrassing and I'm self-conscious and don't know what to do or ask for. I'm thinking maybe I should turn and bolt for the door.

A small lady comes forward and says, "How may I help you?" in almost perfect English.

"This place was recommended to me to get a massage," I answer and add, "I have never had a massage before."

She smiles, explains the routine and passes me off to another small lady in a bright pink and red robe. That lady speaks very little English. She takes me to a dressing room and indicates that I should take a shower and follow the signs to the massage area. I put all my clothes in a locker, and the key to the locker I place on my wrist. After showering, I grab a large American sized towel and wrap it around my waist. Then I head to the massage area.

There are tubs that look like cubes coming out of the floor, each about three feet square and three feet high. Each one is steaming with water vapor. The lady in the pink and red robe indicates that I should enter one of these tubs. The water is hot and I sink down to my chin as the lady prepares a table that resembles what we use in the emergency room to receive patients, but this one has a rail above it down one side. It has a plastic top and she covers it with another large towel and places a small pillow on one end. After about ten minutes, she comes back and gets me out of the tub. I try to keep covered as I get out. I'm as red as the lobster I ate in Sidney and feel as if I have been parboiled.

I lay face down on the area she has prepared as she situates a towel over my mid-section. The next thing I feel is her small, but strong, stubby fingers working into the flesh around my neck and head. At first I tense up, but soon my body gives way to total relaxation. I close my eyes as she moves from one point to another and I imagine that my body has been changed into a floating glob of Jell-O. After my feet are done, I think it's over, but I'm not sure I can move out of this relaxed state. I look around and my masseuse is climbing up the end of the table at my feet. She signals me to lay my head back down. Then she holds onto the rail and walks all over my back, using her weight and toes this time to collapse any resisting areas. All good things must end. She climbs down, gives me a shake and says, "You go now."

I reluctantly gather myself up and head to the dressing room, knowing that tomorrow is a new day and that I will be back in Vietnam.

I have discovered that I need to be careful about what I ask for.

Since mid-November, I have been tightly tethered to the company compound inside the base-camp, except for my leave to Japan. This is not me complaining, but life was much more exciting and interesting serving the MEDCAP team than filling sandbags, repairing bunkers and doing whatever menial maintenance work that comes up. The truth be known, I really miss MEDCAP duty. It was the only thing that really gave me a sense of accomplishment during my tour of duty in Vietnam.

When I return from Tokyo I have a little over two weeks before I am scheduled to return to the States. I have been boxing up all the things I've accumulated over the past fourteen months here, like extra combat boots, poncho liners, and a few other items, and shipping them home.

I want to make one last trip to Tan Son Nhut, where a big PX is located, to purchase a few things and take advantage of my active duty military status that will soon be ending. I contact Captain Miller and ask for permission to take his jeep there two days before my scheduled departure. He's a good guy and grants my request. Rivera, another short-timer buddy of mine, wants to go, too, so we're all set.

We leave out the next morning, lax in our preparation. We pass out of the main gate wearing baseball caps (no helmets) and fatigues (no flak jackets). We are not carrying M-16's for protection. This is the first time in my tour I've been off the base-camp totally unprotected. You would think we were going to the corner drug store to pick up a few things and then coming right back.

We make it to the PX in 45 minutes with no problems and do our shopping. Depositing our bags of freshly purchased goods in the back of the open topped jeep, we start our journey back to Dian. In Saigon many of the major intersections have roundabouts which sometimes require you to stop before getting into the flow of traffic. While we were stopped at one such roundabout in slow heavy traffic, a Vietnamese teenage boy jumped off the curb, grabbed one of my bags and started running up the street behind me. I reacted by jerking on the emergency brake, throwing the transmission into neutral, and bolting after the thief. As I did, I yelled over my shoulder to Rivera, "Stay put. I'll be right back."

I gained quickly on the boy. He knew it and threw down the bag. I picked it up and started walking back towards the jeep. The streets around me were surging with traffic, filled with the acrid smell of exhaust from the small two cycle engines of motorcycles and Lambrettas, cars, and large diesel trucks. The sounds of impatient drivers honking their horns and the squealing of their brakes added to the noise of all the engines. Vietnamese on bicycles and pedestrians are crowded on the sidewalks and edges of the streets. It suddenly occurred to me that I'm an idiot and that I may be at the wrong place at the wrong time. I quickened my pace back to the jeep and thought to myself, "You stupid SOB, if you're fortunate enough to make it back to the jeep, jump in it and go directly back to Dian and don't stop for anything."

I have been in-country for nearly fourteen months living by the rules and now, within days of going home, I know my guard is down and I've taken way too much for granted.

I hop into the jeep and wind it up. Rivera looks at me and says, "Are you in a hurry."

Keeping my eyes on the road I answer, "Yep."

I don't think I was ever as happy to see Dian's front gate as I am today. The guard waves us through and I feel again like I'm going to be home in a few days.

After Greg left a few months ago, he sent Steve and me a letter describing the process of mustering out of the Army, so I have some idea what will happen in Oakland when I finally get there.

On January 13th I head to Long Binh on the early morning ambulance run with all my gear. After checking in my M-16 and a few other things that require my signatures on a small pile of papers, a group of us on the same flight are sent to the waiting area for our plane.

By mid-afternoon we are loaded into a Braniff International 707. The stewardesses are well perfumed as they walk down the aisle. All of the passengers are wearing light weight jungle fatigues and paying particular attention to the stewardesses as they walk by. Home is getting closer.

Soon we're up and away, crammed into the cabin like sardines in a tin. It can be said that the Army does not spend any money on extra room and comfort for military travel.

As the sun is starting to set, we are soon cruising. It's really beautiful in this friendly sky. Instead of going around the world, as we did on the flight to Vietnam, we are going up and over and refueling in Anchorage, Alaska, on our return trip.

We land in Anchorage in a snow flurry and park about a hundred feet from the terminal building. As we wake up and stiffly start moving around, we are told to deplane during refueling. In the last six or seven hours we have gone from eighty degrees to ten below and are still wearing jungle fatigues. I wrap the scrap of an airline blanket about my head and shoulders and get in line to make a dash to the terminal. When I leave the door onto the stair landing, it's like hitting a wall of ice and air as my lungs get a dose of it. I go down the stairs and into the terminal building just on instinct, as my senses are numb.

It only takes a few minutes and a cup of hot coffee to regain my senses. It's the middle of the night and dark outside, but I understand it's dark about twenty hours a day here this time of year. After we get loosened up and fill up on sandwiches, it's time to challenge the cold and get back into the plane. Getting back on the plane doesn't seem nearly as bad as getting off, and we are soon up in the air again, heading toward Oakland.

Oakland is a blur. They are processing soldiers in and out of the country by the thousands. We arrive early in the morning and hit the ground running. We take our bags into a large room with bleachers on three sides. We set down all our bags and are divided into groups. One group goes to breakfast; my group goes to get fitted for dress greens. I can't believe the Army is going to send me home in a Class A uniform that will only get worn once.

After the fitting, we file through a clinic for our final physical exam. I guess they want to make sure we are not carrying some exotic disease home with us; the way some people abuse themselves, I can understand why. Breakfast, I find out, is a steak dinner or whatever else you can imagine. After eating one of the best meals the Army has ever fed me, my group and I get a re-up talk.

We are all tired and most of us just want to go home. I don't think anyone has ever stayed in the service based on this re-up presentation. Next, an Army chaplain comes in and tells us what a good job we did in serving our country. All during this time there are different groups moving in and out of the main room. As in all Army operations, there is a lot of waiting in lines with our groups, but someone has got this operation down pat.

A representative from the Veterans Administration shows us a short film and explains many of our benefits. The one that most interests me at this time is 36 months of higher education benefits.

The pay line is always welcome. This is the first time in over a year I've been paid in greenbacks and it is the biggest payday ever as I receive pay for twenty-one days of unused leave. When I was in Vietnam, I was paid in Military Payment Certificates and I would keep twenty bucks or so each month and send the rest home to the bank.

I can't believe it - by mid afternoon our dress greens are altered to fit, and we are soon wearing them.

Since it's cold in much of the country, we are allowed to get a used overcoat for the trip home, if we want. I never look a gift horse in the mouth. I pick one out even though it seldom gets cold enough in Houston to need it.

There are piles of papers to sign. By the end of the afternoon I have the magic DD-214. It's the one sheet of paper that indicates my separation from the service. I am being delivered to Oakland International Airport, armed with a ticket home. There is no one to say goodbye to here. I feel kind of odd leaving this part of my life in such a flurry.

12

Back in the Lone Star State

Landing at Houston International Airport seems to me almost surreal. Exiting the door of the plane, the first thing I notice is the bright Texas sun. The cool January air makes the whole outside feel like air conditioning, a welcome change from Vietnam. After walking down the stairs of the plane the first thing I do is to kiss the tarmac, saying to myself, "Thank you, God. Hello, Texas".

I hear my name and look up. My sister Kay, my welcoming committee of one, is running my way. We greet with a big bear hug. It already feels really good to be home. There is no brass band to welcome me, but I couldn't be happier!

The family is starting to move out. Kenneth and Becky are off to Stephen F. Austin State University; Peter is on active duty at a naval air station in Pennsylvania; Louis is working and going to Alvin Junior College; Kay is working in Houston. Stephen is a senior in high school and Paul is a junior. Arthur, Richard, and Molly are in elementary school. Mom and Dad are still home.

The first weekend that I am home, all the family gets together, except for Peter, and I talk to him on the phone. It's seldom in one's life that you get to be the center of such a celebration, and for me it's a very special time. It's a time for renewal of family ties and friendships interrupted. It's also a time to look forward and tighten up loosely developed plans for my future.

Finally back home in Danbury to stay, I waste no time in trying to get my life back on track.

I didn't know what was more important, getting a set of wheels or getting a job, so I did both.

Dow Chemical in Freeport was always hiring in some capacity and some friends of mine encouraged me to apply. I borrowed the family car and drove the twenty or so miles to Dow to fill out a job application. After I was done there I dropped in at Clyde V. Lee's car dealership and checked out the Pontiacs and Oldsmobiles. After looking around there I headed to Angleton and looked at the Chevrolets.

This wasn't the first time I'd considered what car I wanted to buy once home. Ford and Plymouth products had already been eliminated from my choices and I knew that I didn't want a foreign car.

A Dow employment representative called me to schedule a physical exam and told me if I passed I could have a job as a sludger in the magnesium production unit. He also told me the pay started at $3.50 per hour. "WOW!" I thought.

Before the service, I had a job working for my Uncle Pete in his flying service. I flagged, drove trucks, and loaded the airplane for a dollar an hour. Flagging was holding up a white flag for the pilot (in this case, Uncle Pete) to see. Generally there was a flagman at each end of the field and each time Uncle Pete passed, both flagmen walked a specified distance on the field, depending on whether Uncle Pete was spraying or fertilizing. This enabled the spray or fertilizer to be applied evenly across the field. Today, flagmen are not required; that operation is taken care of by GPS's and on-board computers.

I also worked for my cousin Francis Peltier, known as "Frenchy," unloading box-cars of fertilizer. Several of us high school guys did that after school in January and February before the spring plantings. There were no forklifts; we unloaded the 80 pound bags with two wheeled dollies, ten bags at a time. The coaches loved it because it kept us all in good shape.

My last summer home I worked for Vincent Hechler, driving a truck hauling rice to the dryers and working in his rice fields.

Working at Dow, I can easily make as much in a week as I made in a month in the Army.

Now I needed to get a car for transportation. I wanted this car to be new, as I thought that it might be the only new car I would ever buy. I also wanted a sporty car, not a family car.

The closest thing to a new car my parents had experienced was a gray four door 1954 Kaiser Dad bought in 1955. It was a used demo and I'm sure he cut a great deal on it because it was the last year model produced in the States. Later on, I can recall when I was thirteen or fourteen the family car engine blew and it was going to cost more to fix it that to replace it. Dad had located an old Plymouth that ran for $125.00. The family coffers were running somewhere near empty so Peter, Kay, Louis, Kenneth and I each pitched in $25.00 to buy the car and facilitate our mobility. Driving was a necessity for all of us kids and I am sure that we were hard on all the junkers we drove.

After looking at all the cars in stock in our local area that somewhat met my criteria I decided on a bright canary yellow 1969 Pontiac Le Mans that sat on the showroom floor at the Clyde V. Lee dealership in Freeport. The written quote was $3,460.00, plus tax, title, and license.

Next stop was the bank to work out the financing. The first thing I found out was-that because I was under 21 and this was my first loan and first real job, I had to get a co-signer to guarantee the note. I was disappointed because I had been own my own now for nearly two years and wanted to be totally independent.

(Note: I have since learned that being totally independent is a state of mind and not physically a real possibility or something I really want be. Without the interdependence of others in our lives, we would be like someone floating alone on a life raft in the middle of an ocean.)

I asked Dad if he would be willing to co-sign the note. He laughed agreeably and said something like, "That banker would be better advised to get you to co-sign on my loans than me on yours."

Dad and I went to the bank, executed the loan documents and then to the dealership to pick up the car. At the dealership the salesman brought out the documents. Surprisingly, the price of the car had gone up about $150. Dad asked to see the written quote that I'd gotten.

I handed him the paper. He compared the two and challenged the salesman saying, "This is not the same deal you quoted my son."

The salesman looked at the quote and invoice and said, "There was a mistake on the quote and the price really should be as shown on the invoice."

Dad looked at the salesman and said, "Your quote is what we based our decision on for buying the car and we have already secured financing based on it. I need to talk to your manager or owner."

The salesman took the paperwork and left us. I could tell Dad was nervous and so was I. I said to him, because I hated confrontation and I wanted the car so bad I could taste it, "Dad, I can pay the extra money. Let's just do it and get out of here."

Dad looked and me and said, "Son, a deal is a deal, and you can't go through life wondering if you're standing on shifting sand or solid ground. If they don't hold to the deal they offered, this is not a company you want to deal with."

When the salesman returned, he told us that he could knock $100 off the invoice.

Dad started rising out of his seat to leave and told the salesman, "That is not the deal you quoted. We came here in good faith to purchase that vehicle based on your quote. Is this how you normally do business?"

The salesman stood up said, "Mr. Peltier, please sit down. I'll be right back."

In few minutes the salesman came back with another man who announced, "I'm Clyde Lee, the owner. Mark here has made a mistake in quoting this car to your son, Mr. Peltier."

Looking at my dad, he said, "He is now making a bigger mistake by attempting to get you and your son to cover his first mistake. We don't do business that way. We would be happy to sell you the car at the quoted price."

We agreed to purchase the car and Mr. Lee left us with the salesman, who nervously and apologetically finalized the transaction.

After we had everything signed, I thanked Dad and told him I'd be along home in a couple of hours.

My first real car - wow, was I happy!

The first thing I did was rolled down all the windows and tooled down the road to Angleton. I figured I'd drive through all my old haunts and see some of my old buddies. It was a bright sunny January day, about 50 degrees outside; after fourteen months in Vietnam it felt like the world was air-conditioned, but after about ten minutes of rolling down the road with the windows down I got chilled, stopped the car and rolled all the windows back up.

Driving through the Dairy Queen in my brand new canary yellow Le Mans, I turned a lot of heads, but I recognized no one. The place was full of high school kids. I was beginning to get the picture. While I was gone for nearly two years, all my friends were either married, away at college, or working.

After driving around for a while longer, I headed home. When all my little brothers and sisters saw me in my new car, they thought that I'd hung the moon. The admiration was nice, but what I would have really liked was to find some young adults about my age to hang around with. So far they were nowhere to be found.

So I went to work.

Dow Chemical put me right to work in the "mag cells", as they did with my father when he returned from World War II.

Magnesium is produced in cells. Each cell is a tank about 15 feet long and about 6 feet in diameter. On the end of each cell is an opening about 18 inches square that provides access to the cell for removing the molten magnesium and cleaning the cell.

The cells are serviced from the second floors of several long buildings that have rows of maybe fifty cells in each building. Inside each cell is a boiling bath of salt water and two rows of 6 carbon rods about 12 inches in diameter and 6 feet long. The carbon rods have large clamps on each one that connect them to large copper buss bars that introduce a very high amperage, low voltage current into the bath. A feedstock of crushed oyster shell is fed into the bath, rich in magnesium. The bath with the electricity running through it reacts with the feedstock and releases the magnesium into the bath where it floats on its surface, while the remainder (sludge) drops to the bottom of the cell.

Once the magnesium rises to the surface, we skimmed it off and transferred it to a crucible mounted on a rail car below at ground level. From there, it went to an area where it was cast into ingots for shipping.

My job as a sludger was to clean the sludge out of a group of five cells. I did that by running a steel rake welded to a 20' long 3/4" diameter solid steel rod into the boiling vat and pulling the sludge to the front of the cell. After that, I took a bucket, which was also welded to the same sized rod, and pulled the sludge up and out of the cells, dropping it into mobile steel containers. There the sludge cooled before it was disposed of in dumpsters.

It was a very hot and dangerous job, but it paid well and if I kept my cells clean, I-could get the job done in as little as six hours.

After a few weeks on the job, I proved to be competent in doing the work and was offered overtime.

I worked what was called the "swing shift". The way swing shifts worked was that I worked one week on the day shift from 7:00 a.m. to 3:30 p.m. Then I worked the next week on the evening shift from 3:00 p.m. to 11:30 p.m. Then the next week I worked the graveyard shift from 11:00 p.m. to 7:30 a.m. Days off were set around a 40-hour work week. For example, I could have Sunday and Monday off one week and the next week be off Sunday, Monday and Tuesday. Overtime was handed out in four and eight hour shifts. The eight hour overtime shifts included a meal.

I worked all the overtime I could get for many reasons, the most important being that it paid time and a half.

My schedule was so crazy with the swing shift. I generally worked when most other people were off. All the girls I knew before were either married, away at school or hiding. (At least I hadn't been able to find them.) I did manage to get together with friends, family and eventually met a few girls to date.

The first thing I did was to buy a used window rattler air conditioner for the Little House. Then I put opaque curtains on all the windows. If I got off work at 7:30 a.m., I needed to sleep until mid-afternoon. The air conditioner provided a cool spot and made enough noise to block out most of the farm noise going on outside.

Because of my odd hours, I spent most of my off time helping out around the farm.

My brother Louis and I had been planning to go to college together in the fall. He had been looking at Texas Tech because they had a good agri-business program. He asked me what I thought of that.

I told him, "I have no clue what I want to major in. I'll figure that out while I'm getting the basic required courses completed. My only requirement is that there are lots of pretty girls wherever we go."

In high school I was never a scholastic standout and was not sure that I'd even finish college with a degree.

"I'm told that the girls are there," Louis answered.

After about a month, Louis and I were talking about it again. He said, "Do you know how far it is to Lubbock?"

"No, am I supposed to care?" I asked.

"Well, it's too far for us to go to school there. How about Sam Houston State University in Huntsville?" he asked.

" My only requirement is still that there lots of pretty girls there," I again informed him.

"I'm sure you will be well pleased," he said.

We filled out our applications and we were soon accepted into the halls of higher learning at Sam Houston State University.

We took a field trip to the University, checked out the campus and the girls and everything passed muster. While we were there, we found a garage apartment and put down a deposit. We were all set to go.

*   *   *   *   *

It was another hot and miserable Texas morning in early September of 1969 that I so clearly remember. I was in Danbury at St. Anthony's Catholic Church. It was packed and there was standing room only. Everyone in the community and surrounding area was giving a final farewell to my dad, Wilburn Mitchell Peltier, age 54. He was born on April 23, 1915, and died unexpectedly on August 29, 1969.

Needless to say, my whole family was devastated.

After the Funeral Mass, I walked with some of the crowd a few blocks to the nearby cemetery. Every one there wanted to offer their condolences, but I just wanted some room to breathe.

Dad had a military type funeral because he was a World War II veteran. He had also served as the Commander of the Danbury Chapter of the American Legion. Some distance away from my dad's grave in a corner of the cemetery, a lone bugler in his dress uniform played the long and mournful notes of taps. Mom and some others in my family sat in the front row under the canopy put up by the funeral home. They were all in tears. Tears ran down my face, too, as I watched Mom receive the United States flag which had draped my dad's coffin only a few minutes ago. The soldiers folded it into a neat triangle and ceremoniously presented it to her. Seven World War II veterans lined up with rifles raised and fired three volleys each, giving my dad, their fallen comrade-in-arms, his well-deserved 21 gun salute.

I looked down at the short funeral program and saw his life reduced to a short column, but his whole life was really reflected in my mother, brothers, sisters, me and all the lives that he had touched who were standing there.

Just a week and a few days ago Mom had awakened me in the middle of the night and told me Dad was having chest pains and that I needed to take them to the hospital. I quickly got ready and we were own our way in minutes. At the emergency room, he was examined, given some medication and placed in a room for observation. Mom sent me back home and told me to take care of things there and bring the car back after breakfast.

He was admitted to the hospital. Things seemed to change very little as we got into a routine with Dad not at home. He seemed to be getting better and we all expected he would be discharged from the hospital at any time.

I had just quit working at Dow and was getting ready to go to Sam Houston State University with Louis to start on a path to get a degree in something, to be determined. Louis, Kenneth and I were in Houston to buy some school clothes when we got the call to go to the hospital. We knew something wasn't right. Our minds went to the worst.

When we arrived, we got the news of Dad's death. Mom had already left to be with the rest of the kids.

A nurse asked us if we wanted to see the body. We said yes, thinking it was protocol. We saw him in the corner of a poorly lit room, draped in a sheet.

It seemed like yesterday that I mustered out of the Army after serving time as a medic in Vietnam. Dad had served in the Army's 93rd Medical Battalion in the European theater during World War II.

I thought to myself as I stood there in that room, "Dad, how can you be gone? I don't feel as if I ever really knew the real you. You never talked about your war experiences except that you had served in France and Belgium. I was waiting for the right time to share with you about my time in the Army, but what I really wanted was for you to share your experiences with me. For those who fought for it, I think freedom has a special flavor the protected ones will never know or understand."

Now that moment was now lost forever.

I was angry.

I wanted so much more Dad, a relationship as an equal, a friend. I wanted to know how he felt about me; I had always longed to be closer to him and not just be someone to be seen and not heard. I have always thought there was plenty of time, but after experiencing Vietnam, I knew better.

Standing there, I could only hope that there is a heaven where he and I could meet and finish together on the other side.

Soon, another nurse came in and quickly ushered us out. Obviously it wasn't protocol.

13

A Herd of My Own

After Dad passed, Louis and I went to Mom and asked her if she wanted us to stay home and help with the transition. She was adamant that we go on to college and made it clear that our education was the key to our future and that the farm was not.

So off to Sam Houston State University we went. Louis was a little ahead of the curve because he was able to get several basic classes completed at Alvin Junior College in the previous spring and fall semesters. I was taking sixteen hours, which was considered a full load.

Soon I had the feeling that time had just stopped. After growing up on the farm where we were never caught up, then being in the Army for nineteen months of regimentation and daily duty at all different hours of the day and night, followed by working the swing shift at Dow Chemical with all the overtime I could muster, I needed to be occupied way more than 16 classroom hours a week.

The Huntsville newspaper, called <u>The Huntsville Item,</u> had an advertisement in the Help Wanted section for a medical assistant needed by the Texas Department of Corrections. The fact that I was a veteran trained as a medical corpsman landed me the job.

With the stroke of a pen, I went from being bored to busy. The job was located 20 miles north of Huntsville at the Ferguson Unit. In that unit all the inmates were between 18 and 25 years old. The medical person in charge was a middle aged man who was a registered nurse. He showed me around and went over all the procedures that were different in the prison. He warned me that the convicts were always trying to con him in some way or another.

The pay was low and my hours were long. I put in twelve hours a day on Saturday's and Sunday's from 7:00 a.m. to 7:00 p.m. and six hours a day on Monday's, Tuesday's, and Wednesday's from noon to 6:00 p.m. Being there 42 hours a week made for long weeks, but all my classes were already scheduled in the mornings so it was a good fit. I mainly dispensed medicine three times a day, making sure the inmates actually took it.

The job had a couple of perks. When I wasn't busy dispensing drugs or tending to minor maladies, I could study. If I was there at breakfast, lunch or dinner time, I could also eat. The food was nothing special, but the price was right.

"Rat was the nickname for one of the inmates who came in every evening with a headache. I administered two aspirins and sent him on his way. I knew he didn't really have a headache, so after about two weeks of headaches I decided to change his medicine. The next time he came in, I gave in a double dose of laxative tablets.

Rat came by the next morning and asked, "Mr. Peltier what did you do that to me for? I was on the pot all night."

"Rat, how is your headache?" I answered.

"What headache?" Rat said.

"See, that medicine did its job," I replied.

That cured Rat for a while. He was just looking for a little attention.

I worked at Ferguson during the fall and spring semesters. In the spring semester I also pledged a fraternity, Pi Kappa Alpha. After that, I decided I could fill my time better than working in the prison, as I had integrated into the college culture of the 1970's.

*   *   *   *   *

Dad and Mom had always talked and dreamed of building a new house. The farm barely made enough to provide enough food, clothing and shelter for our family, though, so a new house was surely not in the cards unless something drastic happened. That "something drastic" did happen when Dad died.

In the late sixties, Mom and Dad took a good look at their family and decided to get a life insurance policy on Dad's life. Mom had gone back to teaching at Danbury ISD and had a policy through the Texas State Teachers Association, so she was taken care of. Fortunately, they took one out on Dad.

So Dad did provide a new house for the family he loved, but he had to die to do it. Not a good tradeoff.

*   *   *   *   *

I knew this girl, who knew this girl.

My sister Kay threw a belated welcome home from Vietnam party for me in the spring of 1970. It was small and laid back. Most of the people there were friends and family that we had known in our teenage years. One of them was Kathy Hester, so I struck up a conversation with her. I had always liked Kathy and before the evening was over, I had asked her for a date. She accepted.

A few days later I got a call from her; she broke the date. As it turned out she was engaged and a date with me just wasn't a good idea. But Kathy had a back-up plan, it was like the "bait and switch" plan that used car salesman use.

"John, I really can't go out with you, but I have this girlfriend who can," Kathy offered.

Since returning from Vietnam I hadn't met anyone who I was really interested in or who interested in me. So I said, "Sure, I'd like to meet her."

The next Friday evening, I drove into the driveway of Miss Janie Huntsinger. I was wearing bell bottomed jeans and a colorful button-up shirt with long pointy collars. I walked up to the door fumbling and nervously thinking, "Here goes nothing." I bravely knocked on the door.

The next thing I knew, I was staring into the face of a cute, petite, blond girl. "You must be John," she said smiling, "and I'm Janie."

"It's a pleasure to meet you," I said cordially.

I didn't know at the time that meeting was going to change my life in so many ways and that all of them would be for the better.

I was welcomed into her home and introduced to her parents, Bill and Kolean. I also met her brothers, Bill, who was my age, and Fred, a few years younger. I didn't meet her sister Cheryl, who was married and lived nearby.

It was a simple date. We went out to dinner at a local restaurant and spent the evening getting to know each other. I left that night with a date for the next week. I liked Janie from the get-go. She was pretty, smart, and active.

In a few months I was hooked - I knew she was the girl for me. We talked about marriage, but she cut me off at the pass.

"Let's graduate from the university. Then we can plan the rest of our lives," she said.

But me, I like to strike when the iron is hot.

She was going to the University of Texas in Austin, and I was attending Sam Houston State in Huntsville. I burned a trail to Austin a lot of weekends early on. She was my first real love.

I also accidentally discovered construction, the second love of my life at the same place and about the same time.

Her dad, Mr. Huntsinger was a construction superintendant for a local developer named Joe Johnson. Her brother Bill also did construction worked there weekends and holidays when he wasn't going to school. I was always looking for work to make extra money for school and was happy when Mr. Huntsinger hired me. I worked with Bill. Bill and I became great friends and it didn't take me long to realize that construction would be my life's work. I just loved to build things.

We started out doing carpentry work in apartment projects. We were soon taking care of all the loose ends that had been overlooked by the other contractors. I loved the work, I loved Janie, and I became a fixture on the Huntsinger couch whenever I could work.

The summer of 1971 I rented an apartment nearby, was working full time with Bill and taking a history course at the University of Houston. At work one day I stepped wrong with a load of lumber on my shoulder and badly sprained my ankle. The company didn't want an injury on their record and continued to pay me for about three weeks until I could go back to work. I didn't mind at all, and it surely helped my grade in the history course.

Janie and I continued to date. We were always busy, water skiing with Bill and their friends or doing other things. We spent time with my family at Danbury and brother Peter's at Galveston Island State Park. The weeks turned into months, and then they turned into years.

I continued to sometimes sleep on the Huntsinger couch and work weekends. One Saturday night late, Janie's "Little Grandma" and "Pa", her grandparents, came in for a visit. Little Grandma noticed my car outside and commented to Kolean, in a loud voice, "Is that bearded boy still hanging around here?" I don't think she approved of my mooching.

(Years later I jokingly confronted her with that incident and her comment and she swore that it never happened, but we got along better after Janie and I started having kids and I was carrying a heavier load.)

In the spring of 1972, I think we were taking each other for granted and we decided to date other people.

That summer I encouraged Mom to go with me to Mexico to take a photography course through Sam Houston State. After Dad was gone, she had taken a real interest in photography and it was my minor at Sam Houston State. It was a six week course and she agreed to take it with me. After about two weeks I contracted some kind of illness that just shut me down and had to come back to Houston for treatment. After I recovered I finish the photography course by shooting pictures of the rice harvest in Danbury.

I stayed with my sister Becky in Houston. Janie was dating someone else, but I begged her to help me through that time, and since she still had a soft spot in my heart for me, she did help. Again, we were together and happy.

I graduated from Sam Houston State in the fall of 1972 with a Bachelor of Science in Industrial Technology.

Getting a job was another story. I was looking for a job in construction. Everywhere I went wanted experience in management, not just a boots on the ground worker. It took me a little over a month to get a job. I had never had that much time on my hands without being properly occupied, and I didn't like it.

Over the next two years, the job took me to Chattanooga, Tennessee, then to Jacksonville, Florida. Janie and I were having a long distance love affair that was not what either of us wanted.

Peltier Sons Rice Harvest 1972

Work ran out in the spring of 1974. Janie flew to Florida to drive back with me. We were a little disconnected and in a rut at the time. After four years of dating we were still talking about our future. I wanted to marry her years before. This time she laid it out with a strong message, "John, we are going to get married or stop dating."

I was surprised when she said that, but promptly replied, "Well, let's get married."

Once we were engaged, there was a flurry of plans to be made, with Janie making most of them.

July 13, 1974, was the date we set.

One weekend during that engagement period we were in Danbury with my family. Uncle Pete and his family were at our house. In the crowd Uncle Pete asked Janie, "I understand you and John are getting married."

"Yes, we are," Janie replied happily.

Uncle Pete commented, "That sounds like good news and bad news."

Surprised, Janie said, "How so?"

Smiling, Uncle Pete answered, "Good news for John, bad news for you."

Everyone laughed, but I think Janie may have been thinking, "What am I getting myself into?"

The wedding went off per Janie's plans. Officiating the service were both Father Jones, the priest I was an altar boy for at St. Anthony's Catholic Church in Danbury, and a Protestant minister that Janie knew growing up. I was a little bleary eyed after the bachelor party my brothers and friends threw for me the night before.

It was a happy time for me. After bouncing across the world in the Army, partying and getting a degree from Sam Houston State and, working out of Texas for nearly two years, I was nearly 26 years old and was ready to settle down.

After dating Janie for four years, marriage was a lot different from the single life. I'm sure looking back I was way too selfish as I adapted to being a husband. More than once I would meet my old college buddies after work for a few beers and get home late. For those times I apologize to my wife.

In 1975, we bought our first house. Janie turned it into a home over the next year. We renovated all the cabinets and the kitchen. Janie was pregnant with Jasie and we ate Church's fried chicken for what seemed like two months while the kitchen was out of commission. Working six days a week, remodeling at night, going to Lemaze birthing classes, and making time for friends and family, I wonder how we survived.

I'm sure my father was not in the room during any of the births of his twelve children. Even after serving as a medic in Vietnam, I was terrified at the idea of being there, but I was trained to be Janie's coach and partner in the birthing of our first child. I had no idea the emotions that would be stirred up in the delivery room as part of the team at the time, but watching and being present during Jasie Anne Peltier's birth, June 17, 1976, rolled over me like a tidal wave of happiness and fulfillment. The tears were rolling down my face when they handed her to me.

In June of 1978 I birthed a different kind of baby and named it Peltier Brothers Construction. At the time I had been grooming Richard to join me when he finished college so "Brothers" was going to work.

The company was making a good profit after our first year end in April of 1979, so I decided to buy a farm. Janie was pregnant with our second, a son who was due in November. I was drawn to the rolling hills west of Bellville, Texas. Whenever I had a chance I was driving the back roads of Austin County. Bill Leathers, a friend from my college days, and I were looking at property and stumbled across 70 acres in Austin County that I really liked. The old farmhouse hadn't been lived in for twenty years. The wood barn was built in 1885, according to the realtor. There was a hand dug well in the front yard. Old implements were lying around. It was my kind of place. Bill thought I was out of my mind.

It's true, "You can take the boy out of the country, but you can't take the country out of the boy!"

How was I going to sell it to Janie? I drove her up there the next weekend.

Every time I spotted a broken down shack by the road, I pulled up to it and said to her, "Do you like this?" The answer was always no.

By the time we got to the place of my dreams, it was looking pretty good, and Janie liked it. We made an offer on it. The offer was accepted, and we closed right after our second child, Josh, was born.

Joshua Edmund Peltier joined us on November 2, 1979, with the same wave of emotion and joy that I had felt during Jasie's birth. I don't think that participating in the birthing experience can ever get routine.

The farm was where I spent most of my weekends. It took months just to get the house in a condition fit for human habitation. We changed out all the old wood windows with aluminum ones. There was poison ivy growing all over the outside walls. I got a double dose; I must have been scratching for months. There was a hand dug well about four feet in diameter and thirty feet deep in the yard, which I quickly filled with dirt to make sure we didn't lose any kids in it. After the house was livable, we spent most of our weekends there. Soon we had a small herd of cattle, along with an unending list of new projects.

In 1981, we decided to build a new house in Spring Shadows. It was a Victorian house on the end of a cul-de-sac. The back yard was literally all swimming pool and I could mow the front yard in fifteen minutes. It worked out really well for me, less than ten minutes from the office, with minimal upkeep, so I could still focus on the farm projects.

MY NEW FAMILY

Wedding Day 1974

College Days

Joshua   Jasie   Justin

Jasie Loves to Fly

Jasie 1982   Josh on Gerti 1983   Justin 1986

Justin Lee Peltier entered the scene on August 29, 1982. He was the last great blessing we had as far as the size of our family. His coming into this world and into my arms was as special as Jasie's and Josh's.

Since the start of Peltier Brothers I was consumed by that endeavor. I would leave the house at 5:00 a.m. and not return until late evenings. It was my brain child and I was driven harder by the fear of failure than the reward of success. Business and I got along very well. I seemed to have an instinct for how to handle various situations and work them to my advantage.

I was living the American Dream and knew it, but wondered why I still felt like I was on empty.

I had a seventy-acre farm, a new house, nice cars, a beautiful wife, three wonderful children, a prosperous business with four brothers as partners and I had just been elected President of the Houston Contractors Association. In the wildest dreams of my youth I could never have scripted such an amazing life for myself. I had filled my life with many things and numerous events, but in my selfishness and independence, they were never totally part of me.

It was like looking through life's window, surrounded by scenes painted by Norman Rockwell, all the while being on the wrong side of the glass.

When I looked in the mirror I didn't like what I saw. I needed a major overhaul. In my ongoing war with God, I thought I had been winning. I could touch and see the spoils around me.

There was never enough; the more I had, the more I wanted. I was living the life I thought everyone wanted.

If I had earned all the trappings of prosperity, then why did I feel so alone and bankrupt? My mother warned us all as we were growing up, "Don't love anything that can't love you back."

I should have listened more attentively, the house, car, boat, farm, nor even Peltier Brothers Construction loves me. But my family does, and it's time I pay more attention to them.

259

Prague 2006

Skiing in Colorado 1993
Elk Hunt 2010
Josh Hunting for Coffiee

I decided it was time to get back to the basics. In my independence I made a pact with myself. I would start by "loving my wife", not in an emotional or physical way but by pragmatically putting her desires, wants and needs in front of my own priorities.

I also cracked the door open to that small space where I stored the remnants of God in my life. It was a dark, dank, musty, bitter hole that smelled of death. I was not comfortable there. I closed the door and retreated.

Along with "loving my wife", I also aligned myself with God's big ten rules. It was becoming obvious to me that "my way" wasn't working very well, so I trusted the God of my youth for direction. I would slip and slide from time to time, but mostly I kept my wheels between the ditches.

Dynamics in my family were changing in the late 1980's. Jasie was having a hard time with relationships at school. I was in the middle of a lawsuit which had the potential to bankrupt my business. We all needed a change.

My brother Arthur told me about a 28 acre tract of land for sale in Tomball. I looked at it and liked what I saw. I had grown up on a farm and yearned to live on some acreage and have animals around.

Generally, to date, the rule of the house had been "my way or the highway", and I knew I was a major part of my problem. I decided not to make the decision by myself to move to Tomball. We had a family meeting and discussed it as an option. I tried to explain about the work of maintaining and living on a farm and that they would all have to pitch in if we the move. I told them to consult with each other and make the decision and that I would abide by whatever they decided. They chewed it over for a few days and came back with an affirmative answer.

We purchased the property in the summer of 1989. We engaged an architect and by the end of the year had plans for our new house. During that time I was busy tearing down the old house and several barns that were on the land. We started construction in December, hoping to be in the house by the start of school in the fall of 1990. I had to commute the kids to Tomball schools for the first six weeks of school in the fall of 1990 before we moved in our new house.

As part of my pact to "love my wife", when we got to Tomball I started going to Tomball Bible Church with her on most Sunday's. I again felt like a fish out of water.

Sometime after that, my brothers Arthur and Peter went with me to a study of the Book of Romans with the pastor of my church. I was still mad at God for the death and destruction he had allowed in a war that had ended fifteen years prior, twenty for me.

During one of the sessions, we came to Romans 6: 23 which read, *"For the wages of sin is death, but the gift of God is eternal life in Christ Jesus our Lord"*.

I mulled that over in mind a lot the next few days.

It finally came to me - we were all sinners and we were all going to die. None of us know when or the circumstances of our death until that time is at hand. I prayed for forgiveness for the way I treated God, my wife, and the rest of my family.

After a while, I finally chalked up my Vietnam experience as a war that men created and administered. It seemed that our ability to kill each other was improving with each generation. In retrospect, I think I was just using the war as an excuse to justify a life where I could justify a "if it feels good, do it" attitude in my life. God allows our free will to lead us down whatever path we choose. While this is true, I'm convinced that the trials in our lives are tests to see if we can seek His face no matter what the situation.

In the early 1990's, I rededicated my life to Christ. While my trials continue and I fail way more than I would like to admit, I am at peace with myself and God.

I have been active in Tomball Bible Church Mission's Team and have served on water well drilling teams in Honduras and Mozambique. Our main objective is to bring the gospel of Jesus Christ through the much needed clean water. Jesus told the Samaritan women at the well, "but whever drinks of the water that I will give him will never be thirsty again. The water that I will give him will become in him a spring of water welling up to eternal life." John 4:14

Mozambique, drilling water well
under the Texas flag.

Water well drilling in Honduras 2001

John Peltier   Mike Bennett   John Qualls

14

PELTIER BROTHERS CONSTRUCTION

When I was a sophomore in college I discovered construction and decided it was to be my life's work. I had no idea then that my decision would have the effect on my life and the lives of so many others that I write about now.

After graduating from Sam Houston State University in the fall of 1972 with a clear view of my vocation and the education to back it up, I found that it wasn't going to be as easy to get started as I first thought it was, but I persisted.

After several months of pounding on many doors and applying for a number of jobs, I finally secured a steady one.

I was turned away from several jobs due to my lack of experience. In one interview, with Hugh Baker at Urbane Construction in Houston, my lack of experience came up again. In complete frustration, I complained to him, "How am I supposed to get experience if no one will hire me?"

"You've got a point," Hugh agreed. "Would you be willing to travel?"

"Definitely!" I answered quickly, without thinking.

He relented and gave me a chance. The company first sent me to Chattanooga, Tennessee, which was just a dot on the map when I headed there to be an assistant superintendent, constructing a Rodeway Inn adjacent to the interstate. I was busy figuring out what the definition of *"assistant superintendent"* was the first couple of months.

Some time later, I noticed that truckloads of framing material would show up, but only about three quarters of them would be unloaded. I called Hugh up and told him, "Something fishy's going on. Sometime's one and one don't add up."

He took care of that issue, but not before he sent me to Jacksonville, Florida, to work a similar job there where we were building a condominium project. That worked out fine for about eighteen months.

In early 1974 Project Manager Jim Cox, Superintendant Ed Sears, and the framing subcontractor, Doris Walker, asked me to partner with them in a new venture. Jim had been negotiating with a large developer to build an apartment complex in the Jacksonville area. The main reason they invited me to be a partner was that I had studied for and passed the test to receive a Florida license as a "Certified General Contractor". Doris put up all the money for the start-up costs and we named the company Huske Builders.

About that same time, the first Arab oil embargo happened. Fuel prices went up and there were long lines at the fuel pumps. We had gas rationing. If the last number on your car license plate ended in an odd number, you could only buy fuel for that car on an odd numbered calendar day; the opposite applied to even numbers. The maximum speed limit was lowered to 50 miles per hour. Jim's negotiations collapsed, along with the rest of the economy, and I headed back to Texas to start anew and marry my first love.

Once in Texas, after I had been searching for another job, I got a call from Richard C. (Dick) Partch, with Fisher Construction. He had gotten my name from another large construction firm where I had applied for a job but was not a good fit. He was looking for a construction estimator, a position for which I had no experience. We hit it off. He was a World War II veteran; I was a Vietnam veteran. He was a member of the Pi Kappa Alpha fraternity in college, as I was also. He hired me on a Friday and I was to go to work on Monday.

I was so excited, a new job, doing a new kind of work in municipal and commercial construction and in a new capacity as estimator.

By Sunday I grew very concerned. There I was, hired as an estimator with a job starting the next morning and I had no idea how to estimate.

I called Dick.

"Mr. Partch, do you remember that I told you that I had never done any estimating before?"

"Yes, but you said you were willing to learn, didn't you?" he asked.

"Yes, sir!" I said.

"Well, I'll see you in the morning," he said.

I must have learned because I stayed with the company for the next three years, and I was living the dream. I loved my job and my life. I was getting a better education in the construction business with Dick as my mentor than I could have received anywhere else, and I was getting paid well for it. Janie and I bought our first house and our first new car and had our first child during that time.

In 1977 Dick began negotiating to build a condominium project in Houston. I went to him and explained that I was really enjoying the municipal and commercial construction and didn't want to be involved in multi-family construction. He, being a lawyer assured me, "John, it's not my intention that you would work on that project."

I was trying to close a door, but Dick left it slightly cracked open.

He was successful in his negotiations and by early 1978, I was his third superintendant on the company's multi-family construction project, which he called Tanglewilde South. My plan had been to be a partner with Dick someday, but after several months of not enjoying my work, I gave Dick my notice. He is still a dear friend today.

After that, in the spring of 1978, I began to think of starting my own construction company, doing the kind of construction work I really liked, not multi-family projects, but public and municipal work.

On June 19, 1978 at the age of 29, with $4,200, a good work ethic and the will to succeed, I founded Peltier Brothers Construction. The other assets of the company were an old short wheelbase, stick shift, hot water six Chevy pickup, a wheelbarrow, a few tools and an office in the third bedroom of my home.

My good friend Bill Burgess had started a business himself, Burgess Specialty Fabricating, a few months before. He was a sheet metal fabricator and I was a contractor, but the business of business was still the same and we counseled each other in those early days. I think that the help we gave each other got us through those first years and for the rest of our lives with a lot less pain than we would have had otherwise.

The *Peltier Brothers* name was one from my childhood. Four of my cousins, Buck, Ronald, Walter and Roy, farmed rice from the 1920's through the 1960's. Their headquarters were about a mile and a half south of us on Hoskins Mound Road. We would go down there in the afternoons from time to time in the 1950's and 1960's and sit around with the group, by then including their sons, and listen to them tell old stories. The main thing that I noticed was how they got along, cared for each other, and enjoyed each other. I thought that if my brothers and I could replicate that someday, life would be good.

At first, I was the sole owner of Peltier Brothers Construction.

My brothers were all doing various things. Arthur and Richard were still in school at Sam Houston, but they worked for me summers and weekends. Richard had already made it clear he wanted to be a permanent part of Peltier Brothers Construction. Peter was working at Texas Parks and Wildlife and had supervised the building of Galveston Island State Park, but he pitched in from time to time when I needed him in my various and diverse projects.

Danny Jones, a superintendant I knew from my days at Fisher Construction, came to work for me after about three months in business to run the field.

It wasn't always easy getting started and building credibility, mainly because payment and performance bonds were (and still are) required for security on nearly all public works projects. I didn't think I was capable yet of meeting requirements to get bonded so I made a deal with David Nunn, of Nunn and Shumway Construction, to bond a project under his name for a 5% fee.

Soon after that an insurance agent named Andy Janda showed up at my house peddling bonds and insurance. He tried to convince me that he could get me bonded on up to $100,000. I just laughed at him. I knew I didn't have enough assets to qualify for that; that was the reason I'd made the deal with David Nunn. But I found out I was wrong. With Andy's guidance and some work, plus a little smoke and mirrors and some snake oil, I could qualify, and I did.

I produced a personal financial statement that listed virtually everything I owned, from the equity in my house and cars to an old motorcycle. Wedding rings, guns, antiques and other questionable possessions went on it. I found out I was worth more than I thought. With Peltier Brothers Construction assets added to that, I was able to start bidding small bonded jobs.

Peltier Brothers started out as a sole proprietorship. Andy steered me to an attorney to get me set up as a "C" corporation. I stayed with Andy as my bonding agent and he became a lifelong friend.

We all have lots of memories of amusing things that happened as we grew, sometimes in strange and unexpected ways.

The summer of 1978 we were doing a project for General Portland Cement Company on the Houston ship channel. I was constantly running to get tools and supplies to keep the job running smoothly. One day while I was at a gas station filling my truck with fuel, the man at the pump next to me noticed that I was a contractor by the way my truck was equipped. He came over and asked me if I was hiring.

I answered, "Yes, we've got a concrete job just down the road."

He related to me that he had a guy named Jose who had been working for him for about a week who was a pretty good hand. He went on to tell me that he was finished with the job and asked me if I wanted to hire Jose, as he nodded at the guy in the back of his truck.

"Yes, I could use extra help right now," I replied.

With that, Jose climbed out of the bed his truck and hopped into the back of mine. I took help wherever I could find it.

One time I recall when Danny Jones was running a job and my oldest brother Peter came by to help out and earn some extra money. Before long, Danny had Peter drilling dowel holes in a concrete wall. He handed Peter an air hammer drill, showed him where to drill the holes and then instructed him, "Take this drill and stop when you get to the '*henway*'."

Peter took the drill and started drilling. After a moment I saw Peter stop, look at Danny and ask, "What's a '*henway*'?"

"About three or four pounds," Danny laughed, before he gave him the depth in inches.

Another time Peter was in town on Texas Parks and Wildlife business, wearing his Texas Parks and Wildlife uniform and driving his Texas Parks and Wildlife truck, when he stopped by a project just to see how things were going. As soon as Peter stepped out of his car, Jose and five other crew members scattered. They disappeared like a covey of quail. It took us two hours to find them and get back to work. After that, Peter was banned from wearing his uniform on our jobs or driving up in that truck.

Near the end of that first year, Peter came to me and said that he'd decided to leave Texas Parks and Wildlife and go into construction.

You could have rolled me over with a feather. "Really? Who are you going to work for?" I asked, very surprised.

"You," he announced.

Still in shock, I answered, "Now that sounds like a plan."

Peter had been helping me out off and on, and I knew he enjoyed the work, but we had never really talked about him coming on board full time. He had nine years experience working for the State and the security that came with it. I was shocked that he would leave, but at the same time with Peter's attitudes and abilities, I knew he would be a great asset to the team.

We set our first fiscal year end date to be April 30th because we had already made enough money to be in the 30% tax bracket. Peter, Danny and I took nice bonuses; the success that year enabled them to pay me to buy into Peltier Brothers Construction at 10% each. At that point, with Peter as a part owner, the word *brothers* in the name of our company became honestly plural.

During the start-up phase of Peltier Brothers, Arthur and Richard were both at Sam Houston, studying for degrees in Industrial Technology. They were a godsend for me as a labor pool. They and their friends always needed extra money and they spent countless weekends working on various projects keeping me ahead of the wave.

In the fall of 1981, right after he graduated, Richard came aboard and shored up the estimating and project management, which was running me ragged. He had always planned on joining me at Peltier Brothers; in fact, he's the one who actually gave me the confidence to use the name Peltier Brothers. Richard became an owner shortly after that in 1982.

After Arthur graduated in the spring of 1980, he went to work as an electrician for nearly three years. I finally convinced him to join us after that. During that time, he did extra course work and studied to receive his Journeyman's Electrical License. His experience in the electrical field added an important component to our field operations. Arthur was offered ownership status in 1983 and accepted.

Peltier Brothers continued to grow.

By 1984 when we were looking for more help managing our projects, Gene N. Elsik, Jr., who had just graduated from Texas A&M with a degree in Construction Science, answered our call. He showed up for his interview in a suit and tie, looking like a fish out of water, but I could tell he had the demeanor and attitude to take care of our needs. Later, we learned that his pregnant wife, Barbara, had been waiting out in his truck during the interview. He told her when he got back to the truck, "I've got to get this job. The regular dress code for this company is blue jeans, leather boots and a collared shirt!" He did get it.

About the same time, Al Mandola, the son of our banker Annette

Mandola at Spring Branch Bank, was doing some site mowing for us. He and I had also been working together buying and selling real estate. Things got slow in real estate, but PBC continued to grow, so Al came to work with us doing project management.

As we were growing, there were times when things got rocky, too.

When we struck an agreement with a friend Don Underwood, a struggling bridge contractor, to help him secure bonding on some bridgework he wanted to do, it was a fateful decision that had a great effect on our company and caused one of our most rocky times.

Peltier Brothers bid several bridge projects to help Don and we did finally get a bid, which we subcontracted to him, per our prior agreement.

The work was going fine until the fall of 1987, when Don asked to borrow one of our cranes. He needed it to set some beams and pour concrete on a bridge deck. His use of a Peltier Brothers Construction crane was not in our agreement, but as the prime contractor on the job, we needed it to move timely. We came to an agreement to send our only available crane to the job. Good crane operators are important and hard to find, but Don assured me his operator was top notch.

In late 1987 disaster struck. It happened when Don's crane operator got off the crane while he was in the process of raising the boom – not a good idea. Matters got worse because the boom kick-out lever, a safety device to prevent the boom from being lifted beyond its limits, was faulty. As a result, the boom was pulled back over the top of the crane and collapsed, with the heavy boom striking the inspector on the project with a near fatal blow. It was tragic, and we were thankful the inspector wasn't killed.

About that same time Danny Jones, who had always liked his Schlitz beer, was enjoying it a little too much; he and Peltier Brothers Construction had a parting of the ways. I brokered a deal for Danny to sell his 10%, with 5% to Gene Elsik and 5% to Al Mandola. The company guaranteed the payment.

With the certainty of a lawsuit against Peltier Brothers Construction because of the crane accident, our stock wasn't looking like a very good investment. We were actually at full risk of going bankrupt because of the accident, but my thoughts were to run the company as if it were going to survive. We needed to do that regardless.

It was a busy time for me. Houston Contractors Association had elected me president in 1987, to preside in 1988. Houston Contractors Association acted as liaison between many municipal contractors and many cities, counties, the State of Texas and various utility districts and authorities. It was an honor to serve.

By April of 1988 we had decided that it would be a good idea to fly a new flag. We started up a new entity we named HEMP Corp. The name was taken from the first letters of Huntsinger (for my brother-in-law Bill Huntsinger who helped us out at that time), Elsik, Mandola and Peltier. (It had nothing to do with the hemp plants from which marijuana derived.) We started bidding and constructing all new work in the HEMP Corp name, paying Peltier Brothers through loans and rentals; all transactions were always at arm's length and above board.

Peltier Brothers was sued as a result of the crane accident, which caused us to be entangled in a hellish lawsuit for nearly five years. I would be the last to tell you that we were in the right because that would be wrong, but we had agreed to lease a piece of our equipment to Don and, even though it was unknown to us, it did have a safety defect.

We had a $1,000,000 umbrella policy that covered that kind of loss. Northbrook, our insurance carrier, had to defend us and could have chosen to offer our policy limits, but instead they chose to fight the case. From what I could tell by talking to several legal and insurance related friends, the lawsuit was likely a mult-million dollar case. If Peltier Brothers Construction had to pay much over the policy limits that could be awarded to the plaintiff in court, it could have bankrupted us.

Even though our insurance company defended us, I was wisely counseled to get Peltier Brothers a separate lawyer, and I did.

I had been told by the plaintiff's attorney that the plaintiff wasn't after Peltier Brothers, but was after the insurance company because when it didn't offer our policy limits. It had exposed themselves and us to much more liability. I really didn't know much about the legal ramifications of that lawsuit, but I did know that the suit was real and it was, on paper, directed at Peltier Brothers and not the insurance company.

We cooperated with the lawyers, courts and our insurance company, but we continued to do our work under HEMP Corp. HEMP Corp was even making a profit. At the same time, we kept Peltier Brothers flat, making very little profit.

In 1990 our business hit an all time low. As a result, we had to furlough most of our hourly men and had to give busy work to a couple of the superintendents just to keep them. We abandoned our profit sharing plan, made everyone fully vested and paid them in full. That was the only money most of them had to live on. Al left the company to get back into real estate full time, so Gene bought his shares.

We all came to the office to work every day and received paychecks every week, but with the lawsuit hanging over us it was like we didn't know who we were working for.

Finally, in the spring of 1992, the lawsuit went to trial. It was a real eye opener for me. I discovered that it wasn't about right or wrong or good or bad. It was totally about the law. In addition, it didn't take me long to figure out that we were being out-lawyered and out-maneuvered on almost every front. The plaintiff's lawyers made our expert witnesses look like "Ned in the third grade" and theirs like Roman senators.

While we weren't the only defendants in the case, Peltier Brothers had the most to lose. At one point in the trial when the plaintiff's lawyer was cross examining another defendant, I could tell the questioning wasn't going the way the plaintiff's lawyer wanted it to go. The next thing I knew that defendant was dropped from the lawsuit.

Peltier Brothers lost the battle in the courtroom, with the judge ordering our insurance company to pay well over our policy limits.

In the end, it turned out that the plaintiff's lawyer's statement to me was true - the plaintiff just wanted the insurance company to pay.

In the summer of 1992, much to my relief, Peltier Brothers was given a total release, without having to be out any money. Our insurance company even ended up reimbursing all of our legal fees.

The ending of that long and grueling lawsuit was like the weight of the world was finally lifted off our shoulders. We knew who we were working for again, and it wasn't the plaintiff. We finished all the projects that were under construction in HEMP Corp and after all the dust settled on April 30th, ended our fiscal year.

Again we raised the flag of Peltier Brothers Construction, Inc., high and proud in 1994. Next we did a stock swap between HEMP Corp and Peltier Brothers. I retained one hundred percent of Hemp Corp and decreased my interest in Peltier Brothers. I still held the major interest in Peltier Brothers Construction, but instead of being an employee of Peltier Brothers, I continued to work as a consultant to Peltier Brothers Construction and employee of Hemp Corp. That gave me a platform for other ventures and investing.

The next year we began making some other good decisions that ultimately affected our success. With the encouragement of our accountant, we decided to change our accounting system and some of our office equipment. Becky Ogden, our in-house accountant at that time, had started with us in 1980 when we had an unwieldy IBM System 32. It looked like a steel desk with a monochrome computer screen built in; the printer was a giant tractor feed that used 11 ½ x 14 inch sheets of paper.

In the mid-1980's, we upgraded to an IBM System 36, which was much faster and easier, but still provided only paper reports. About the same time, Becky and her husband decided to go full time into the antique business, so I had to find a new accountant to run the new software, all based on a new personal computer format.

A woman named Jackie Hoang showed up for an interview. She had an accounting degree from the University of Houston and was somewhat familiar with the new software; she also seemed to be all about business. She had come to the United States from Vietnam when she was thirteen, had learned English well and had made the USA her home.

Being a Vietnam veteran, I had great respect for her, knowing some of the hardships she had likely endured. I offered her the job, but she didn't just take it immediately. She went home, consulted with her husband and got back with me the next day with a few more questions. Only then did she take the job. It appeared that the job was just as important to her as it was to me.

With Jackie in charge, we loved the new system. It was fast and accurate and we didn't have to print out a report to check on a detail.

Over the years, Jackie has turned out to be my right hand. Sometimes I think she knows my mind better than I do.

Another *brother* was added in 1997. That year our brother Stephen took early retirement from a 23-year career at Dow Chemical to join us at Peltier Brothers and start a second career. He packed his family and all his worldly goods, moved to Tomball, and made himself the fifth brother in the company. His experience in safety, metal fabrication and piping made him a great and much needed asset.

In addition, the fact that all of his four children (Jeremy, Jennifer, Jeffery and Jacob) eventually graduated from Texas A&M with degrees in Construction Science affected the company in the long term. Jeremy, Jeffery and Jacob have become partners. Jennifer went to work for Cemex, one of our largest concrete vendors and has been a great help in liaison and scheduling our concrete pours in a timely manner.

Peter was elected president of Houston Contractors Association for the calendar year of 1998. This was the second time two brothers had served as president of HCA. Fifteen years later in 2013 Richard Peltier served as president and it was the first time three brothers had held the office.

Wilburn Mitchell Peltier (Will), the son of my brother Louis and the namesake of my father, worked summers for Peltier Brothers, with the intent of eventually coming on full time. After graduating from Sam Houston in the spring of 1998, he came aboard. He learned estimating from Richard and project management from Gene. He has learned those areas well and has helped make Peltier Brothers a more profitable company.

In June of 1999, the Houston Business Journal named Peltier Brothers Construction number thirteen of the top fifty family-owned businesses in the Houston area. I wasn't aware that family-owned businesses were going the way of the horse and buggy. I had always believed it was blessing if you worked with people that you care for who in turn care for you. If the people are your family, the blessing is multiplied.

As one of those top fifty family-owned businesses, we were treated to a nice dinner and awards ceremony and given a comprehensive write-up in a special edition of the Journal. It was good publicity for the company, too.

Because of Texas tax laws and the preferential treatment they gave to partnerships (over corporations), in 2002 Peltier Brothers Construction applied for and was given partnership status. But even though being a Texas partnership was advantageous for Texas tax laws, we elected to continue to pay federal taxes as a corporation.

It seems nothing stays the same and that time marches on. In 2004, Peter formally retired from full time employment at Peltier Brothers. I say that because I am writing this over ten years later and he still maintains an office with the Company and has worked as a consultant on many of our projects since then.

Partly as a result of Peter's retirement, but mostly because they had earned the right, in the same year Stephen and Will were given the opportunity to become partners in Peltier Brothers. The existing partners voted them in unanimously and they accepted.

Our nephew Will's presence ushered in a new era at the Company. He was proof that all the harassment he got as a kid from his uncles could be overcome, to the benefit of us all.

In the summer of 2002, another nephew joined the company when Stephen's oldest son, Jeremy T. Peltier, came aboard. He had also been working for Peltier Brothers for many years, beginning in the summer of 1994 when he was as young as fifteen and got his driver's license. At the time, he rode with me (and drove when I needed rest) to deliver materials to a project we had in Charleston, South Carolina.

Peter was there constructing two caissons 150 feet deep. Will and one of Louis' other sons, Bryan, went out to Charleston that summer to work and live with Peter.

In January of 2002 Jeremy came to work full time at Peltier Brothers, armed with a Construction Science degree. Gene was very happy to have another Aggie whoop in the office.

Jeffery H. Peltier, the second of Stephen's Texas Aggie sons, graduated in 2006 and wanted to come to work for us, too, but we were a little lean in work at the time, so we encouraged him to find a job with a local construction company. He found work with Lockwood, Andrews and Newman as a field inspector. As it turned out, it gave him a little different perspective on the construction industry. By January of 2007 our work picked up and we were able to hire him to work on several field projects. He had a good feel for planning and scheduling projects.

Jacob A. Peltier, Stephen's third and youngest son, followed the same trail set by his older brothers. It was his destiny. I remember one time when Jake was only 7 or 8 years old and our families were on vacation together in Yellowstone Park. I asked Jake what he wanted to be when he grew up. Without even thinking, he blurted out, "I want to be a Peltier Brother!"

Jake graduated from Texas A&M in December of 2008, and like it was at the time for Jeff, work was down to a trickle. During his senior year in college, Jake had interned with Balfour Beatty and they offered him a job upon graduation. He accepted and worked there doing municipal building work for nearly three years. In May of 2011, we offered him a job and he accepted. In December of the following year, he was formally and finally invited to be a Peltier Brother.

During that time, I had been contemplating pulling in my horns and turning over the reins of Peltier Brothers to this next generation. After much planning and praying, we worked out an exit strategy that seemed it might just work. At the end of 2013, I entered the semi-retirement mode.

For the first six months there was little difference. I went in four days a week and my phone still rang fairly often. By 2014, I cut it down to three days a week and my phone got quieter. Around April of the same year, with the year end books coming to a close, my expertise and experience seemed to be needed less and less. I was really happy after the final tally when the year ended on a very positive note.

I don't think I'll ever be able to completely let go of this company that I founded. I do hope, though, I can always keep an office there, maintain a presence and hopefully be able to give some useful advice once in a while to the competent partners who have taken over and are carrying on.

And I will always stay in touch with the many business associates I've worked with over the years as a result of Peltier Brothers; some of them have become lifelong friends and I am grateful for that.

15

A RATTLER'S TALE, May 11, 2007

It was South Texas brush country, twenty miles outside of Freer, where nearly everything in the landscape will stick you, sting you, or bite you. With nights so clear that the stars nearly touch the horizon in every direction, and its wild and raw natural beauty, we were drawn there like moths to flame.

My brother Louis and I had just finished setting up the last protein feeder pen, and were driving the jeep to the far west end of the property to check out two game cameras.

It was the last day of winter 2007; spring was right around the corner, and so was a five foot diamondback rattlesnake lying still near the edge of the road. I stopped the jeep within ten feet of the snake. It just laid there like one long line. Jeb, my dog, had been snake trained but I commanded him to stay clear as he hopped from the jeep. While Louis took its picture, I pulled out my Colt 45, model 1911 pistol.

"The only good rattlesnake is a dead rattlesnake," was standard code for this ranch.

I said to Louis, "Back me up." He readied a Ruger carbine ranch rifle with a full twenty round clip.

I thought to myself, "I wish I had my small 22 caliber rifle now. That skin would make a nice belt."

I took aim at its head and squeezed off the first shot – an inch high. It jerked its head back. The sound was deafening as Louis started laying in a few rounds and I continued firing. The snake had been hit several times and started to retreat quickly. Louis riddled its body with bullets before it could move more than a couple of feet.

The snake laid still in a twisted mass. "I don't think we could put together two hat bands from what's left of this hide," I said. "Get the camera and we'll get an 'after' picture."

With my empty 45 in my right hand, I reached to grab the snake behind its head with my left. When my hand was within ten inches of the "dead" snake, it closed the distance between its head and my hand like a lightning strike.

"The SOB bit me!!" I cried out.

"No!" Louis yelled. He turned and unloaded the rest of the magazine into the rattler.

I could feel the hot poison coursing up my arm; I instinctively put the bite area of my hand in my mouth, sucked at the poison and spit several times. It was futile, and I knew I was in big trouble.

I scrambled into the passenger side of the jeep. Louis loaded up Jeb and while racing back to camp made a phone call to his son, "Will, John just got bit by a rattlesnake. I need you to find the closest place that can treat snake bites. Then do whatever it takes to arrange the quickest transportation there."

By the time we made it to camp, eight to ten minutes later, I was feeling unsteady.

"I was worried about you falling out of the Jeep," Louis told me later. When we arrived in camp my truck was still hooked-up to the trailer we had been using earlier. Louis quickly unhooked the trailer, threw a few things in the truck and started it. "Where are you going?" I blurted out.

"Stay put!" he yelled back.

He roared the truck around and stopped one step away from where I was sitting in the jeep. He came to me and said, "Be steady getting into the truck. If you fall, I'm afraid I won't be able to pick you up."

Together, we transferred me to the truck, then Louis drove as if we were being shot from a cannon. The first six miles were dirt roads. The speed, the bumps, the constant swerving to find smooth parts of the road, and mainly the venom, made me nauseous. Louis, the rest of front cab area, and I were soon dripping with a healthy coat of fresh vomit. With my seat belt attached, I could feel myself deliriously pitching and rolling from that pivot point like I was on a bad roller-coaster ride.

I knew that I was in the hands of God and others. My body was retching, quaking and trembling in its fight to overcome the venomous bite, but somehow my mind was at peace, knowing that I could do nothing for myself and feeling comfort in the hands into which I had been placed.

A cop friend of mine once told me, "You can beat the rap, but you can't beat the ride." This was to be the ride of my life.

When we reached the paved road the ride smoothed, the speed increased, and Louis was driving hell bent for leather.

I looked up and saw that we were following a police car. Later, I saw another emergency vehicle's flashing lights. As we got closer to the flashing lights ahead, I could see an ambulance on the side of the road with its rear doors open. We pulled in close; an EMT helped me out of the truck. My pistol was still hanging on my hip. I was surprised at the great effort it took as I pulled it from its holster and laid it on the seat where I had been sitting, noticing the EMT backing off.

They rolled a gurney next to me, helped me onto it, securely strapped me in place and loaded me into the rear of the ambulance. The ride resumed. After taking my blood pressure, the EMT struggled to remove my wallet from my back pocket to verify insurance and identification.

The EMT continually asked questions, "What is your name? Are you married? How many kids do you have? What are their names?"

Every time my eyelids seemed heavy, she would blast me with another question.

Time passed, but I had no concept of it. At some point the ambulance stopped. I saw Louis's worried face looking into the back of the ambulance at me. I don't remember being in pain at that time.

"The HALO Flight is a few minutes out," someone announced. In 1987, HALO-Flight Inc., a nonprofit charitable organization, began air ambulance service to provide the fastest and safest emergency air transportation and medical care for residents and visitors of South Texas.

Soon I heard the old familiar sound of a chopper coming in to land. Memories of my time as an Army medic forty years ago and half a world away flew through my mind. I knew that this time the ride was for me.

They hustled the gurney from the ambulance to the chopper in the darkness. The flashing lights, the engine noise of the chopper, the wash of its rotors, the police and EMT onlookers, and the garbled barking of radio transmissions somehow made me feel as though I had entered a carnival midway.

A small, pallet-like bed jutted out from the side of the aircraft, and they elevated my gurney to the same level, transferring my carcass to it as gently as was possible. The berth was hard and one size too small. It rotated into the rear bay, sliding forward and locking into place. I felt like my feet were in the cockpit with the pilot and my body from the waist up was in the EMT work area.

The ride went airborne as we ascended into the cool black sky. Again a cuff was attached to my right arm so that my blood pressure could be monitored constantly.

The next thing I remember, I was rolling into a brightly lit room with a mess of faces looking down at me. Later, I discovered I had arrived in Corpus Christi at the Corpus Spohn Hospital.

"Are you allergic to anything?" one asked.

"No," I moaned quietly.

"ARE YOU ALLERGIC TO ANYTHING?" she badgered.

"No," I said louder.

"Are you sure?" she asked again.

After a moment, I replied, "Rattlesnakes."

That drew smiles and laughter, and things seemed to lighten up a notch or two.

The tee-shirt I was wearing disappeared quickly with a few snips of the scissors and my jeans and underwear vanished off the ends of my feet. They moved me to a bed and almost immediately I threw up all over the place. While someone was cleaning me up, my right arm was busy giving up blood for testing and getting an IV drip, which I'm sure included life saving antivenin. I was wired to a monitor with buttons that were glued to my chest.

After those first few minutes in the ER, my memory faded.

Not knowing exactly what had happened in the ER, two weeks later while Louis and I were at our nephew's wedding I asked him, "Can you tell me what it was like in the ER when you got there?"

He thought for a moment and said, "I got to the hospital at about 8:00 p.m. and asked if I could see you. The receptionist called the ER and then told me to check back in ten minutes. After about five minutes had passed, a young nurse escorted me to the ER and introduced me to the doctor in charge. Your body was raging and shaking in uncontrollable convulsions. Your face was grimaced with pain. I asked the doctor if he could give you something to relieve your pain and he said, 'He can live with the pain, but not without blood pressure'."

Then the doctor told Louis that he was giving me adrenaline to get my heart racing and something else to constrict my blood vessels to get my blood pressure up. He couldn't give me pain killers because they would dilate the blood vessels.

Over the next few hours my blood pressure improved and stabilized; then I was given small doses of morphine as I complained of pain.

Sometime later, days or hours, I don't know, the doctor came in and told me that I had visitors.

I was surprised and happy to see my wife Janie, my two sons Josh and Justin, and my brother Stephen. I welcomed them and then drifted back into the safe haven of sleep.

During the time Will was making arrangements for me, he was also getting the word out to my family. The first person he called was my brother Stephen, whom he asked to go tell Janie personally. He didn't want that message delivered when she was alone. Then he called my sons Joshua and Justin.

When Stephen got to our house he found Janie's cell phone laying on the counter blinking with missed calls.

When Justin got the call he was walking out the door with some friends to go to dinner. He told them what happened, then bolted out and drove to our home in Tomball, calling Josh and Janie on the way.

Josh later told me this story, "There is nothing scarier than receiving two voicemail messages, one from Will, in a serious voice, saying 'Josh, call me as soon as you get this.' Then one from Justin saying, 'Josh, call me. Something happened to Dad.' I immediately called Justin and learned that you had been bitten by a rattlesnake."

Josh had been at a crawfish boil with his girlfriend Anna, who was a coworker of Ellie, the daughter of my wife's best friend. As soon as he got off the phone with Justin, he told Anna what had happened and left for home. Ellie, who was sitting across the table from them, immediately called her dad and told him about the snakebite. Her dad, Rich, looked up across the dinner table at our pastor's house and said, "Janie, did you know John was bitten by a rattlesnake?"

Janie and the boys converged at the house to find Stephen waiting. He insisted on driving them the four and a half hours to Corpus Christi. As Stephen drove, three cell phones were busily engaged, getting the word out and asking for prayers. One of those calls was to my daughter, Jasie, who was then living in Switzerland.

When they were within an hour or so of Corpus, Louis called and gave them the news that my blood pressure had been stabilized. The news was a great relief for everyone and a wave of calmness swept through the car.

The next morning arrived with a nurse poking me with a needle to take some more blood samples. Janie was dozing uncomfortably in a small straight-backed chair. It warmed my heart just to see her again. In the ICU no visitor was supposed to stay overnight. She didn't arrive until the wee hours of morning, so they didn't push her out.
This whole episode marked the end of a record about which I had often boasted: it was the first night I had ever spent in a hospital for treatment in my life. I will add that I was really glad to be there.

My mind was still fuzzy and my left arm was throbbing, swollen several times its normal size, and, as I examined it, it was easy to say it was UGLY. As ugly as it was, I was very thankful that it was still attached to my body and that the prognosis was good. The doctor was concerned about possible compartmentalization that could lead to paralysis and/or gangrene, plus the loss of appendages. He paid close attention to the swelling and the next day he did a procedure called a fasciotomy. It entailed cutting three deep gashes in my hand and forearm, allowing my arm to decompress and relieve pressure on my nerves.

During my three days in ICU the care was excellent. I never felt like a piece of meat being passed around a butcher shop. I have a saying about my wife, "If she liked it, I love it."

I felt like Dee, my day nurse, treated all my wants and needs in a similar fashion. Al, the night nurse, the doctors, the vital sign takers, and blood drawers all seemed interested in the same goal: getting me well as quickly and efficiently as possible.

During the next three days in a regular room, cabin fever began to settle in, even with the great company and playing card games one-handed, I wanted to get back to Tomball to convalesce. The doctor made an extra effort, coming by Tuesday evening to check on me, which allowed for a Wednesday morning discharge.

I'm on the mend and the ride continues. The doctor at the wound center in Tomball told me that because my basic health was good my wounds are healing rapidly. The fingers on my left hand are numb and tingling; he says the nerves grow slowly and it might be a year before most of the feeling returns.

If it weren't for the technology of the cell phones and computers, my brother Louis who brought me out, and his son Will, who orchestrated the emergency team, I might not be writing this story.

An invisible support group materialized around me. It became very visible as the incident unfolded through personal visits, phone calls, emails, cards, flowers, and countless prayers.

In the eyes of my children, I'm sure I had been the picture of good health, independence and resourcefulness. I think they were shocked at how quickly that picture of their father changed when they saw me on the brink of death and totally dependent on others for survival.

It gave me great pride and satisfaction to witness their response, circling their wagons around Janie and me and standing ready to do whatever it took to shield and protect us.

My daughter Jasie kept in constant contact with us and kept everyone updated by chronicling the events on her blog site. Her fear of losing me later turned into anger towards me once my survival was assured; she hated that I might engage in any action that could cause my untimely departure from this life. She soon got over it since I'm still around.

I am humbled by the number of people who care about my well being. However, I don't recommend testing your support group by messing around with rattlesnakes.

The snake was doing exactly as nature intended. I learned that it was not uncommon for snakes to bite after they appear to be dead. Pit vipers instinctively strike, even after their heads have been removed. I am told they will even strike with the blunt end of their body.

And me? Well, I got a taste of what it's like to be the prey instead of the predator, and I will forever be wary of "dead" snakes.

16
AN ESSAY ON GRASS AND WATER

I am at a retirement party for Anderson. This is strange because I haven't seen him or even thought of him since 1968. He looks the same, only different. Now there's a little paunch around his belly, his face sags around the edges, his movements are deliberate, and his hair is thin and graying.

It's a large office filled with people I don't know and I can't figure out why I am here. As I glide through the crowd, I see everything in snapshots.

"Bishop?"

He turns with a quizzical look on his face, "Peltier?"

We had always addressed each other by last names.

I survey the room and recognize several guys I had known in my Army days. Sasser, Juenemann, Stewart, Salines, Della, Looney, some I knew well. Some I had known just in passing. Something didn't fit. I knew all of them, but they didn't know each other - the timing didn't work.

The sound of rain on a tin roof startles me. I wake up.

It isn't rain, but a rattling air conditioner. I am at the deer lease, and it's 4:30 on Saturday morning. I roll out of bed, stumble over Jeb, my Chocolate Lab, and start a pot of coffee.

My brother Louis comes into the kitchen at about 5:30. I offer him a cup of coffee and he asks, "What are you doing?"

"I had a weird dream about some Vietnam buddies. I think they were on my mind because of my memoir class and I was just making a few notes."

"No shit?"

"No shit."

"Bullshit!"

"Louis, I'm trying to write about something I know about."

"Cow shit."

"Cow shit?"

"Sure, you've been in and around it all your life. You have some under your toenails that will never wash out."

I'm in a memoir class with women and I'm the only guy. I call them "The Harem."

My first thoughts are that neither the Harem or my wife will like it, but I've always been a little contrary.

"Okay, I'll give it a shot just for fun."

Here goes nothing!

* * * * *

COW SHIT

There is a great misconception in the world about cattle ranchers. Most folks think that a rancher's main job is rounding the cattle up, vaccinating, deworming, castrating and branding them. The truth of the matter is their primary job is feeding them, and that means that a lot of forage is required. Depending on the quality of the forage, climatic conditions, body condition, gestation, and calf requirements, a mature cow requires fifteen to twenty five pounds of forage per day. Then add to that another seventy five to one hundred fifty pounds of water. Subtract from that what it takes to maintain the cow's body condition and provide milk for a calf or fetus, and it becomes apparent that those cows have created quite a lot of manure.

Growing up on a farm and ranch, we were in constant contact with those silky green piles deposited indiscriminately by the many bovine creatures that roamed the area. We were confused about what to call ourselves - "farmers" since we raised rice or "ranchers" since we raised cattle. One thing for sure, we were taught not to be afraid of those green piles because they were only grass and water, and if some of it got on you, with very little effort, you could clean it off.

Unless it was the cold of winter around the house, we were barefoot. If we stepped in a cow pile inadvertently, the common saying was, "You cut your foot."

Fresh cow patties were nice and warm and make your skin soft and green and pretty smelly. As kids, we considered bottling the stuff to replace women's mud pack facials with "cow patty packs".

We held my little sister down once and tried it out. It left her face soft and green and our butts red and pained.

Manure does have a couple of upside potentials. When a cow patty is completely dry, you can burn it in a campfire. Cow chip tossing was a rage before Frisbees. It does make a great "tea" for fertilizing vegetables and flowers when you steep dried chips in water.

Fresh manure doesn't burn really well, but it does burn. At Halloween each year in Danbury, there was always at least one prank where a pile was scooped into a brown paper bag, placed on the front porch of the principal's house, and the top of the bag set on fire. After a knock on the door, the prankster disappeared into the dark with his buddies and watched the scene as the principal opened the door and stomped the fire out.

We always had a cow we milked twice a day. The routine was to call the cow to the pen, put sweet feed in its trough, clean the udder, sit on a five gallon bucket, press our heads hard into its flank to keep it from kicking unexpectedly, position the milk bucket between our knees and then start milking. Sometime if we got too relaxed, the cow would "kick the bucket". If we were quick, we could move the bucket out of the way and save the milk. If the cow was quicker than us, the bucket went flying. When the cow's hoof went into the bucket, we knew what the coating was on the hoof, grass and water. That created a quandary, do we throw it out and be short of milk, or do we just take it in, strain it like we always did and put it in the refrigerator?

****

Cattle Habits:

1. Anytime you gather the cows for any reason, they start raising their tails and spraying manure everywhere. The consistency goes from soft as mud to runny as water.

2. Anytime you move a group of cattle in a trailer, they coat the bottom of the trailer with about inch of *grass and water.*

3. Every time a cow's hoof comes in contact with a hard surfaced road, sidewalk, patio or whatever, their reaction is to lift their tail and make a deposit.

4. Cow are curious. They test every gate, especially the one to the back yard. Once in, they make a bee line to the flowers and shrubs, eat what they can, trample the rest, then make multiple deposits in the area.

Definition of a gate: A hole in the fence that cattle can get out of.

****

My most up close and personal experience with this fecal matter was when I took a course at Houston Community College in determining pregnancy in cattle. That information is important for managing a herd. We learned about their plumbing layout and the process of palpation. In that process we wore a long plastic "glove" on our dominant hand that covered our arm to our shoulder. The cow's head was securely held in a steel head gate for the protection of both you and the cow. The glove was well lubricated and we pushed into the rectum through the anus to about our elbow.

Obviously, the cavity is filled with fecal material and the cow is pushing to remove the newly introduced foreign object. The foreign object is looking around to find the cervix with his fingers through the rectal lining. The fecal matter is streaming out the rear around the arm. Most of the time you must cup you hand and pull out quantities of the material to allow for a better feel.

Once the cervix is located, you feel the uterus. If it's small and you can hold it in your hand the cow is "open", not pregnant. Between sixty and ninety days after conception, the uterus drops over the pelvic brim into the abdominal cavity. After six months you can feel the formed calf. Once the fetus has fallen over the pelvic brim, in order to feel the calf, you must push in all the way to your shoulder.

Generally by this time you have the full effect of the fecal matter.

Your face and nose are in close proximity to the source, and there is a splattering of it in your face, hair and clothes. As the palpator, your focus is in your fingertips; all the while the cow's internal muscles are pushing, squeezing, and fighting your every move. The constant pressures tire all the muscles in your arm, hand and fingers. You don't care about the cow shit.

At the end of the class there was a "hands on" seminar at the Farm and Ranch Club near Bear Creek Park. Cows were brought in from being open to all different stages of pregnancy. Our assignment was to estimate the length of term of each. There were about ten guys and two gals in the class. I was the second in line to palpitate one particular cow. Ron, a classmate, had palpitated it just before me. Right after I pushed in to feel around, Ron hollered at me, "Is it a heifer or a bull"?

I immediately knew why he asked. The calf was fully formed and its front feet were entering the birth canal. I hollered back, "I can't tell. Every time I try to push past the head, it starts sucking my thumb."

Taken by surprise, one of the girls asked, "Really?"

*   *   *   *   *

Some final notes, there are no winners in a shit slinging fight.

You always get some on you, most of the time before the fight begins.

When you stir shit up, it generally creates a big stink.

Well, enough of this bullshit.

For a free sample call 1-800-SHIT-HAPPENS.

Eat more beef and drink more milk!

July 30, 2005

Epilogue

Now it's 2017.

Janie is still beautiful and loving after over forty years of marriage.

I look around. All my kids have college degrees and are married. I have ten grandkids and one more on the way.

In the house where we grew up, Mom had a row of her babies' pictures in the living room. These pictures took on the name of "Mom's Wall". I think in her mind those pictures represented the only legacy she cared about and that whatever accomplishments those souls produced she would be a part of them. As number five, I was able to see the line of pictures grow to eleven. (Leo Patrick, our brother who died in infancy, never had a picture.)

Later, as Mom aged and had to move into a series of nursing homes, we moved those pictures along with her. We took great care to hang them neatly in a line from oldest (Peter) to youngest (Molly). They were always a topic of discussion with the healthcare workers and the many people she met in those homes.

She always liked to show us off when we came to visit. Sometimes she would introduce me as, "Number Five on the wall."

For her 90th birthday I put together a DVD slide show depicting a glimpse of her life. While I was showing it on the television in her room, a nurse came in and started watching it with us. She took me aside and asked if I would be willing to show it to all the people in the home, which I gladly did. I was amazed at the response. Mom became an overnight celebrity of the home.

I knew her time was short and I wanted her to see my rendition of her life. I had always thought it sad that when a person dies they have a slide show of their life at the funeral for everyone else to see. So I decided to make it mostly up so she could preview it and offer any comments of any other things she might want included in it.

Florida 2015

Weddings

Josh & Anna

Jasie & Tanner

Justin & Kit

MOM'S WALL

Peter Carl   June 27, 1942

Katherine Matilda   September 25, 1943

Louis Mitchell July 28, 1946

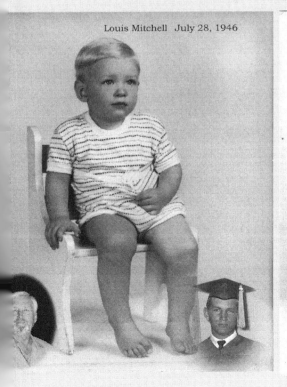

Kenneth James   October 16, 1947

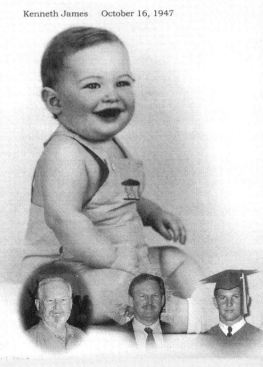

MOM'S WALL

John Eldridge   November 15, 1948

Rebbeca Susan   December 31, 1949

Stephen Thomas   Feburary 16, 1952

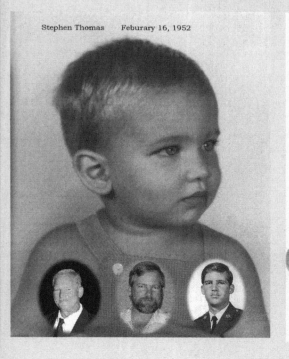

Paul Anthony   June 23, 1953

MOM'S WALL

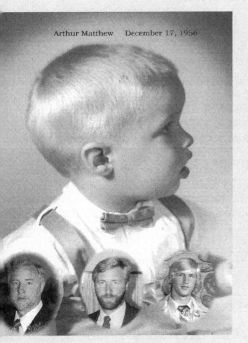

Arthur Matthew   December 17, 1956

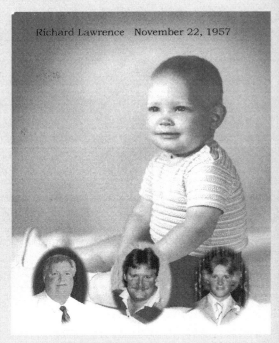

Richard Lawrence   November 22, 1957

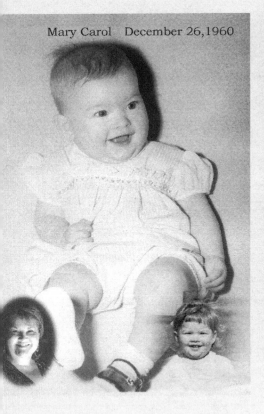

Mary Carol   December 26, 1960

Mom and Dad   1965

A little over nine months later, with nine of her children and several spouses holding hands around her bed and praying for her as she crossed over into the arms of Jesus, she left us.

Barbara Ida Peltier, April 7, 1918 - January 28, 2009

At the time of her passing, she left a legacy of eleven children, forty two grandchildren and twenty four great grandchildren. At Mom's passing, there were 24 great grandkids. The number of souls continued to grow and as of the writing the number is 60 and three more in the oven.

Peltier Brothers Construction has far surpassed my dream of just providing a living for me and some of my brothers and many employees. I have initiated an exit strategy from Peltier Brothers that eventually will pass the baton to the nephews. I have been semi-retired for two years and the company has done quite well, so well that the nephews beat their chests and tell me how good they're doing. I have to remind them of who picked and trained them. (I lie so well - sometimes, I think they believe me.)

Over the years I've been involved in several other businesses, mostly with my family.

I joined Al Mandola and Kerry Emmott in several residential real estate developments. The first, in 1996, was Hunters Creek, which was nearly 480 acres, followed in 1997 by Stone Lake, which was 223 acres with a 20 acre lake in the center for detention. In 1998 we did Bridal Creek, which was 115 acres. In 2001, we started Huntington Woods, which was 33 acres. I enjoyed all that work, too.

In 2000 my brother Louis and I bought 176 acres with Austin Bayou frontage near Danbury and next door to his home. We developed that property into home sites of over one acre each. We named the sections Bayou Oaks and Bayou Oak Estates. We developed Bayou Oaks along existing county roads. For Bayou Oak Estates, we built a concrete curb and guttered road that snaked into the property and ended in a cul-de-sac. The 55 acre tract was going to be developed at the end of the cul-de-sac across a drainage ditch, but we were approached by an individual who wanted the whole thing for his estate and we accepted his offer. At present we have five lots left to sell. That's been a fun ride, too.

In 2000, my friend Mike Bennett and I bought the first franchise issued by a company known as Uretek USA. The business used polyurethane to lift and stabilize concrete foundations and other structures. I invited my sister Molly to be Office Manager and David Jackson, a longtime friend from

Sam Houston State, to be Sales Manager. They both accepted. As a result of her work with Uretek, in 2003 Molly was elected president of Woman Contractors Association. Maybe construction was in my family's DNA all along.

Uretek was a good business, with lots of roller coaster rides. I had the opportunity to sell my interest in 2012 and did. Now Molly runs the day to day operations; her new partners are well satisfied with her at the helm.

In 2004 my friend David Giles and I gave birth to another company, which I named TerraFirma Earth Technologies. David had longtime experience in the construction dewatering business and I had experience of the business of business. We initially set out to bring in my daughter Jasie as owner and figurehead for what was called a "Woman Business Enterprise" in the City of Houston, but that didn't work out. Consequently, my son Joshua came in as a principle in the venture; he had worked with them from the start using his computer skills.

After several years in the business, we began looking for a way to expand our operations. David had a friend who worked with MORETRENCH, a large dewatering company out of New Jersey; fortunately, they were looking to expand in our direction. In 2010, they purchased TerraFirma. David and Josh continued to work for them. I wanted to start working myself out of that business so, for me, the sale was a good opportunity to exit TerraFirma.

In 2012, MORETRENCH decided that the TerraFirma part of the business was not profitable enough to pay its proper load and offered it back to us previous owners in a very attractive deal. I declined to be part of the deal, but David, Josh and David's brother Mike took it on. They are continuing to do well in the business as of this writing.

Now, looking back over all the time that has passed since that day on June 19, 1978, when I was 29 and stepped out into my own business, I can truly say that it's been a great journey!

It gives me satisfaction to think about what an impact Peltier Brothers Construction, Inc., has made on me and so many members of my family, plus many others who have become part of the family. Then I pause to think about how many future generations may be affected. Who knows?

Exiting business has been a double edged sword for me; I miss the challenges and excitement of the hunt, but my family is still there and I am ready and able to help when the need arises.

Now I get to work on "special projects". My latest and greatest is the Papa Haus, a structure I've built at our farm. It's a tall structure in the woods.

Papa Haus 2015

Papa Haus 2015

It's main purpose is to provide a retreat for the grandkids to be able to get away and listen to the quiet and beautiful nature that abounds in its setting. I wanted to put the Papa Haus down by our creek, along the west boundary of our farm, but the boundary line is in the middle of the creek.

Since I couldn't put a fence in the middle of the creek, I created a long triangle of land along the creek, separate from the pasture. To do that, I put a fence out about ten feet out from the creek at one end and about forty feet at the other end. That created a great space for the Papa Haus.

Peltier Brothers had a 10' X 12' galvanized frame for a landing that had been incorrectly fabricated. The fabricator didn't want it, but when I saw it, I immediately envisioned it as a platform for a structure in that creek bottom.

I also found four 6" I-beams, 12' long, which I used for legs and a used galvanized stair assembly that was 10' high. With all those, I had the starting point for a structure. We took it all to the farm and started welding it all together. I put together a plan for a two story observation building on top of the platform. We placed the front of the structure on the fence line and the rear about 15' to the edge of the creek bank.

My brother Peter has a portable sawmill set up at his farm up in East Texas, so we cut all the framing material out of pine and red oak planks for the siding. We prefabricated all the walls we could in Tomball, where Janie and I live, and took the panels to the farm, using our boom truck to set them on top of the 10' high platform.

It took the whole of 2015 to get it all up. With a lot of (physical) help from my banker and good friend Steve Rife and many others, we fitted and cut until it was complete. I love the Papa Haus and hope many generations down will get to enjoy it.

I feel busier now than I've ever been. Between projects at the farm, grandkids, Peltier Brothers, property management, travel, mission work, and writing this book, my days are full.

The pursuit of happiness described in our Declaration of Independence worked out well in my life.

Thank You, Lord.

THE END

The Thundering Herd 2015

Front: Molly, Becky, Kay
Back:
John, Kenneth, Stephen,Louis, Paul, Richard,Arthur, Peter

Made in the USA
Lexington, KY
04 October 2017